STUDIES IN MUSICOLOGY

Lavergne of Chapel Hill

GLEN HAYDON

STUDIES IN MUSICOLOGY

ESSAYS IN THE

HISTORY, STYLE, AND BIBLIOGRAPHY

OF MUSIC

IN MEMORY OF GLEN HAYDON

Edited by James W. Pruett

Foreword by Charles Seeger

GREENWOOD PRESS, PUBLISHERS
WESTPORT, CONNECTICUT

Library of Congress Cataloging in Publication Data

Pruett, James W   comp.
    Studies in musciology.

    Reprint of the 1969 ed. published by the University of
North Carolina Press, Chapel Hill.
    Includes bibliographical references.
    Includes index.
    1. Musicology--Addresses, essays, lectures.
I. Haydon, Glen, 1896-1966. II. Title.
[ML3797.1.P78 1976]   780'.15   76-7574
ISBN 0-8371-8883-0

Originally published in 1969 by the University of North Carolina Press,
Chapel Hill

Reprinted with the permission of the University of
North Carolina Press, Inc.

Reprinted in 1976 by Greenwood Press
A division of Congressional Information Service, Inc.
88 Post Road West, Westport, Connecticut 06881

Printed in the United States of America

10 9 8 7 6 5 4 3 2

To the memory of

GLEN HAYDON

(1896–1966)

Kenan Professor of Music

The University of North Carolina at Chapel Hill

FOREWORD

The nearly fifty years of Glen Haydon's interest in musicology spanned approximately the time of the growth of the discipline in the United States from its first tentative beginnings to a maturity recognized at home and abroad. He was the outstanding member of the first small class in the subject, an introduction only, offered in an American University (1917–18). Two years earlier, the Head of the Harvard Department of Music had written me that he had discussed the new word "musicology" with his colleagues and that "we do not think much of it." No less an oracle than President Charles W. Eliot had already snorted "Musicology! Next, it will be Grandmotherology."

At that time, the only organization in the United States for serious students of the history of music was a New York Chapter of the old S.I.M. (Société Internationale de Musique), soon to be a casualty of World War I. The membership comprised O. G. Sonneck, W. S. Pratt, Carl Engel, Adolf Weidig, Leo S. Lewis, Otto Kinkeldey and a few others. In my innocence, I had thought I was the first to use the English equivalent of *musicologie, Musikwissenschaft,* etc., then in established currency in continental Europe. But on my first visit to the Library of Congress I discovered that Sonneck had already filled a whole drawer of cards under that subject-heading. Pratt's article "On Behalf of

Musicology" was published that same year (1915) in the first issue of *The Musical Quarterly*.

During the 1920's, feeble and sporadic efforts were made to revive or supplant the small S.I.M. Chapter, but nothing came of them until in what was almost an act of desperation a group of five men formed the New York Musicological Society, whose annual *Bulletin* (1931–34) is now a collector's item. It prospered with the specific intention eventually to form a national society. This was done in June, 1934, under the name of the American Musicological Association (later, Society) with Otto Kinkeldey as President. By June, 1936, there were three chapters: Greater New York, Western New York, and Washington-Baltimore.

Haydon read a paper, "The Problem of the Dissonance," at a meeting of the last-named on March 23, 1935, was elected to the Executive Board of the Society for 1936 and President, 1943–44, holding other offices at various times. Meanwhile, he had taken part in the brief life of the American Society for Comparative Musicology, an affiliate of the Gesellschaft für Vergleichende Musikwissenschaft, which was, in turn, a casualty of World War II. By 1934, he had been invited to head the Department of Music in The University of North Carolina, where, as Professor of Music, he formed and until his sudden death led one of the best university departments of music in the country.

Glen Haydon was born in 1896 in Inman, Kansas. After grammar and high schools in Hobart, Oklahoma, he entered the University of California at Berkeley, graduating in 1918 with a major in music. During 1918–19 he served with the 363rd Infantry, 91st Division of the American Expeditionary Forces (AEF) in France and later with General Pershing's General Headquarters Band. He played clarinet professionally for many years in and around San Francisco. From 1920 to 1925, he was instructor of band, orchestra, and woodwind instruments in the Berkeley High School, meanwhile receiving a degree of M.A. from the University of California in 1921. After two more years of study and travel in Europe, he became instructor and, later, Assistant Professor of Music in his alma mater, serving as Chairman of the Department of Music from 1929–31. But it was not until 1931 that he obtained leave of absence and undertook what was for him the turning-point in his career, final preparation of a doctoral dissertation (University of Vienna, 1932), *The Evolution of the Six-Four Chord*.

Perhaps it is hard for the student in musicology today to understand a fourteen-year gap between the baccalaureate and the doctorate, especially when chairmanship of a department intervened. It was, however, only in 1930 that the first chair of musicology was created (at Cornell, for Kinkeldey). For some years afterward, library and duplication services were still at a minimum, except at three or four of the largest institutions—the Library of Congress, New York Public, and Harvard University. Departments of music in colleges and universities and conservatories of music knew little or nothing of European musicology and were not friendly to attempts to introduce it. Music educators in the public schools and the music profession at large were, to the extent they heard mention of the word, mostly hostile even in the 1940's. Formation of the national society (1934) and the appointment to university positions of a half dozen well-known European historicomusicologists who had participated in the International Congress of Musicology in New York (1939) and had been stranded there by World War II about summed up the efforts to support the discipline from inside.

Of equal or, perhaps, greater help was the support of musicology from outside the university. First to be mentioned must be the Music Division of the Library of Congress, which under the guidance of four able Chiefs (Sonneck, Carl Engel, Oliver Strunk, and Harold Spivacke), built one of the greatest collections of music and musicological materials in the world; second, the American Council of Learned Societies, which set up a Committee on Musicology in 1927, encouraging and supporting acceptance of musicology by academic bodies; and finally even the Department of State, under whose auspices a Conference on Inter-American Relations in the Field of Music (1939) was placed in charge of musicologically-minded persons. From that time on, foundations as well have given increasing support to musicological endeavor.

Haydon was an active participant in the conference-to-conference, committee-to-committee planning and working-out of many of these developments through active membership in a baker's dozen professional organizations. In most of them he held office and chaired committees, among them the Music Educators National Conference, the Music Teachers National Association (President, 1940–42), the National Association of Schools of Music, the North Carolina Music Teachers Association (President, 1937–40), the College Music Society, and the Music Library Association.

As may be noted, Haydon's published writings fall under three principal heads: the history of the fine or professional art of European music, with special reference to the Italian Renaissance; the "theory" of that idiom, which is to say the propaedeutics known as "harmony," "counterpoint," etc.; the organization of the practice of music-teaching in American schools, colleges, and universities. Not being a specialist in the history of the European professional idiom, I shall leave to others consideration of the titles in that aspect of its study. With respect to the theoretical works, I can, however, state with assurance: there is general agreement that his *Evolution of the Six-Four Chord* and *Introduction to Musicology* were pioneers in their day and must still be regarded as basic references for contemporary students in Europe as well as in America.

I should like to register here, especially, an appreciation of Haydon's activity in the hurly-burly of music-professional organization of which he has left a partial record in the occasional papers I classed under the third heading. Musicologists of the future will pay attention to the writings under the first two headings, but they will probably ignore the third. Yet many of the conditions of future music activity and musicological study and research in the United States have been and continue to be laid down in the free-for-all give and take of music-organization.

A unique characteristic of the "state of music" in the country today is the operation of two trends that might be considered incompatible. On the one hand, there is a vast diversification and diffusion of music activity throughout the population, for which there is no known precedent. Comparatively stable traditions of music, long inherited, cultivated, and transmitted more or less discretely within a social class structure that has modified only slowly the basic distinctions of city and country, rich and poor, learned and unlearned, are in daily confrontation with each other. Where, before 1900, change in these traditions occurred comparatively slowly through individual initiative, it is now effected rapidly by mass communications. As a result, fragmentation of old genres and syncretization of new, still too evanescent to be labeled "traditions," is the rule. To what extent the idioms of professional, popular, and folk music of 1900 will be recognizable as existent in 2000 is a question.

On the other hand, these same mass communications—public education, inexpensive print, radio, phonograph, tape, and television—are producing a confrontation of old and new ways of *talking* about music in which change, though equally rapid, is of the opposite kind—leveling rather than separating, synthesizing rather than fragmenting them. Music educators in the schools no longer blanch at the word "musicology." Musicologists admit that tribal, folk, and even popular music idioms are worthy of serious study. The result is a very gratifying diminution of separative and divisive trends between lower and higher education, between learning and doing, between music and the rest of the humanities. Where, at the turn of the century there was utter incomprehension between the adepts of the various interests, there now seems to be at least a promise of a common language in which the undeniable diversity of musical experience can be dealt with in musicological terms understandable by everyone concerned. But in the academic set-up in the Western world, which has reflected and made use of this more rapid change in many fields, consequently widening their scope and devising working relationships between the opposing trends of fragmentation and integration in them, musicology has lagged. The historical orientation of a study of the monuments of the professional idiom of European music still dominates. No organized method for dealing with the present of that idiom has been developed. It is not concerned with the trends that lead to its immediate future. It has so structuralized both its research and its pedagogy bureaucratically that we have, *de facto,* instead of one, unified study of the music of man two sharply differentiated discipines. The one academically established as "musicology," the other still seeking establishment as "ethnomusicology"—an obvious misnomer, for it comes much closer to comprehending the total field than does the established study. By the same bureaucratic structuralization, ethnomusicology is now in danger of becoming divided, within the few universities in which it has been accepted, into two opposite disciplines: one, an anthropological, that deals with music primarily in nonmusical terms from outside-inwards; the other, a musicological, that deals with the same materials primarily in musical terms from inside-outwards. Thus, unfortunately, the old trend toward fragmentation has outrun the new toward integration.

I have dealt summarily with this state of affairs in several papers and need not repeat myself here. Suffice it to say: agreement seems to be increasingly widespread that both splits are pernicious. No one will deny that in any large field of scholarly endeavor specialization requires various approaches and objectives, and that methods of study must vary in detail. But as yet no concerted plan has been widely enough agreed upon for healing the splits. Bukofzer's argument for two separate musicologies in the first report "Les Colloques de Wégimont" (Bruxelles, 1956) was sufficiently discredited by Brailoiu in an appended statement. There would be no more point to separate Western and non-Western musicologies than to separate Western and non-Western linguistics. And still less, to an anthropology of musicology pitted against a musicology of anthropology. The sooner Western music-historians take off their blinders of Europophilism —as practically all other Western historians have done—and go to work upon the history of non-Western musics (and their own popular and folk musics, which are now ethnomusicological data) and ethnomusicologists (hopefully, anthropological as well as musicological, and some of them non-Westerners) summon the courage to go to work upon the ethnomusicology of the music of the West, dealing with it as a whole—its professional as well as its popular and folk idioms—the better it will be for all concerned. The term "ethnomusicology" will still be valid and useful to designate an *approach* to the study of music in its social-cultural context. But the term "musicology" should cease to be considered valid to designate only the historical orientation in the study of but one of the multitude of music idioms in the world, even if its adepts would still like to regard it subjectively and ethnocentrically as the best of all possible musics merely because it is their own, or equally subjectively, but egocentrically, as the best merely because they like it more than any other. The musicality of man is too big a matter for its study to be cut up into a congeries of fortuitously divided pigeonholes. There may be more truth than is fashionable to admit, nowadays, in the ancient mystical belief that music unites what language tears apart: that it may be one of the best ways in which man may know and feel the oneness of things, just as through language he may know and feel their manyness.

CHARLES SEEGER

Institute of Ethnomusicology
University of California
at Los Angeles

ACKNOWLEDGMENTS

Indebtedness to the Alumni Annual Giving funds and the University Research Council of The University of North Carolina at Chapel Hill for aid in publication of this book is gratefully acknowledged.

Mrs. William Jenner of Chapel Hill, North Carolina, executed the musical examples.

The Reverend P. Alfonso Raes, S.J., Prefect of the Biblioteca Apostolica Vaticana, graciously supplied the illustrations from the Capella Sistina codexes for the contribution by Father José M. Llorens.

CONTENTS

AM	*Acta Musicologica*
CouS	C. E. H. Coussemaker, *Scriptorum de Musica medii aevi nova series*. 4 vols., Paris, 1864–76
JAMS	*Journal of the American Musicological Society*
MD	*Musica Disciplina*
Mf	*Die Musikforschung*
MfMg	*Monatshefte für Musikgeschichte*
MGG	*Die Musik in Geschichte und Gegenwart*. Kassel, 1949–
MQ	*The Musical Quarterly*
PMTNA	*Proceedings of the Music Teachers National Association*
RbM	*Revue belge de Musicologie*
RMI	*Rivista Musicale Italiana*
SIMG	*Sammelbände der Internationalen Musikgesellschaft*
VfMw	*Vierteljahrsschrift für Musikwissenschaft*
ZfMw	*Zeitschrift für Musikwissenschaft*

STUDIES IN MUSICOLOGY

AN UNKNOWN PRE-MADRIGALIAN

MUSIC PRINT IN RELATION TO OTHER

CONTEMPORARY ITALIAN SOURCES

(1520–1530)

Knud Jeppesen

RISSKOV

Translated by Lilian P. Pruett

By 1514 the steady stream of Petrucci's frottola editions seems to have come to an end whereas the secular publications in new editions by his Italian competitor Antico continued through several more years. The fourth book of frottole (RISM 1520[5])[1] apparently was the last of these; this item may, however, go back as far as 1517 (RISM 1517[2]), and possibly to 1513 (RISM 1513[1]).

Musico-bibliographically speaking, the decade of 1520–30 appears to be characterized by a diminishing of secular songs in Italian prints while Masses and especially motets increase significantly; in France, on the contrary, Attaingnant's chanson editions begin in abundance only from *ca.* 1528. It is particularly noteworthy, however, that in this period there appeared in Italy for the first time prints containing sacred as well as secular compositions, but not—as was often earlier assumed—indiscriminately mixed; rather, the sacred pieces are followed by a concluding section of secular songs. The oldest collection of such a combination may be the *Motetti novi e chanzoni franciose . . .* (RISM 1520[3]), followed by the *Motetti e canzone libro primo* (RISM 1521[6]). In the abecedarium B of the Colombina (f. 272′) one finds the entry: *Moteti e canzone libro primo Jo. mouton et pluriu(m) alioru(m) authoru(m). n°. 21 7307. R. 1520.*

---

1. RISM = *Répertoire International des Sources Musicales*. Volume I: *Recueils Imprimés XVIe–XVIIe Siècles, Liste Chronologique* (Munich: Henle, 1960). All further references to this bibliography are made by similar numbers.

This description, even though somewhat more detailed, coincides generally with the only other known copy of the collection, owned by the Pierpont Morgan Library in New York, and with the *Fior de motetti. . .*[2] Likewise, RISM's *Motetti et carmina gallica* (*ca. 1521*[7]) is identical with the entry in the abecedarium B (f. 272′) of the Colombina reading *Moteti novi e ca(n)zone franzose de Iusquine et altri. V. 1524* ☐ *6169* (both having the same text incipit, "Nesciens mater,"[3]) and is therefore later by three years than RISM assumes.

Also important is a print preserved in Palma and unknown to RISM: *Messa motteti Ca(n)zonni Nouamente sta(m)pate Libro Primo.*[4] Only the superius survives, but it suffices to identify the edition with the entry found in the Colombina: *Missa moteti canzoni li° p° n° 15 7780. R. 1526.* Finally, we may mention in this connection the collection *Libro Primo De La fortuna*[5] which opens with five motets followed by nineteen secular pieces, first canzone, then finally villotte. Unfortunately, the *Fortuna* print bears no date and the Colombina apparently also lacks any information concerning the matter. We may estimate the date given in RISM as being a few years too late; more on this later.

Let us consider more closely the editions which are most important in this context. The *Motetti e canzone* . . . of the Morgan Library belongs to a collection of four partbooks on paper, oblong, *ca.* 16.2 x 11.5 cm., bound in sixteenth-century brown pressed leather, containing the following prints:

1. *Motetti libro primo* (A. Antico, Venet., 1521)
2. *Motetti libro quarto* (*ibid.*)
3. *Missarum liber primus* (RISM 1521[1])
4. *Missarum diversorum authorum liber secundus* (A. Antico, Venet., 1521)
5. *Motetti e canzone libro primo* (without printer's mark or date)

---

2. RISM [*ca.* 1526] assumes that this was printed in 1526, but a copy, once available in the Colombina Library in Seville, appeared in Rome in 1523.

3. Unicum in Bologna, Civico Museo Bibliografico Musicale (CMBM), formerly the Liceo Musicale "G. B. Martini," R. 141(2), alto part only.

4. Unicum in the Cathedral of Palma, Mallorca, without colophon and date, but printed by Nicolo de Judici, who dedicated the collection to an unnamed noble patroness.

5. RISM [*ca.* 1530[1]], unicum in Bologna, CMBM, R. 141(4), without printer's mark, alto part only.

All these books were acquired by John P. Morgan; the previous owner was Lord Ashburnham who, in turn, had purchased them from the Burnham Abbey (Bucks). They appear as item 1762 in *The Libri Library Sale Catalogues* (London, 1859). The copy appears to have been temporarily in German possession; in any case, at the beginning of the bass partbook we find the inscription: "2175 / 7 alte Gesangbücher / 7 bd." One copy of the *Motetti e canzone* . . . seems once to have been in the possession of the famous Fugger family of Augsburg.[6] Unfortunately, indications of the date of printing and printer are missing in the Fugger inventory which dates from the year 1568, as they are in the Morgan Library copy; the former lists only: *Muteti Et Canzoni Lib. 1°*.

Alfred Einstein, in 1939, was the first to call attention to this significant collection.[7] He rejects the thought that this may be an Antico print, in spite of the fact that the surviving copy is bound together exclusively with Antico prints, as mentioned earlier. The character of the notation clearly opposes such an assumption. His own surmise that the book may have been printed by Giunta or perhaps Scotto[8] is, however, still unconfirmed. Of the four partbooks the superius and bass have 16 pages (one gathering of 8 sheets each) whereas the alto and tenor had 18 pages (2 gatherings of 9 sheets) of which one leaf is now missing in the tenor partbook; it is therefore probable that at one time the printer's mark and the date were given on the missing pages which, it appears, must have been available in the Colombina copy. Occasionally a somewhat confused foliation in Arabic numerals is found (recto, upper right corner) in addition to the sheet signature (recto, lower right corner) which runs continuously in the superius from AII–VIII, in the tenor from BII–IX, in the alto from CII–IX, and in the bass from DII–VIII. Only the superius shows correctly numbered pagination; in the alto the count appears as 9–12–11–11–13, in the tenor, 14–12–13–17, and in the bass, 11–14–14–14.

---

6. Gf. R. Schaal, "Die Musikbibliothek von Raimund Fugger d. J., *AM*, XXIX (1967), 129.

7. Alfred Einstein, "A Supplement," *MQ*, XXV (1939), 507 ff.

8. Alfred Einstein, *The Italian Madrigal* (3 vols.; Princeton: Princeton University Press, 1949), I, 135.

The inside of the title page in each book shows a complete table of contents listing the 21 pieces of the collection ordered as they appear in the print. The script of the text is gothic throughout with "Petrucci-like" richly embellished initials (as though by strokes of a pen), such as are mostly found in Italian music printing of this time. On the other hand, the noteheads are less ordinary: they are somewhat broad and bulky, with irregular stems more or less heavily drawn. Furthermore, there are four staves per page, not five, as is most often the case in similar Antico collections.[9]

To begin with, the contents of the collection consist of sixteen motets, partly of Netherlandish origin and partly—and this is most important—by Italian masters of the early sixteenth century who are otherwise rarely represented, such as Fra Rufino, Don Michel, Costanzo Festa, and Bartolomeo Tromboncino. Whether or not the obscure Thomas Martini was an Italian is uncertain.

Five secular songs follow, three by Rufino, which together with two motets by him make him the most heavily represented composer in the collection. The oldest source to which our print seems to be related is Petrucci's second book of laude (RISM 1508[2]), in which the same "Ave Maria," listed in our print as "Nr. 14, B. T.", appears anonymously on f. 33'–34.[10] From older sources we meet, in addition, the motets "Helisabeth beatissima" of Co. Festa,[11] "In illo tempore" by Andrea de Silva,[12] "Sicut lilium" by Brumel,[13] and "In omni tribulatione" by Moulu.[14]

There follow then five more secular songs which appear quite progressive and which could hardly date from much earlier than ca. 1515–20. Particularly noteworthy is a villotta by Fra Rufino, "Venite donne belle," which is built upon one or more folksongs. The other pieces clearly approach the madrigal. All sources

---

9. Cf. the facsimile of the cantus, p. 14, in Einstein, footnote 7.
10. The same piece appears moreover in the MS Panciatichi 27, f. 146'–147, also anonymously (Florence, Biblioteca Nazionale).
11. Bologna, CMBM, MS Q. 19, f. 52'–53.
12. Antico, *Motetti libr.* II, 1520, no. 11, anonymous.
13. *Ibid.*, no. 12, anonymous.
14. Antico, *Motetti libr.* IV, 1521, no. 14.

which contain concordances with these secular songs [15] exist in partbooks and are fully texted in all parts. Numbers 1, 3, and 4 of the Italian pieces have been published in modern editions.

The collection *Messa motteti Ca(n)zonni* . . . (brought to my attention by the Rev. R. Caldentey Prohens, librarian of the Cathedral Archives in Palma, Mallorca, in the spring of 1963) was, as previously stated, hitherto unknown. The superius partbook, the only one that is still extant, is bound in leaves of an old ecclesiastical parchment manuscript whereon is noted: Bibl. Cat. 377, Palma (Mallorca). The book consists of 16 leaves, paper, obl., 15.9 x 10.6 cm., 4 gatherings of 2 sheets, on which we find a foliation in Arabic numerals running from 1–16 as well as a sheet numbering A–D, both recto, upper and lower right, respectively. The only fairly complete and clear watermark is a half-moon which shows similarity but not exact agreement with Briquet 5211, Vicenza 1526.[16] The notation with four staves per page is technically well-executed, although the note-heads are not always exactly placed on the lines; the text script is gothic, with the exception of the dedication which is set in Roman script, and shows the usual pen-stroke initials, again excepting the dedication. On the inside of the title page is the table of contents organized according to the three forms contained in the collection. The dedication follows: "Alla Ill. Signora la S. Maria Constanza Contessa / die Maniere, Patrona sua obserua(n)dissima / Nicolo de Judici. S. D." This Nicolo is the one who in collaboration with Andrea Antico printed a collection of frottole in 1517 (RISM 1517[2]) and who, after Antico's departure from Rome, continued to work by himself, as it now appears.

The collection opens with a Mass, *Mesa de paraninphus*, ascribed by the table to *P. molu;* in this print composers' names are given only in the table of contents. The Mass appears to be unknown; in any case, the Moulu article in *MGG* does not mention it. On the other hand, the model for the Mass, the four-voice

---

15. That is, the following sources: Bologna, CMBM, MS Q. 21; Florence, Biblioteca Nazionale, MS Magl. XXIX, 164–167 and 111; Venice, Biblioteca Nazionale Marciana, the famous villotta MS (IV, 1795–98).

16. Charles Marie Briquet, *Les filigranes* (4 vols.; Leipzig, 1923).

motet *Paraninphus salutat* by Loyset Compère, is preserved in several sources, of which the oldest may be the small print, *'Altus liber secundus,* Bologna, CMBM, R. 141(1) (RISM 1521⁴).[17]

The opening Mass is followed by a section of four motets. The first and third—*Omnes sancti tui* by Hadrie(n) and *Benedicat tibi dominus* by Gascogne, respectively—are unknown to me, while the second, Verdelot's *Tanto tempore,* was very widely-known and appeared in print as early as the first book of the *Motetti del Fiore* (RISM 1532¹⁰). Among the motets is placed the single French chanson of the collection, Josquin's *Cuor langoreux,* a five-voice composition, with the quintus deriving canonically from the highest voice.[18] Finally, the table of contents lists among the motets an *Ave regina quatro sopra dui in tenor,* a work which is missing in the music part, but which was presumably identical with an anonymous composition of the same title in *Motetti novi et chanzoni franciose a quatro sopra doi* (Venezia, Antico, 1520, f. 6'–8; cf. RISM 1520³). The remainder of the collection consists of seven so-called canzonas; the term should not be understood in the strict literary-formal sense, but more simply as referring to pieces with Italian texts. Among these are three by the otherwise unknown Ant. Pretin.[19] Two of

---

17. In the first edition of *Die italienische Orgelmusik am Anfang des Cinquecento* (Kopenhagen, 1943), p. 56, I pointed out that this print must be identical with the following entry in the catalogues of the Colombina: *Moteti numero 16. libro secundo diversorum authorum. prim(u)s Jo. mouton et ultimus anton de viti. 6215. Ro. 1521* ⬜⬜. The same observation was later made by F. Lesure ("Les Anonymes des Recueils du XVIᵉ S.," *Fontes Artis Musicae,* II (1955), 38), evidently without knowledge of my remark.

Rubsamen as well touches upon the possibility that R. 141(1) may be identical wi:h the second book of Antico motets, also without knowledge of my reference [Walter Rubsamen, *Music Research in Italian Libraries* (Los Angeles, 1951)]. From a comparison of R. 141 with the copy of the Antico motet collection held by the Universitätsbibliothek Munich (RISM 1520¹ which, by the way, makes no mention of the alto partbook in the Colombina, cf. Jeppesen, *ibid.,* among others) it becomes apparent that the two prints have absolutely no connection. In spite of this RISM persists in treating the print R. 141(1) as probably identical with *Motetti libro secundo, Venezia* (*sic*), A. Antico (RISM 1521⁴).

18. The new edition of this work in the *Werken van Josquin des Pres* (Amsterdam, 1925–   ), "Wereldlijke Werken," p. 1, is based on sources of which a print from 1545 appears to be the oldest.

19. It remains uncertain whether he is the same man as *N. alias il pretino* who is known only as a singer at St. Peter's in Rome in 1539; cf. Franz X.

the songs, *Laere grauato* and *Mia benigna fortuna,* are settings of sextains of Petrarch.[20] The music of the first piece is found as No. XVII of Ms. B. 2495 in the Istituto Musicale Cherubini (Firenze), anonymous and without the alto part; that of the second piece appears in the bass partbook, Ms. γ L. M. 8, Bibl. Estense (Modena), f. 19'–20, also anonymous. Both sources may have originated between 1530 and 1540. The poem, *Questa umil fera,* set by Marcheto (Cara), is also by Petrarch (sonnet 119). The composer listings of *Rugerius* and *Seco(n)do fa re,* with the songs *O cor ne gli amorosi lacci* and *Gli e pur bella,* are completely enigmatic. Possibly, however, the former is identical with the Cesare Ruggiero who was organist at S. Petronio in Bologna at the beginning of the sixteenth century.[21] Verdelot's madrigal, *Madonna quando io v'odo,* is particularly important as it represents the earliest printed piece of the composer as well as of the category, the date of appearance thus being set at 1526. The piece is found also in CMBM, Ms. Q. 21, which served as the source for the new but anonymous edition of it by C. Gallico.[22] At the end of the publication we encounter two more anonymous secular compositions, *Ben ch'el ciel fortuna amore,* and *E quando andaratu al monte.* The latter is perhaps the most interesting piece of the whole collection, being a *centone,* a chaining-together of quotations from popular songs:

Example 1

Haberl, *Bausteine für Musikgeschichte,* III (Leipzig, 1888), 89. This study also appears in *VfMw,* III (1887) as "Die römische 'Schola Cantorum' und die päpstlichen Kapellsänger bis zur Mitte des 16. Jahrhunderts."

20. Nos. 3a, strophe 1, and 9a, strophe 1, respectively.

21. Cf., among others, Hieronimo Casio de Medici, *Libro intitulato Cronica* (Bologna, 1525).

22. C. Gallico, *Un Canzoniere Musicale Italiano del Cinquecento* (Florence, 1961), p. 183.

As mentioned earlier, the notes and rests in this print are not always placed clearly on or between the lines and unfortunately there is no possibility of making corrections through collation with other partbooks since these are missing. Those are, however, minor matters which in no way question the clear relationship to the respective folk melodies. Eight such songs are drawn upon, some rather popular, but one unknown musically and textually. The opening quotation of Example 1 belongs to one of the well-known pieces and the identity of Example 1(a) with the villotta of the same name by Jo. Ba. Zesso, found in Petrucci's seventh book of frottole, f. 55', is self-evident: [23]

Example 2

The song, apparently still alive at the end of the nineteenth century, accompanied herdsmen through four centuries as they drove their cattle into the mountains in springtime.[24] The melody de-

---

23. New edition in A. W. Ambros, *Geschichte der Musik* (Leipzig, 1911), V, 534. Note that the third note of the tenor, bar 7, in the Petrucci original correctly reads d'.

24. Cf. Emilio Lovarini, "Le Canzoni popolari in Ruzzante," *Il Propugnatore*, Nuova Serie I (1888), 291.

rives from a well-known Gregorian psalm intonation and was used in connection with a number of different texts.[25] The oldest source transmitting the melody is Giovanni Ambrosio's book of dances (*ca.* 1460) where it appears as a *ballo* entitled *Voltate in ça Rosina*. It occurs also with the text *Margaritum,* as in Example 1(c). In the Venetian dance book the melody has the text *Margaritum,* and that only. A textual variant with completely new music is seen in Lodovico Fogliano's *centone, Fortuna d'un gran tempo,* found in Petrucci's ninth book of frottole (f. 38') where the third word reads *father* instead of *mother.*

Example 2a

Related in situation but not in melody is Example 1(b), which clearly resembles the quotation in *La Bataglia Taliana* (1552) by Mathias Fiamingo in the third part of his madrigal, *Una leggiadr';* incidentally, in a textual *centone* of the second half of the sixteenth century [26] the incipit is given more fully as *Tosa to mar te chiama l'hora e tarda:*

Example 3

There follows a piece—presumably a carnival song—which compares closely to the upper part in a manuscript held by the Bibliothèque Nationale (Paris), Ms. Res. Vm[7] 676, f. 92'–93:

25. Cf. Knud Jeppesen, "Ein altvenetianisches Tanzbuch," *Festschrift Karl Gustav Fellerer* (Regensburg, 1962), p. 251.

26. Cf. S. Ferrari, "Documenti per servire all'istoria della poesia semipopolare cittadina in Italia dei secoli XVI e XVII," *Il Propugnatore,* XIII (1880), 432 ff.

Example 4

Fa – ti   be – ne a   sto   me – schi – no   Nu – do   ce – co   sor – do   e   mut –   to
non di   pa – ne   non di   vi – no   Non di   car – ne   de ri – fiù   –   to

Do   ma – don – na   (do   ma – don – na) un bo – chon – ci   –   no   di   quel

vo   –   stro   quo – ni – am   quo – ni – am   quo – ni – am

Su   –   pra   Co   –   lo – run   a   –   men.

It is found also in the famous Pixérécourt manuscript [27] and in the Colombina in Seville.[28] In the latter the piece occurs twice, once in a musically slightly varied version (f. 115'–116) and once in a completely new musical setting which seems to have no relation to the folkmusic material (f. 111'–113). Following this is a brief quotation from a song by Josquin Dascanio (des Prez), *El grillo e bon cantor,* whose only other source is Petrucci's third book of frottole (1505, f. 61'–62):

Example 5

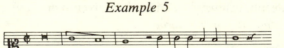

El   gril   –   lo   el   gril–lo e bon can – tor

It is perhaps questionable whether we are dealing here with an adaptation of a genuine folksong or with art-music which was later absorbed into folkmusic. We may make the same observation as regards Example 1(f) with respect to the frottola of the same name by Antonius Rossetus Veronensis in Petrucci's second book (1505, f. 28):

---

27. Bibliothèque Nationale (Paris), F. fr. 15123, f. 116'–117.
28. Codex 5–1–43.

Example 6

Che   più fe – li – ce   sor – te

Clearly from the realm of folkmusic is the following, which appears in the centone, *L'ultimo di di maggio:* [29]

Example 7

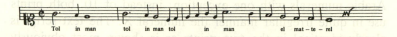

Tol   in man   tol   in man tol   in   man   el mat – te – rel

The same is doubtlessly true of the last quotation, *La bertuncina.* The melody to this piece seems to be completely unknown and has no connection, as one might possibly assume, with the ballo, *La bella berssanina,* number 11 in the Venetian dance book. Rather, it may perhaps be related to the dance, *Bertonzina,* which is mentioned without inclusion of the music in a poem about the woman who was fond of dancing.[30]

In the search for sources which might be related to the Palma print, there seems to be only one that merits serious consideration, namely, the *Libro Primo De La fortuna,* already mentioned. The chronology of this print, which is especially important for the early madrigal, has caused musical bibliographers many a headache in the course of time. First, Vogel [31] (1892) thought that 1535 might be the most probable date of printing. Einstein (1945), in his new edition of Vogel, questions such a late dating and suggests 1530 or 1529 instead. A still earlier dating is supported by Torrefranca [32] who suggests first (p. 123), that the print may be at least fifteen years older than indicated by Vogel; second (p. 401), that it must have been printed around 1515; and third (p. 409), that it appeared at the latest in 1515—all of

---

29. Bologna, CMBM, MS. Q. 21, No. XXXXVIII, II.

30. Mantua, Biblioteca Communale, MS. A. I. 4, f. 280.

31. Emil Vogel, *Bibliothek der gedruckten weltlichen Vokalmusik italiens* (Berlin, 1892), II, 379, 627. Reprinted with Alfred Einstein's revision and enlargement (originally in *Music Library Association Notes,* II–V, 1945–48) by Georg Olms (Hildesheim), 1962.

32. Fausto Torrefranca, *Il Segreto del Quattrocento* (Milan, 1939).

this without documentation. Upon comparison of this print with that preserved in Palma, it becomes surprisingly obvious that the two might almost be described as twin prints.

Let us consider first the typography of the text in the two sources. It is gothic throughout with the exception of the dedica-cation in the Palma print (the Bologna print lacks a dedication) which is set in Roman type. The *Tabulae* are in both cases set in gothic type, while in both folio references are made in Roman numerals. It is striking that despite this the foliation appears in Arabic numerals with one exception: instead of 10, both prints use in quite irregular manner the numeral X. The text script is clearly identical in the two prints as is shown most obviously through minute comparison of the very complicated and artfully executed initial letters; only the initial *P* displays some small dimensional displacements, but such displacements may be observed within the same print as well.[33] To be sure, the two papers do bear different watermarks (the head of an ox in *Fortuna*, Palma a half-moon as already described), and they also differ in format (*Fortuna:* 15 x 12 cm., Palma: 15.9 x 10.6 cm). On the other hand, both partbooks contain 16 pages (4 gatherings of 2 sheets), and the sheet foliation is the same, running alphabetically from superius to bassus. The similarity is equally clear as concerns the actual printing of the notes. Both prints use four staves of the same width and height per page. The type for the notes, heads as well as stems, and—not of least significance—the *custodes* are of the same kind. The flat signatures are identical in both prints, a little bit too small to fill a space completely and therefore appearing sometimes too high or too low. In both prints the stems of the notes upon the third line are—practically without exception—drawn in upward direction while the stems of notes above or below this line are going respectively down or up-wards,[34] a characteristic which is quite useful in correcting notes which are not clearly placed on the staves, as is frequently the case in both our prints, especially in the Palma copy.

33. Cf. *Fortuna,* ff. 6′ and 10; Palma, ff. 4′ and 7.

34. In other prints from this period we find less consequential evidence in regard to this fact; for instance, in the *Libro primo de la Croce* (RISM 1526⁶), the stems of notes on the third space and fourth line are variously placed either upwards or downwards. Especially in the prints of Petrucci does one frequently observe such haphazardness.

Tabula

P.mola	Mesa de paranin pbus	ii
	Motteti	
Uadrie	Onnes sati tui quesumus domine	v iii
Uerdelot	Zanto tempore	x
Fascogne	Benedicat tibi dominus	x
Josquin	Cuuor laguer x	x i
	Aue regina quatro sopra vui in c.uor	
	.Lazoni	
Ant.pretin	Belta come la vostra	x i
Rugerius	Ocor neglia morosi laci streto	x ii
Ant.pr.tin	Laere gruato e leportuna nebia	x iii
Ant.pretin	Mia begnin fortuna	x iii
Marcheto	Questa bumil sera	x iui
Secodo fa re	Hic pur bella questa bella	x iiii
Uerdelot	Ma cona quado io vodo	x v
	Ben chel ciel fortuna amore	x v
	E quando andaratu al monte	x vi

Messa motetti Ca(n)zonni Nouamente
sta(m)pate Libro Primo

By courtesy of the Cathedral Archives, Palma, Mallorca

P. molu. *Mesa de paraninphus.*
ibid., f. 3′

"sento tal con forte"
Altus Libro Primo De La fortuna, f. 11′

Si per bizaria   cbe regna   tutta nfain

te signoxa mia   nõ steli in   fãtafia   cbe ognor   non fuffe

to   Do barba   nicollo   prcsteme la vra putta

domã velarëvero   ff

"E si per bizaria"
ibid., f. 12′

On the whole, there are so many important correspondences between the two prints that one may safely assume that the *Fortuna* print also originated from the presses of Nicolo de Judici in Rome, and approximately at the same time as the Palma print, that is to say, *ca.* 1526. The fact that these collections thus together transmit the earliest printed madrigals of Verdelot hitherto known gives further support to the above observations and represents perhaps, chronologically viewed, the most important result of this study.

THE MUSICAL CODEXES OF

THE SISTINE CHAPEL

WRITTEN THROUGH THE GENEROSITY OF

THE PAULINE POPES

José M. Llorens
BARCELONA, INSTITUTO ESPAÑOL DE MUSICOLOGÍA
Translated by Helen Daniel

From study of the musical codexes in the Vatican Library, compiled expressly on papal commission, it may be concluded that the most important and significant contribution to the repertory of the Cappella was made by those pontiffs who took the name of Paul. The aim of the present article is to show the merit of those pontiffs who procured for their Cappella codexes of musical and artistic value. I offer this study in memory of the late illustrious musicologist and friend, Glen Haydon, researcher in the musical collections of the Vatican, who contributed many interesting studies and excellent transcriptions.

The musical codexes of the Pontifical Chapel prior to the second half of the fifteenth century have been completely lost. Repeated sackings, transfers from place to place, and lack of care, particularly of those manuscripts not in active use, explain the irreparable loss. Of their former existence there remain only references and inventories in which is found evidence of the use of Roman chant, plainsong, and polyphonic music. Thus, one reads in the *Historia Bibliothecae Romanorum Pontificum tum Bonifatianae tum Avinionensis* of Cardinal Francisco Ehrle, first, and of Mons. A. Pelzer, afterward, various descriptions of the musical codexes which existed in that library. There are mentioned in all 25 antiphonaries, 7 graduals, 2 books of motets, 5 prosarios, 2 offices of the Feast of Corpus Christi and another dedicated to the blessed Lambert. It is also known that Paul I

(757–67) sent to Pepin an "antifonario" and a "responsoriale." [1]

Nevertheless, it is evident that the College of Papal Singers did not enjoy the stability necessary for the establishment of its own *scriptorium* until the last quarter of the fifteenth century, after the Exile of Avignon and the so-called Western Schism. (For a complete and detailed account of all cited codexes see my work, *Capellae Sixtinae codices,* Biblioteca Apostolica Vaticana, 1960.)

THE CARDINAL PIETRO BARBO: POPE PAUL II (1464–1471)

Pietro Barbo, elected Pope on September 30, 1464, assumed the name of Paul II. He wished to emulate the Medici dynasty in every aspect of artistic activity and was an enthusiastic collector of coins and ancient artifacts, his anterooms constituting a museum of importance.

The Pope, satisfied with his new and magnificent palace built in the center of the city, established there his habitual residence as well as the pontifical exchequer. It may be assumed that, since the Papal Chapel lacked good collections of plainsong, the Pope contributed the magnificent examples which he had had compiled for his Chapel of St. Mark (Venice) when he was a cardinal. These books, designed for the lectern, are the most ancient preserved in the present collection of the Sistine Chapel; they bear the library numbers 5, 6, and 12. From the inscriptions which appear on f. 207 of no. 5 and f. 233 of no. 12, it may be inferred that these codexes were composed for the Chapel of St. Mark probably during the years 1451–64 when Cardinal Barbo was its titular head and perhaps nearer 1458, when the Chapel was expanded and embellished.

In churches, chapels, and cathedrals Gregorian chant enjoyed a certain prestige, which in bookmaking terms was translated

---

1. Fr. Ehrle, *Historia Bibliothecae Roman. Pontificum tum Bonifatianae tum Avenionensis . . .* I (Roma, 1890). A. Pelzer, *Addenda et emendanda ad Fr. Ehrle Historiae Bibl. Roman. Pontificum . . .* I (Bibliotheca Vaticana, 1947). Higinio Anglés, "El tesoro musical de la Biblioteca Vaticana," in *Collectanea Vaticana in honorem Anselmi M. Card. Albareda a Bibliotheca Apostolica edita* (Città del Vaticano, 1962), I, 23.

into the general use of parchment—a more noble and lasting material—and in a rich and beautiful ornamentation. As for the musical content of these codexes, it has at the present time little importance, consisting as it does of music understood and sung in a form radically different from the original. For this reason these codexes are more interesting to the liturgist, historian, and critic than to the musician.

> *Ms. 5.* 220 ff.; ff. 1–208, parchment, 209–20, paper (late addition); 550 x 390 mm.; maximum frame 510 x 380 mm., minimum frame 260 x 255 mm.; tetragrams: 2–6 per page.

A note written on f. 219ᵛ says: "Archangelus Cribellius Cappellae Pontificiae Cantor donavit MDCII." I believe that this means merely the delivery of the additional pages on paper (ff. 209–20), which contain a detailed index of the contents prepared by Crivelli for the more effective use of the codex.

The anonymous clerk makes it known (f. 207) that he has finished the compilation of the Gradual at the behest of the aforementioned cardinal: "Ad honorem Dei Reverendissimus in Christo Pater et Dominus domnus Petrus Barbo tituli Sancti Marci praesbyteri Cardinalis Venetiarum scribi fecit hoc presens Graduale." However, at the outset (f. 5) the term *Antiphonarium diurnum* is used. It is a Roman gradual, with the repertoire suitable for the Mass Propers of the feasts of the liturgical year and the saints' celebrations, concluding with some parts of the Mass Ordinary for all liturgical classifications.

Within this manuscript the calligrapher and miniaturist in fruitful collaboration have successfully produced a truly beautiful codex. The limitations imposed on this article, which must also consider other manuscripts, compel the description to be brief and concise. The codex uses Renaissance gothic letters, larger for words set to music than for spoken text. There is a notable uniformity in the contents. Minium is used for titles, incipit and explicit. Gold is used more extensively in the initial capital letters of the sentences, numerous on each page. In accord with the technique of the miniature and its manner of using gold, the capital letters form the base of the color decoration. But the place where this unknown miniaturist has applied his art with the greatest diligence is in the large initial letters drawn at the beginning of each of the festal seasons celebrated, showing the image of the commemorated saint.

The first initial (f. 5), which is the most beautiful of all and which covers the entire page, centers the figures in a frame within the letter "D," the initial letter of the text *Dominus secus mare Galileae.* This is the sole instance of lettering in gilded outline entire words accompanying the music. The figure of the Savior, standing on the broken rock of the seashore, with a castle showing in the far distance, indicates to the apostles Peter and Andrew, his brother, the spot for the miraculous catch of fish. The most characteristic feature is the clear-cut beauty of the men and the scene—like a splendid frontispiece. The border of the page is characterized by decorative floral elements dotted with numerous little balls of gold glowing like tiny suns. In the center of the lower margin, in the circumference of which are entwined the orles of the cardinal's hat, there appear the arms of the cardinal with the inscription *Petrus Barbus Venetus Cardinalis Sci. Marci.*

In striking prominence and like well-set precious stones, the miniaturist has traced very fine and elegant initials on a gilded background representing the scene of the Presentation of Jesus (f. 13), St. Agatha martyred (f. 17), the apostles Philip and James (f. 31), the feast, *In inventione S. Crucis,* with four persons attending St. Helen (f. 33), Zacharias offering the ritual incense (f. 34^v), the birth of St. John (f. 38^v), the apostles Peter and Paul with keys and sword, respectively (f. 43^v), St. Paul (f. 45), the deacon St. Lorenzo with the instrument of torture (f. 51), the Assumption of Our Lady (f. 53^v), the Birth of the Virgin (f. 57), the Dedication of the Church of St. Michael (f. 62^v), All Saints, glorified social classes (f. 67^v), St. Clement as pope (f. 69^v), and the arms of Cardinal Barbo (f. 70).

Ms. 6. 223 ff.; 530 x 380 mm.; maximum frame 505 x 370 mm., minimum frame 380 x 260 mm.; tetragrams: 1–7 per page.

In comparison to codexes 5 and 12, manuscript no. 6 appears to be of an inferior artistic quality and as though the work of a different miniaturist. Written also for the use of the Cardinal's chapel, it contains text and chant for the holy offices for Sundays and ferial days and for certain other holy days.

The figure of the psalmist, King David, appears frequently as a decorative note. The first large initial "B" of the Psalm text, *Beatus vir,* shows David accompanying himself on the trapezoidal psaltery in praise of the Lord, who looks down from the top of the miniature. A border in brilliant and varied colors features him again at the beginning of f. 4^v. The rest of the ornamentation serves as a picture frame in the center of which appears the coat of arms of the Cardinal upheld by two angels. This design is repeated (f. 39) in the initial of *Dominus illuminatio mea* except that here the angels appear on their knees looking up toward a blazing burst of light. David is again shown with the insignia of a king on f. 54^v.

The illumination of the initial "D," divided into two parts, of the text *Dixit insipiens in corde suo* (f. 69^v) shows the contrasting figures of Homo sapiens and insipiens together with the Barbo arms. For the psalm, *Salvum me fac Deus quoniam intraverunt aquae,* the miniaturist places in the two sections of the large initial "S" the figure of David covered by the waters looking toward the eternal Father (f. 85). Again, the same king surrounded by four musicians holding rebec, psaltery, flute, and trumpet illustrates the text *Exultate Deo.* The presence of singers forming a chorus may be noted in f. 123. Finally, for the beginning of Sunday vespers, *Dixit Dominus,* the miniaturist has taken the theme described in the psalm, namely, God, the Father and his Son, Jesus Christ, with the emblems of the Cardinal. Brilliant, vivid coloring with some incrustation of burnished gold is found in all the miniatures. The writing and the rest of the ornamentation, initials, titles, and incipits are similar in style to that of the calligrapher of codex no. 5.

Ms. 12. 234 ff.; 535 x 395 mm.; maximum frame 530 x 385 mm., minimum frame 395 x 250 mm.; tetragrams: 4–6 per page.

There is no doubt whatever that this manuscript complements no. 5, and was written by the same unknown scribe who states (f. 233): "Ad honorem Dei Reverendissimus in Christo Pater et Dominus Petrus Barbo Titularis Sancti Marci praesbyter Cardinalis Venetiarum scribi fecit hoc presens Graduale suis expensis."

(Cf. also f. 207 of *Ms. 5.*) Codex 12 contains the *Proprium Missae de Tempore* and *de Sanctis* from the first Sunday in Advent until the second Sunday of Passion as well as the *Ordinarium Missae* for different classes of celebration.

The figure of the Psalmist in a prayerful attitude before God the Father, surrounded by angels, appears again in the first initial of f. 4. This illumination with gilded outlines is the largest in the manuscript and belongs to the text *Ad te levavi animam meam.* The rich ornamentation which surrounds the miniature and the borders includes representations of fruit and flowers on panels of gold from which are suspended little gilded balls, like suns. In the lower center is found the Barbo crest, which is repeated frequently in the larger initials. The colors used are brilliant and vivid with a fine variety of shading. A very beautiful painting of the apostles SS. John and Peter appears incrusted on gold with the figures placed on either side of the letter "I," prominent in the text of their feast day (f. 44ᵛ). There follows (f. 47ᵛ) the scene of the Slaughter of the Innocents within the initial for *Ex ore infantium.* It ends with the figure of St. Thomas, the martyr, invested with the insignia of bishop. These miniatures are adorned with ornamental elements varied in color and of a vivid intensity. As concerns the calligraphy of the miniatures and that of the other initials of the text, the observations made in reference to the previous two codexes apply here as well. Barbier de Montault [2] mentions the following miniaturists and calligraphers who served the popes: Simon Onorato, during the years 1454–56, Nicholaus Presbyter and Clemens de Urbino, for the years 1458–64, Giacomo de Fabiano and Austino Patrizio together with the copyist Andrea da Firenze in the biennium 1462–64.[3]

THE CARDINAL ALESSANDRO FARNESE, POPE PAUL III
(1534–1549)

The enthusiasm which Paul III felt for sacred music, whether plainsong or polyphonic, is clearly revealed in the codexes written at his command. Of the whole collection which is today

---

2. Mgr. X. Barbier de Montault, *Oeuvres complêtes,* I, *Inventaires ecclésiastiques, Tome Premier, La Chapelle Papale* (Rome, Poitiers, 1889), p. 268 ff.

3. Eugène Müntz, *La Bibliothèque du Vatican au XVIᵉ siècle. Notes et documents* (Paris: E. Lereux, 1886), pp. 8, 73, 75, 97, 104.

preserved in the Sistine Chapel the most significant contributions, in terms of content as well as beauty, were compiled during his pontificate. The repertoire included here shows the degree to which, under the protection of Paul III, composers oriented sacred polyphonic music toward those aesthetic standards which the Tridentine Reform was to approve and favor. The tendency, begun earlier, to humanize an art which, because of its dry and arid liturgical style was moribund, is here accentuated in a more vigorous rhythm. It was at the court of Paul III that the Christian rebirth of beauty through the wedding of art and religious feeling was prepared, an ideal which in sacred music would mean the synthesis of liturgical spirit with the cultural manifestations of artistic sentiment.

Codexes of Gregorian Chant. Six codexes of Gregorian chant written for the chapel of Paul III are preserved (nos. 2, 3, 8, 9, 11, and 28). All are on parchment with numerous drawings and beautiful miniatures; they contain the repertory for the liturgical use of the Mass and Office.[4]

Ms. 2. 209 ff.; 560 x 417 mm.; maximum frame 560 x 417 mm., minimum frame 215 x 275 mm.; tetragrams: 2–6 per page.

The scribe has left a record of his work on f. 208: "MDXXXV. Galeacius Haerculanus, Clericus Bononienses, Scriptor S. D. N. D. Pauli PP. III eiusdem Pontificatus anno primo, hunc librum in Palatio scribebat." Another, in his turn, for ff. 145–51, "Archangelus Cribellus Magister Cappellae scribendum curavit. 1601." These last pages simply transcribe the text for Holy Friday vespers.

The complete manuscript is an antiphonary for the Triduum Sacrum (Maundy Thursday, Good Friday, Holy Saturday) of Holy Week. It contains three sumptuous pictures with corresponding borders which circumscribe the entire page. The first painting (f. 3) represents the Supper of Our Lord with properly worked out perspective and expressive countenances of a fine color. The border is formed by stylized monsters and floral

---

4. José M. Llorens, "Miniaturas de Vincent Raymond en los manuscritos musicales de la Capilla Sixtina," in *Miscelánea en homenaje a Mons. Higinio Anglés* (Barcelona, 1958–61), I, 475–98.

themes, elements suggesting the arms of Pope Farnese, little angels, and a bust of the pontiff.

Another miniature of singular beauty (f. 74) shows the figure of Jesus bearing the cross on the road to Calvary. Accompanying Jesus is a throng psychologically portrayed in his facial expression. The medallions of the picture, which is centered on the page, represent the following scenes of the Passion of the Savior: Prayer in the Garden, Betrayal of Judas, the Arrest, the Judgment, Flagellation, Crowning with Thorns, Ecce Homo, Pilate, Road to Calvary, Crucifixion, Calvary, Descent from the Cross, Burial, Resurrection, the Women at the Sepulchre, the Apparition to Mary Magdalene; little angels waving banners with inscriptions complete the ornamentation.

Comparable style and quality are evident on f. 153, which shows the burial of Jesus: the lifeless body of the Savior rests in the arms of Joseph of Arimathea. The fainting Virgin Mary is supported by the Apostle John and two pious women, while Mary Magdalene, on her knees, kisses and perfumes the feet of the Master, drying them with her long hair. Another smaller miniature which completes the lower part delineates the letter "C" with stylized drawings of birds' beaks. In the borders are abundant allusions to the Farnese arms with the motto, ΔΙΚΗΣ ΚΡΙΝΟΝ, birds symbolizing immortality, little animals, and insects. They must all be attributed to the famous papal miniaturist Vincenzo Raimondi, whose style of Michelangelesque imitation is patently evident here. The remaining initials, finely flowered, appear in gold on a multicolor background.

Ms. 3. 143 ff.; parchment; 635 x 435 mm.; maximum frame 590 x 415 mm., minimum frame 390 x 290 mm.; tetragrams: 2–6 per page.

The hands of the miniaturist and calligrapher of Ms. 2 are seen again in Ms. 3. The scribe gives evidence of his work having been completed (f. 142ᵛ): "Galeatius Herculanus Clericus Bononiensis, Anno V Pontificatus S. D. N. Dni Pauli III hunc librum ad usum suae Sacrae Cappellae scripsit, anno Domini Nostri Jesu Christi MDXXXVIIII." Another scribe (f. 66ᵛ) had the task of filling folios 60–66ᵛ: "Leopardus Antonotius, Praesbiter Auximanus scribebat anno MDCLIV aetatis suae 65, tempore pontificatus SS. D. N. D. Innocentii PP. X anno pontificatus sui XI. Existente Magistro Cappellae pro tempore R. D. Dominico Salamonio."

This Roman *Graduale* includes the Proprium Missae from Passion Sunday until the Vigil of Pentecost. On f. 2 Messer Vincenzo uses the initial "I" to represent two associated scenes from the life of the Savior: the enemies of Jesus with stones in their hands and the Master who passes unharmed among them. In the corners of the border are four medallions: the adulterous woman accused, the Resurrection of the Son of Naim, Jesus talking to the scribes and Pharisees, and the fourth remains in black, unfinished. The effigy of Paul III, emblems and symbols from the arms of the Pope, with fruits, birds, insects, and inextricable knots constitute the ornamental motif of the border. Of equal size is the miniature of f. 93 whose theme is the Savior's Resurrection and the stupefaction of the soldiers guarding the sepulchre. Decorating the margins around the picture are similar floral elements, stylized human heads with medallions for the four virtues, a bust of Paul III wearing *capa pluvial* and tiara with emblems and symbols from his coat of arms. The remaining initials are in gold on a blue and red background.

> *Ms. 8.* 130 ff.; parchment; 650 x 440 mm.; maximum frame 630 x 420 mm., minimum frame 390 x 285 mm.; tetragrams: 5–6 per page.

The similarity between this codex and no. 9 indicates 1545 as the approximate date of origin. It contains a Roman *Graduale* for Lent. The calligraphy indicates the hand of Federico Mario Perusino, the scribe for codexes 9 and 11. The single large miniature of the manuscript occupies an entire page. In the center of the initial "C" is shown the Eternal Father admonishing the first parents, Adam and Eve, following their sin; the Tree of Life, the serpent, and spade and pick complete the drawing. In the bands of the border medallions show the bust of Paul III with papal insignia, while shields and symbols with themes of flora and fauna complete the ornamentation. The remaining initials are traced out with fine drawings and gold upon a red and blue background.

Ms. 9. 111 ff.; parchment; 655 x 450 mm.; maximum frame 635 x 420 mm., minimum frame 395 x 285 mm.; tetragrams: 3–6 per page.

Ms. 9 contains the second part of an antiphonary (the first part is in no. 11) which covers the period from the first Saturday after the Octave of Epiphany up to but not including Advent. Three distichs from the mediocre talent of Euriolo Silvestri de Cingoli announce (f. 110ᵛ):

> Liminibus Jani clausis clementia Pauli
> Pontificis iussit thura cremanda Jovi.
> Praebeat ut castis faciles concentibus aures,
> Dum veniam placido poscimus ore Deum;
> Idque ut commodius fieri per saecula possit.
> Hunc scribi librum iussit: et aere suo.

And further:

> Sedente Paulo III. Pont. Max. opt.
> Anno XI secunda Octob. M.D.XLV.
> Federicus Marius Perusinus scribebat.

The five large miniatures, however, belong to Vincenzo Raimondi. The first (f. 2) represents the alliance of Jehovah with Abraham and the other patriarchs. It shows a magnificent initial in a frame, which taken as a whole recalls the mural on the ceiling of the Sistine Chapel depicting the Creation of Adam. Two cornucopias and beaks of rare birds with intertwining ribbons form the edge surrounding the initial. The border, which in turn surrounds the entire page, contains medallions with the likeness of Paul III, arms, and a rich ornamentation with elements of flora, fruit, and fauna. The second (f. 6) appears without edge or border; it shows the risen Christ holding in his left hand the Cross, as though it were a standard. Two soldiers sleeping in front of the tomb complete the drawing. Another (f. 59ᵛ) represents the Ascension of the Savior before his astonished apostles and disciples. The theme of the fourth miniature (f. 71ᵛ) is the Holy Trinity: Father and Son uphold with their right hands the Holy Spirit. Birds and stylized flowers complete the ornamentation. The last miniature (f. 78) represents a Eucharistic symbol with traces of an inferior artistic quality and was most likely executed by a different artist. The other numerous capital initials appear finely flowered in many colors.

> *Ms. 11.* 99 ff.; parchment; 653 x 460 mm.; maximum frame 610 x 415 mm., minimum frame 595 x 400 mm.; tetragrams: 4–6 per page.

This codex has been intensely studied by León Dorez in his work, *Psautier de Paul III* (cf. footnote 10). As a final rubric to the codex Euriolo Silvestri da Cingoli composed the four following distichs (f. 99^v):

> Ad lectorem
> Si te forte mouent lector speciesque decorque
> Scire quis hunc librum iusserit aere suo
> Exscribi et pingi, minima haec, ne noscere cures
> Orsa sed ingentis maxime cerne animi.
> Italie pacem, Sanctissima foedera Regum
> In Turcas classem, iustaque bella feros.
> Et Vaticanas moles et suscipe Templa.
> Qui facit aeterna haec, haecque caduca iubet.

And in continuation:

Sedente Paulo III Pont. Max. Optimo. Kalendas Aprilis MDXXXIX. Completum Federicus Marius Perusinus scribebat.

The manuscript is an antiphonary of the feast days of the saints for the whole liturgical year. Rich in both number and quality of miniatures, *Ms. 11* reveals the hand of Messer Vincenzo. On f. 1, the figure of St. Andrew, in an attitude of motion and bearing on his shoulders the Cross, occupies the principal part of the miniature. The border is formed by ornamental sketches intermingled with elements from the Farnese escutcheon. In the center of the lower part appear the emblem and device of the Pontiff. The border contains seven little figures of the virtues: prudence, justice, fortitude, temperance, faith, hope, and charity, while in the corners one finds the four evangelists.

The initial of each one of the feast days designated in the antiphonary shows the figure of the saint celebrated, as follows: f. 1ᵛ, St. Andrew saluting the Cross; f. 5, St. Lucy; f. 8ᵛ, St. Inez and an angel; f. 11ᵛ, the conversion of St. Paul; f. 15, the Purification of Our Lady; f. 17, St. Agatha; f. 21ᵛ, the Annunciation; f. 24, the Holy Trinity with an aureole of saints; f. 28ᵛ, the apostles Philip and St. James; f. 32, St. Helen; f. 34, the Nativity of St. John the Baptist; f. 36ᵛ, Zacharias in the temple; f. 43ᵛ, St. Peter and St. Paul; f. 47ᵛ, the Visitation of Our Lady; f. 52ᵛ, St. Peter saved by the Angel; f. 56, Our Lady of the Snow; f. 64, the Assumption of the Virgin; f. 69ᵛ, the Nativity of Mary; f. 72, the Exaltation of the Cross; f. 77ᵛ, the Archangel St. Michael; f. 85, St. Martin; f. 88, St. Cecilia with five angel musicians; and f. 94ᵛ, St. Catherine. The other initials—rich in color—appear finely adorned with flowers.

Ms. 28. 127 ff.; parchment; 660 x 440 mm.; maximum frame 610 x 420 mm., minimum frame 470 x 290 mm.; tetragrams: 5–6 per page.

This writer of the Cappella left a sure record of his work on f. 126ᵛ: "Galeatius Herculanus, Clericus Bononiensis, anno septimo Pontificatus S. D.N. Dni. Pauli Pape tertii hunc librum scripsit anno Domini MDXLI."

The manuscript corresponds to a Roman *Graduale* for the season of Pentecost. It contains a large, full page miniature with border—a work by Raimondi—which represents the Descent of the Holy Spirit at Pentecost. Four medallions in the corners of the border show the four virtues: prudence, justice, fortitude, and temperance, while two other medallions adorn the center at both sides with the image of Paul III in prayer. In the center of the lower margin two nude angels hold the complete papal escutcheon. Stylized flowers, little animals, birds, and insects constitute the remaining ornamentation. The other initials are in gold on blue and red.

Polyphonic codexes. The codexes which contain polyphonic music written during the pontificate of Paul III for his Apostolic Chapel bear the numbers 13, 17, 18, 19, and 24. Codexes 20 and 64 are probably from the same pontificate, the latter only after f. 14. The same cannot be said of codex 61, although it was so considered by F. X. Haberl.[5]

The compositions included in these codexes are classed as follows: 20 Masses, 32 motets, 8 Magnificats, 30 hymns, 14 antiphons, 3 Sequences, and 4 Benedicamus. Named composers are represented in addition to anonymi. The following is a tabular arrangement of the contents:

Table 1

	Masses	Motets	Magnificats	Hymns	Antiphons	Sequences	Benedicamus
Anonymous	1	2			2		
Arcadelt		8			2		
Argentil	1						
Beausseron	1				2		
Brumel		1					
Brunet						1	
Conseil		1					
De Silva		2					
Desprez		3			1		
Escobedo	1	3					
Festa			8	30	1		4
Galli		2			1		
Gascogne	2						
Hesdin	2					1	
Isaac		1					
Jachet	1	1			2		
Le Bel					1		
Lhéritier					1		
Lupi	1						
Misonne	1						
Morales	3	3			1		
Mouton	3						
Ortiz		3					
Piéton	1	2				1	
Richafort	1						
Sermisy	1						

    5. Fr. X. Haberl, *Bibliographischer und thematischer Musikkatalog des päpstlichen Kapellarchives im Vatikan zu Rom* (Leipzig, 1888), p. 66.

Of the 20 Masses only 5 parody secular themes: "Min vrien-dinne" by Lupus, "Pour quoy non" and "En satazin" by Gas-cogne, "Tristezas me matan" and "Mille regretz" by Morales. Relatively few, when we consider that in *Ms. 45* of the pontificate of Clement VII, which preceded that of Paul III, six of the 12 Masses contained in the Ms. are chanson parodies. In *Ms. 51,* belonging to the period of Innocent VIII (1484–92), the pro-portion is 11 out of 17 Masses. This is a clear indication of the strict spirit of the reform in sacred music. The compositions seem free of enigmatic canons except in the Mass "Mille regretz" by Morales where, in the Sanctus and Agnus, we find enigmatic verbal directions indicating the solutions to 3 canons: at "Mul-tiplicatis intercessoribus," "Duplicatam vestem fecit sibi," and "Breves dies hominis sunt." A canon appears in the antiphon "Salve Regina" by Desprez where the canon indication reads "Qui perseveraverit salvus erit."

The polyphonic codexes of Farnese's pontificate, like those of Paul V, are on thick, nubby paper prepared by hand, with a few thin sheets included at the beginning of some codexes.

Ms. 13. 185 ff.; paper except f. 2, parchment; 630 x 460 mm.; maximum frame 530 x 380 mm., minimum frame 400 x 350 mm.; pentagrams: 10 per page.

One can dimly see in this codex the hand of the writer Johannes Parvus.

Contained in *Ms. 13* are Masses by Argentil (1), Escobedo (1), Jachet (1), Misonne (1), Mouton (3), and one anonymous setting; also motets by Arcadelt (2), Beausseron (1), Escobedo (2) and Morales (2).

The four initials "K" of the Kyrie for each of the four parts, arranged in traditional choirbook format on the verso and recto of two leaves (f. 3ᵛ–4), show the style of Appollonio Buonfra-telli. In them appear, finely ornamented, the escutcheon and figure of Paul III with a variety of colors. The remaining initials, with line drawings, may be attributed to the pen of the callig-rapher.

Ms. 17. 143 ff.; paper; 665 x 495 mm.; maximum frame 620 x 440 mm., minimum frame 410 x 400 mm.; pentagrams: 10 per page.

This is the work of the papal clerk Johannes Parvus and of the miniaturist Vincenzo Raimondi.

The repertory of *Ms. 17* includes the principal composers of the first half of the sixteenth century from the Franco-Flemish, Spanish, and Roman schools. On the Masses appear the names of Claudin (1), Gascogne (1), Hesdin (1), Morales (2), and Richafort (1). On the antiphons, Festa (1), Fremin (1), Jachet (1), Jehan (1), and Morales (1). Illuminated initials—"K"— for the four parts are included (f. 3ᵛ–4). In the first appears the figure of St. Paul surrounded by stylized figures while in the second are drawn the Farnese shield and crest; the other two repeat symbols from the pontifical shield with the inscription *Pacis et iustitiae cultor,* while the marginal bands of both folios are formed by geometrical drawings in blue on gold ground. The remaining initials, with linear calligraphical drawings, may be attributed to the copyist.

> *Ms. 18.* 197 ff.; paper except ff. 3–4, parchment; 650 x 460 mm.; maximum frame 540 x 390 mm., minimum frame 160 x 350 mm.; pentagrams: 10 per page.

Ms. 18 was written in the year 1539, probably by Johannes Parvus. Only 2 antiphons in the Ms. are of unknown authorship; all other compositions belong to Constanzo Festa, the composer most frequently appearing in the codexes of Paul III. This manuscript includes 30 hymns for various festal days, 8 Magnificats, and 4 Benedicamus. In the hymns, polyphonic music alternates with Gregorian chant. Vincenzo Raimondi reveals his art in the four initials on the parchment sheets (f. 3ᵛ–4), on which the letter "Q" is embellished in each of the four voice parts. The first is bordered and shows the complete escutcheon of Paul III in the center; rainbow, lilies, and the Farnese blazon appear in the second, keys in the third, and the inscription *Paulus III. Pontifex Max. Anno V* in the fourth. In the lower margin of f. 3ᵛ may be read *Constan. Festa in Advent. D. N. I. Melos,* while on f. 4 are seen two red lions supporting the fleur-de-lis. The remaining initials at the beginning of each composition come from the pen of the amanuensis.

Ms. 19. 168 ff.; paper; 650 x 500 mm.; maximum frame 625 x 480
mm., minimum frame 460 x 460 mm.; pentagrams: 10 per page.

Although without date, this manuscript belongs to the pontificate of Paul III, as may be deduced from the decoration of
several pages with the shield and emblem of the aforesaid Pope.

The collection comprises 6 Masses, by the following composers: Beausseron, Gascogne, Lupi, Morales, Piéton, and Hesdin; 7 motets by Brumel, Arcadelt, Johannes de Ferrara
(Johannes Galli), Maistre Jehan (Johannes Galli), Josquin
Desprez, Morales, and one anonymous; and 2 antiphons—one
each by Beausseron and Lhéritier.

The four first initials (f. 3ʳ–4), which correspond to the letter
"K" of the Kyrie in the four respective vocal parts of the *Missa
de Beata Virgine* by Beausseron, give evidence of Vincenzo Raimondi's hand. The lines of the upper initials are traced with
folded ribbons and those of the two lower with vines. In addition, the first bears the image of Our Lady giving the breast to
her divine Son, and the others show the shield and emblem of
Paul III. The ornamentation in them all is characterized by elements of flora and fauna. The remaining initials are of notable
proportion and with their lines traced in black.

Ms. 24. 151 ff.; paper; 647 x 450 mm.; maximum frame 570 x 405
mm., minimum frame 425 x 365 mm.; pentagrams: 10 per page.

This is the collection which contains the oldest repertory of the
entire group belonging to Farnese's pontificate, even though the
Ms. bears a relatively late date, 1545 (f. 100). The 26 compositions are by the following composers: Arcadelt, 6 motets and 1
antiphon; Desprez, 3 motets; Consilion, 1 motet; Escobedo, 1
motet; Hesdin, 1 sequence; Brunet, 1 sequence; Isaac, 1 motet;
Jachet, 1 motet and 1 antiphon; Oritz, 3 motets; Piéton, 2 motets
and 1 sequence; Andreas de Silva, 2 motets; and by an unknown
composer, 1 motet. The motet, *Corona aurea,* by Arcadelt was
created especially for the coronation of the Roman pontiff and
his anniversary. This codex is lacking in miniatures having only
initials with broad calligraphic tracings in black.

THE WRITERS OF THE PAPAL CHAPEL OF PAUL III

Not all of the codexes bear the name of the writer of the text and of the music. During this period the same copyist did the text and the musical notation, although much later a differentiation was made through the terms *harmoniographus* and *ortodographus*. Of three regular copyists in the Cappella, two were employed for Gregorian, the third for polyphonic notation. Both the notation and the text appear in all the codexes with large, clear, and elegant characters. The names signed here agree with those found in the books of the Tesorería Secreta and of the pontifical exchequer on the monthly payrolls, being listed after those of the singers. In fact, on February 1, 1534, Galeazzo Hercolano first appears in place of Aloysius Cassanensis.[6] Hercolano served as writer until January 1, 1548; his colleague was Federico Mario de Perugia. This entry will serve as an example: "Adi 28 febraro 1545 ▽ (escudos) quindeci pagati a ms. Federico et a ms. Galeazzo scrittori di Capella di N.S., sono per rigatura di carte, inchiostro, vernice et altre cose per lor servicio."[7]

Federico outdid Galeazzo in beauty and neatness of penmanship. He began his official duties in September, 1538, occupying the vacancy of Johannes Occhon.[8] When Hercolano stopped writing, the whole task of copying fell upon Federico, double work paying a double stipend. Federico received, moreover, twelve escudos for the purchase of "inchiostro, vernice, genabrio et altre cose appartenenti al suo esercitio."[9] Federico was without doubt the most esteemed calligrapher in Rome. Consequently, the Pope turned over to him the writing and ornamentation of the *Psalter*,[10] for which Raimondi did the miniatures: ". . . e per comprare oro macinato per fare lettere maiuscole al detto Salmista."[11] Federico was employed moreover by the Cap-

---

6. Roma, Archivio di Stato, *Mandati Camerali,* v. 864, f. 204.

7. *Ibid.,* v. 1293, f. 8.

8. *Ibid.,* v. 870, f. 171.

9. *Ibid.,* v. 1291, f. 52.

10. Léon Dorez, *Psautier de Paul III. Reproduction des peintures et des initiales du manuscrit latin 8880 de la Bibliothèque Nationale, précédée d'un essai sur le peintre et le copiste du Psautier* (Paris: Berthaud Fréres, 1909).

11. Roma, Archivio di Stato, *Tesorería segreta,* an. 1540–1543, f. 41.

pella Giulia and by Mons. Alfonso Oliva for the Church of St. Augustine of Rome and for the Augustinian Convent of Acquapendente. His work ceased in 1554, the year of his death.

Federico was followed by Johannes Parvus, or Johannes Petit de Seulis. The latter is always considered as the writer of *canto figurato*. The codexes which he wrote for the Papal Chapel are extremely numerous, as he spent a long life devoted to the service of the Popes. Although he did not hold an official title until May of 1540, there are recorded some previous payments to Johannes Parvus: "A di 16 agosto 1538, 25 pagati a Ioanni Petit, scrittore di Capella per alcune spesse fatte per la detta Capella." [12]

In addition to the writers, there are frequent references to *Loysi ligatore dei libri* and *Martino cartolaro*. In fact, "A di 22 maggio 1545. ▽ (escudos) undice a mo. Aloysio ligatore de libri per ligatura di un libro grande di canto fermo in carta pecora con soi fornimenti de ottone et ligatura di un altro libro grande di canto figurato per servicio de la Capella." [13] Only once is Juan Escobedo mentioned as a writer of *musica figurata* with the amount of 12 escudos by way of "mancia." [14] This Spanish copyist entered the service of the Cappella in 1554, remaining until his death in 1566.

THE PAPAL MINIATURIST

The presence of the miniaturist is evident in all the codexes of the Cappella of Paul III with the exception of *Ms. 24*. He was not, however, as were the scribes, considered a member of the Cappella. Consequently, he did not participate in the monthly salary nor in the benefits and privileges accorded his fellows. He did, however, receive a suitable recompense for the work accomplished, for example:

"A di 22 di giugno ▽ (escudos) cento et vintisette a messer Vincentio Raymondo, miniatore della capella et Sacrestia di N. S. quali sono per resto della summa delli ▽ 457 quali se li pagha per conto saldo di tutti quelli libri miniati et stimati da fra

12. Léon Dorez, *La Cour du pape Paul III d'après les registres de la Trésorerie secrète*. Collection F. de Navanne. (Paris: E. Lereux, 1932), p. 239.
13. Roma, Archivio di Stato, *Mandati Camerali*, v. 1293, f. 11.
14. Léon Dorez, *La Cour du pape Paul III . . .* , II, p. 134.

Bastiano, piombatore et mastro Perino del Vaga, pittore, presente il R. Monsignor de Ascisi, Mastro di Capella." [15]

The first pope to include the miniaturist in his household was Paul III, who chose Vincenzo Raimondi, whose appointment was made official by a special mandate of May 27, 1549.[16] Prior to this, Raimondi had already been paid 1,743 escudos for work on the musical codexes for the Cappella of Pope Farnese. None of the miniatures described are signed by the artist. Nevertheless, payroll entries and other notes from the papal archives have permitted us to trace Raimondi and to recognize the unmistakable style of an artist who, in the judgment of Benvenuto Cellini, best realized the miniaturistic art of painting.

Worthy of mention, in addition to these books of music, are those no less beautiful ones belonging to the Papal Sacristy of Paul III: Missals, lectionaries, psalters, and others for liturgical use. Of great interest is the account of these found in Monsignor Barbier de Montault's inventory of all the objects in the Sacristy of Paul III in the year 1547. Within the great variety of items listed one notes the many books artistically decorated for the use of the pope, prelates, and high dignitaries who officiated in the Cappella. The finger marks and edges worn by much handling attest to frequent use. These books are now scattered among various museums and libraries in England, the United States, and France.

These remarks would be incomplete without alluding to the second volume of Masses, no. 180, printed in Rome, 1544, by the brothers Valerio and Luis Dorico; the composer, Cristobal de Morales, dedicated the volume to Paul III, his protector. In the frontispiece the Spanish composer is depicted offering his work to Paul III, who receives it from him with satisfaction, bestowing upon him his blessing.

CARDINAL CAMILO BORGHESE, POPE PAUL V (1605–1621)

Paul V always took a particular interest in the increase and splendor of liturgical ceremonies. He presided at public religious

---

15. Roma, Anchivio di Stato, *Tesorería segreta,* an. 1545–1548, f. 92.
16. José M. Llorens, *Miniaturas de Vincent Raymond . . .* , p. 476.

functions which were celebrated in the city, with greater frequency than his predecessors, and through his presence infused them with new vigor, a characteristic which was commented on by contemporaries. The cantors of the Cappella were carefully selected, and in not a few cases through the personal intervention of the Pope. Among other references is that of Orazio Barzotti of Rome, secretary from the year 1614:

"Primo di novembre. Doppo il vespero si congregarono li Sig. cantori in Cappella de Xisto 4 li quali furno no. 18 per dare la cotta al Sig. Cosimo Corselli, fiorentino, basso il quale doppo d'havere cantato un terzo in presentia di N. S. al vespro di tutti Santi, la mattina alla messa un quarto et el giorno una lettione de Morti si compiacque N. S. d'ordinare subito al R^{mo}· Sig. Paolo Alaleona (Master of ceremonies) che chiamasse il Sig. Paolo Facconio (maestro di cappella) et dicesse che era piaciuto a N. S. il detto Basso, ma che voleva che lo ricevessimo secondo le nostre Constituzioni et uso." [17]

In order to fill the vacancy of Felice Anerio a competition was arranged among eighteen singers, of which only two were chosen, but with the proviso:

"Havendo comandato Sua Santita che sinche non erano stati sentiti da lui non si facesse altra risolutione." [18]

This condition was met in Vespers I and Mass of All Saints, Ludovico Petrosti, contralto, and Giovanni Falbo, basso, being chosen.[19]

The codexes written for the Chapel of Paul V are numbers 7, 25, 33, 43, 47, 52, 59, 68, 77, and 91. All are on heavy paper and contain polyphonic music except no. 7, which is written on parchment and consists of Gregorian chant. The composers represented are: Felice Anerio, 1 psalm; Octavio Catalani, 1 psalm; Archangelo Crivelli, 6 Masses, 1 motet, and 2 psalms; Teofilo Gargari, 3 psalms, and 1 offertory; Rogerio Giovanelli, 2 psalms; Johannes Mouton, 1 motet; Romulo Naldi, 1 Magnificat; Giovanni Maria Nanino, 1 motet; Flaminio Oddi, 4

17. Roma, Biblioteca Vaticana, *Diarii Sistini*, v. 32, f. 47^v.
18. *Ibid.*, v. 33, f. 35^v.
19. *Ibid.*, v. 33, f. 35^v.

Masses; and Palestrina, 13 Masses, 5 motets, and 38 offertories. The supremacy of him who was considered "Princeps musicae" is quite evident.

> *Ms. 7.* 51 ff.; paper; 593–420 mm.; frame 420 x 280 mm.; tetragrams: 3–6 per page.

This is the handiwork of the papal scribe Josephus Dosius, as is noted on f. 2: "Paulo V Pont. Max. Nicolao de Fanis Monteneanen. existente Magistro Cappellae, Josephus Dosius Placentinensis scribebat anno Domini MDCXIX." Contained in *Ms. 7* are Gregorian chants for vespers on ferial days. The larger initials are in red and blue without adornment and from f. 13 on they remain unfinished. The smaller initials and titles are frequently in red; in addition, in some empty spaces, there are ornamental tracings in black. The binding is contemporary with the manuscript, with wooden boards covered with leather, clasps and bosses of metal. The insignia of the Pope are engraved on both covers.

> *Ms. 25.* 166 ff.; paper; 560 x 405 mm.; maximum frame 500 x 287 mm., minimum frame 475 x 283 mm.; pentagrams: 8 per page.

This is a manuscript bequeathed by the author to the Cappella. The following quotation is from f. 2: "Archangelus Cribellius presbyter Bergomensis Cappellae Pontificiae ex legato dicavit, Hercule Ferruccio magistro pro tempore existente, Dominicus Brancadorus scribebat MDCXVII." This is confirmed in the Diario of the 5th of May, 1617: "Il detto Sig. Archangelo ha lasciato per testamento cinque messe esse quale voleva stampare, alla Cappella che le tenghi per sua memoria, con patto che si faccino copiare in buona forma a spesse delli heredi, non havendo esso havuto in tempo di stamparle, ha fatto anco un'opera pia che ha lasciato tutto il suo per amor di Iddio in diversi luoghi pii, cosa degna di eterna memoria." [20] This note was added by the secretary Lorenzo Marubini da Castiglione, a Florentine.

The volume in question contains Masses: *Credo maius* in 4 voices, *Petrus Apostolus, a4, Sumens illud ave, a5, Euro gentil,*

---

20. *Ibid.,* v. 36, f. 14.

a5, Domini est terra, a5, and *Canite tuba in Sion, a6.* Brancadoro chose to adorn the Ms. in an unprecedented way. In the ornamental bands which are interlaced in each of the initials of the cantus, altus, tenor, and bassus parts of the last Mass (f. 128ᵛ–162) he inserted names and country of origin of the singers active at that time in the Collegio. The remaining bands show figures with flowery lines in black.

> *Ms. 33.* 112 ff.; paper; 725 x 515 mm.; maximum frame 725 x 460 mm., minimum frame 480 x 385 mm.; pentagrams: 8–10 per page.

Here we have a model which was submitted in competition for the position of papal writer, as is indicated on f. 2: "Paulo V. P. M. Horatio Griffio Cappellae Magistro pro tempore motetta conscripta a variis amanuensibus decertantibus de munere scribendi in Pontificali Sacello Anno MDCX." The contents comprise 3 motets by Palestrina, 1 motet and 1 psalm by Crivelli, 1 motet by Nanino, 2 psalms by Felice Anerio, 1 Magnificat by Naldi, and 4 unsigned psalms. The initials are simply traced in black. The binding is similar to that of *Ms. 25:* wooden boards covered with skin, with clasps and bosses of metal, and escutcheons of Paul V and of the cardinals Jaime Serra and Antonio Gallo appearing on both covers.

> *Ms. 43.* 161 ff.; paper; 558 x 415 mm.; maximum frame 530 x 375 mm., minimum frame 220 x 300 mm.; pentagrams: 4–8 per page.

Domenico Brancadoro is the writer of this manuscript dating from the year 1619 (f. 75). It is a collection of 38 offertories selected from the two editions printed "apud Franciscum Coattinum" in Rome, 1593, and "apud Angelum Gardanum" in Venice, 1594. The initials are adorned in black. The binding is of contemporary skin-covered wooden boards with clasps and bosses of metal.[21]

> *Ms. 47.* 165 ff.; paper; 550 x 400 mm.; maximum frame 520 x 355 mm., minimum frame 210 x 320 mm.; pentagrams: 8–9 per page.

This is again the work of the writer Domenico Brancadoro, with the date 1616. It contains 6 Masses by Palestrina; three of

---

21. Roma, Biblioteca Vaticana, *Cappella Sistina,* v. 549, 595.

them—*O admirabile commercium, Memor esto,* and *Octavi Toni* —were newly copied by Tomas Altavilla in 1708. The initials are in black. When the manuscript was restored in 1724, it was bound with wooden boards covered with leather, with clasps and bosses of metal.

> *Ms. 52.* 99 ff.; paper; 515 x 375 mm.; maximum frame 500 x 360 mm., minimum frame 290 x 287; pentagrams: 6–9 per page.

For this we are indebted to another papal writer, Ippolito Fersino, working during the years 1612–13 at the behest of Stefano Ugerio. It is another collection of 3 Masses by Palestrina with the initials likewise adorned in black. This manuscript, owing to wear caused by constant use, has mended borders and margins. The binding is of the period with boards of heavy paper covered in parchment.

> *Ms. 59.* 60 ff.; paper; 590 x 410 mm.; maximum frame 480 x 375 mm., minimum frame 420 x 320 mm.; pentagrams: 6–8 per page.

Seven psalms are contained in this Ms., three by Teofilo Gargari, two by Ruggiero Giovanelli, one by Giovanni Crivelli, and another by Ottaviano Catalani. The order of these compositions was rearranged in 1632 according to a note on f. 2: "Quae diversis temporibus fuerunt conscripta existente pro tempore magistro Capellae R. D. Aldobrando Trabochio in unum fuerunt collecta. Anno Domini MDCXXXII." The first two psalms by Gargari (f. 3–14), written by Dosio, bear the date of 1620; there follow those by Giovanelli and by Crivelli, copied by Brancadoro in 1617 (f. 33ᵛ–34), and finally that of Catalani, also the work of Brancadoro. The initials are ornamented in black. The contemporary binding is of boards of heavy paper covered in parchment bound with clasps.

> *Ms. 68.* 114 ff.; paper; 570 x 410 mm.; maximum frame 485 x 310 mm., minimum frame 250 x 280 mm.; pentagrams: 8 per page.

Brancadoro wrote *Ms. 68* in 1618. Four Masses by Palestrina are contained here. The initials have calligraphic adornment in black.

Ms. 77. 108 ff.; paper; 460 x 370 mm.; maximum frame 444 x 315 mm., minimum frame 377 x 300 mm.; pentagrams: 4–10 per page.

Rearranged in the same year as *Ms. 59,* 1632, there are collected in this volume 2 unsigned motets, the first of which can be ascribed to Mouton, and 4 Masses by Flaminio Oddi, as indicated on f. 1: "Quae diversis temporibus fuerunt conscripta existente pro tempore magistro cappellae R. D. Aldobrando Trabochio in unum fuerunt collecta anno Domini MDCXXXII." At the end of each Mass the composer, Flaminio Oddi, signed his name and added: *Laus Deo et eius Genetrici.   1611.* In the first Mass, *Sicut lilium inter spinas,* he wrote this dedication: "D. D. meis observandis Musicis et Cantoribus Cappellae Pontificiae 1612." The initials to f. 4ᵛ–5 are adorned with tracings while the rest appear only in black. The binding is from the date of the collection, with boards of heavy paper covered in parchment.

Ms. 91. 35 ff.; paper; 800 x 530 mm.; maximum frame 716 x 435 mm., minimum frame 355 x 414 mm.; pentagrams: 6–11 per page.

This codex is composed of three works written in different years. The works are 2 Magnificats by Teofilo Gargari and 1 unattributed motet, *Beatus Laurentius,* which is now identified as by Palestrina. The first composition, by the hand of Dosio, dates from 1620, the year in which Gargari served as *maestro di cappella;* the second also was copied by Dosio, at the beginning of the pontificate of Gregory XV, in 1622; the third was copied for Cardinal Francesco Barberini by Leopardus Antomotius. The initials, as usual, are in black.

Ms. 31. 124 ff.; paper; 720 x 490 mm.; maximum frame 610 x 430 mm., minimum frame 475 x 260 mm.; pentagrams: 8–9 per page.

The ascription of this manuscript to the Pauline Popes is questionable. There is no date, but the hand of Lucas Orpheus Fanensis, who died in the year 1608, is recognizable. Taking everything into consideration, *Ms. 31* could belong to the pontificate of Clement VIII (1592–1605). The composers included are Giovanelli with 2 psalms, Nanino with 5, Crivelli with 2,

Felice Anerio with 2 psalms and 1 Magnificat, and Gargari with 1 Magnificat. This manuscript was probably the last written by Orfeo in the Cappella, since he left it unfinished. In fact, ff. 1–2 were left blank for the frontispiece and index, an omission remedied by a later scribe. Since these compositions do not belong with certainty to Paul V's pontificate, I have not included them in the total number previously mentioned.

Numbers 171 and 172, which Haberl ascribes tentatively, certainly belong to this period, but they were not written for the papal chapel nor through the munificence of Paul V. Notes written in the initials of ff. 18 and 19 are quite clear: *Collegii Germanici Pater Harmann Oberker et Johannes Thomas Cunonius.*

THE COPYISTS FOR PAUL V

The renaissance of the miniature toward the second half of the fifteenth century, rivaling its elder sister painting, ends in our codexes with the outstanding contributions of Vincenzo Raimondi and of his collaborator Appollonio Buonfratelli. From that time on miniature artistry declines and dies; it is the moment at which predominance of printing is established. Consequently, the importance of the miniaturist is minimized. The illuminators of initials limited themselves to flowery tracings in color or black, very similar to those reproduced by the printing presses.

Hence, Paul V did not have a miniaturist in his chapel, although his scribes continued to produce works of painstaking calligraphy. Scribal appointment was obtained through competition; there survives an account on this subject from the *Diario:* "Venerdi a di 20 di xbre 1619. Finita la messa si cominció la congregatione, si disse el Veni Sancte Spiritus con l'orationi solite e di poi il Sig. Mastro ordinó alli scrittori quello che havevano da fare et da scrivere et da li a poco comparse il Sig. Biasio Stocchi qual vien puntato come farò più a basso. Scritto che hebbero ciascheduno di loro le loro mostre furno chiamati dentro tre periti et furno tutti tre di opinione che fusse la meglio quella del Sig. Giuseppe Dosio, et il Sig. Mastro disse che il Sig. Cardinale Borghese gli haveva detto che ogni volta de detto Sig. Dosio fusse idoneo haveria tanto piacere che havesse il loco sicome ne fece fede il Sig. Gio Domenico Puliaschi familiare di Sua Sig^a. Illma. il quale raccomandava a tutti detto Dosio. Finalmente fu preso viva voce dandogli ciascuno il voto a voce publica cominciando il Sig. Mastro, di poi il decano gradatim sino al fine, ognuno disse essere il meglio e cosi hebbe da tutti il voto publico et detto Sig. Dosio piglio allora il possesso datogli dal Sig. Mastro e ringratiò tutti dal favor fattoli." [22]

Let us point out first, in chronological order, Lucas Orfeo de Fano. In 1587, he was already a scribe for the Cappella, and, as he was anxious to sing with the chapel singers, he asked repeatedly to be admitted there. Cardinal Gallo favored his application: "A di 7 giugno 1587 l'Illmo. Sig. Cardinale Gallo nostro protettore ci ha mandato a dire che pigliamo m. Luca da Fano nostro scrittore della Cappella per cantore sopranumerario il qual dice non voler niente dalla Cappella se non che lo lassiamo cantare con la cotta. Non è stato ne provato ne esaminato ma solamente datoli la cotta." [23] The secretary Nicolò Fanti registered in the *Diario,* vol. 28, f. 58, the death and funeral of Orfeo: "Ultima d'ottobre 1608 il Sr. Luca da Fano laborat in extremis." (f. 58^v) "Prima Novembris 1608: Hoggi è morto il Sig. Luca da Fano circa le 22 hore. N. S. l'habbia in Gloria. 2 Domenica: Doppo l'offitio s'è datta sepoltura a Luca da Fano in Sto. Honofrio fu accompagnato da tutto il Collegio di cantori e dalli mastri delle ceremonie conforme al solito."

Orfeo was succeeded by Giuseppe Antonello within a few days (f. 59): "Marti 4 Novembris 1608. A hor. 15 e mezza il Rdo. Collegio de Cantori si congregó nella Capella di Sisto dove celebrò messa bassa il Sr. Arcangelo Crivello, doppo la quale il detto Collegio havendo havuto in consideratione l'ottima sufficienza dello scrivere in canto figurato del Sr. Giuseppe Antonello et considerando aver inoltre altre buone qualità de detto soggetto et haverlo fatto diligente che in Roma non n'era di meglio soggetto nello scrivere di questo, si risolve pigliarlo per scrittore di capella, come meglio si potrà veder nell'istromento fatto per mano del Sr. Archangelo nostro notaro." The name of Antonello

---

22. Roma, Biblioteca Vaticana, *Diarii Sistini,* v. 38, f. 58^v.
23. *Ibid.,* v. 16, f. 29.

disappears from the records in 1613 and in its place we find Ippolito Fersini or Persini. The volume corresponding to the year 1612 is lacking and thus it cannot be known with certainty when Antonello's scribal activities ceased.

Fersini, in his turn, served until 1617, when he was replaced by Domenico Brancadoro, who had as his assistant and collaborator Giuseppe Dosio. Brancadoro died December 3, 1619, and we are told about his funeral Mass by Domenico Tombaldini in the *Diario,* vol. 38, f. 55: "Domenica à di 8 di xbre 1619. Il Sig. Mastro propose se si doveva andare collegialmente a fare l'essequie al Sig. Domenico Brancadoro gia defonto scrittor della Cappella del canto figurato e fu risoluto, che per essere stato lui solicito e diligente si doveva andare a cantarli la messa per l'anima sua e si andara martedi per essere il settimo doppo la sua morte. Disse anco che il concorso si farà alli 20 di questo presente mese, cioè dello scrittorato. (f. 55ᵛ) Martedi a di 10. Si andò a far l'essequie alla bona memoria del scrittor di canto figurato ms. Domenico Brancadoro a Santa Caterina delli Funari."

And so, as had been announced, on December 20, 1619, the competition to fill the vacant place of the scribe took place. (The text has already been transcribed.)[24]

For the copying of Gregorian chant, from long before the pontificate of Paul V, the Cappella had counted on the services of Luigi Mercato. Because of his precarious health, in 1620, it was decided to combine the duties of Luigi Mercato with those of the polyphonic music copyist in the person of Dosio; *Diario,* vol. 39, ff. 46–47: "Adi Pᵒ d'Agosto 1620. Finita la mesa il Sʳ. Mastro prego tutti li SSʳⁱ compagni che si fermassero un pocho per ragionare d'un negᵒ.(zio) importante al serve.(izio) e reputatᵉ(ione) della nostra Cappˡᵃ et essendo cosi tutti congregati il sopraᵒ(detto) Sʳ Mastro mese in consideratione a tutti che dovendosi scrivere in bellissima forma li canti fermi riformati dal detto Sigʳ Mastro per ordine del Collegio, ne potendo durar questa fatica il Sigʳ Luigi Mercati come vecchio et infermo, ne trovandosi al presente soggetto alcuno che possa dar maggior sodisfatione si nella scritura, come nella meniatura (cosa neces-

---

24. Cf. pp. 42–43.

sarissima alla reputatione della Capp[la] come si vede da libri antichi) che l'Sig.[r] Giuseppe Dosio nostro scritore del Canto Figurato il quale può molto bene esercitar l'uno et l'altro uff°. si per esser manieroso et sufficientissimo in ogni sorte di canto, si anco per che scrive presto et bene et volentieri.

Però concluse che li pareva molto ben fatto quando tutti fussi stato con bona sodisfatione di tutti confirmarlo nella sostitutione del Canto fermo cum futura successione giachè il detto Sig[r] Dosio esercita et scrive continuamente i Canti fermi, che bisognano per la Cappella. Et se bene questo par che sia novità per esser anticho stile, che li scrittori siano due persone, cioè uno per il canto fermo et l'altro per il canto figurato non di meno non ha far difficoltá alcuna per esser il sopra detto Sig.[r] Dosio scritor così celebre et per dar esso solo maggiore sodisfatione alla Cappella che due scrittori.

Dichiarando che non si intenda mai per nissun tempo, che alcuno possa prettender di haver tutti due questi uffitij, se però non havesse le med.[me.] circunstantie et qualità che ha il detto Sig[r]. Dosio al quale però di dia questo altro carico del canto fermo pro hac vice tantum. A questa proposta del Sig. Mastro tutti li Sig.[ri] Cantori viva voce, nemine discrepante per esser molto bene informati delle qualità di questo soggeto acconsentirno et si contentarono di confirmarlo nel detto canto fermo protestando che per l'avenire ciouè dopo il Sig[r]. Dosio intendono che la Capp.[la] habbi due scrittori, ne mai si acconsensi in nesun altra persona sola se non si vedrà effettivamente per esser che fusse meritevole et atta à essercitar l'uno e l'altro uffitio con sodisfatione, et reputatione dalla nostra Cappella.

Il Sig[r]. Mastro ringratiò tutti e partiti che furono se n'ando dal Sig[r]. Cardinale del Monte Prottetore a darli conto di tutto questo fatto et S. S[ria]. Illma. per esser ben informato del valor di questo homo, lodó la proposta del Sig[r]. Mastro, et insieme la resolutione di tutta la Cappella."

In the preceding account is mentioned the task of writing *in bellissima forma li canti fermi riformati dal detto Sig. Mastro*. In the chapel archives there is no manuscript conforming to this description. There does exist, however, *Graduale de Sanctis iuxta ritum Sacrosanctae Romanae Ecclesiae cum Cantu, Pauli V*

Pont. Max iussu reformato. Romae ex Typographia Medicea, anno MDCXIIII.[25]

Saint Paul recommended to the Colossians and to the Ephesians, "loquentes vobismetipsis in psalmis, et hymnis et canticis spiritualibus, cantantes et psallentes in cordibus vestris Deo." The pontiffs who took the name of Paul during their times in office brought to fruition this desire of the Apostle through the medium of the worthiest and most expressive musical language which the art of their time offered. By preference they devoted attention to liturgical chant, called Gregorian by antonomasia, a legacy of the Old Testament in its form and a legacy of the New Testament in its expression; a legacy which from Christian Rome has spread with the faith, and reaches our time with its characteristics of artistic goodness, holiness, and catholicity. For the codexes containing this precious and sacred repertory, these Popes procured the noblest material, parchment, and the richest ornamentation, the miniature. And, in conclusion, they held unaccompanied polyphony as being the most artistic and sublime medium of elevation expressed through the simultaneous joining of voices "ad Dei gloriam et animarum salutem."

---

25. Roma, Biblioteca Vaticana, *Cappella Sistina,* v. 347, 348. Concerning this edition it is well to note that, in spite of its title *Iussu Pauli V,* it never had an official status. The editor Raymondi had to be satisfied with an entirely personal breviary, authorized in 1608, wherein he is recognized as originator and editor. These were years during which chapel masters "corrected" and adapted Gregorian chant to their own taste much to the detriment of the true musical sense of chant.

Cappella Sistina, codex 2, f. 153

Cappella Sistina, codex 6, f. 123

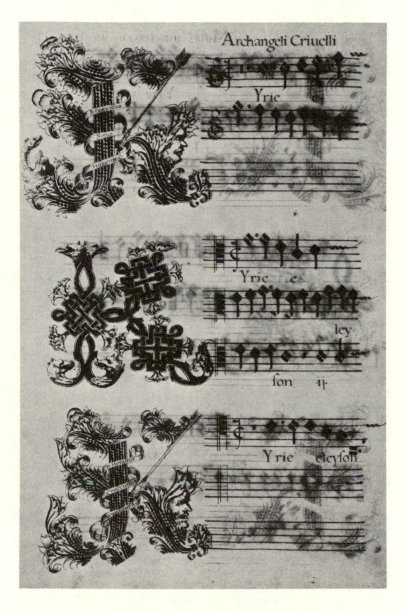

Cappella Sistina, codex 25, f. 128′

Cappella Sistina, codex 611, f. 1'

A CATALOGUE OF

TYE'S LATIN MUSIC

John Satterfield
ELMIRA COLLEGE

Several musicologists have listed the extant works of Christopher Tye and the manuscripts which contain them. Printed lists meant to be complete are by Eitner,[1] Arkwright,[2] and Noble.[3] Weidner has recently revised the catalogue of Tye's instrumental music,[4] while the English music by Tye seems still to need a new examination; my present purpose is to present a catalogue of the composer's Latin music, resolving differences among earlier catalogues and correcting errors in them. The revision presented here comes from a transcription of all the complete Latin pieces by Tye[5] and from an inspection of the actual manuscripts during January, 1965.

Fragments and pieces wanting one or more parts do not appear in the catalogue. All of the sources are in England; apparently

1. Robert Eitner, *Quellen-Lexikon* (2. verbesserte Auflage; Graz, Austria: Akademische Druck-u. Verlagsanstalt, 1959), IX, 479.

2. Christopher Tye, *Mass to Six Voices, "Euge Bone,"* ed. G. E. P. Arkwright ("The Old English Edition," No. X [London: Joseph Williams, Ltd., 1893]), pp. 28 ff.

3. Eric Blom (ed.), *Grove's Dictionary of Music and Musicians* (5th ed.; New York: St. Martin's Press, 1954), VIII, 626.

4. Robert W. Weidner, "The Instrumental Music of Christopher Tye," *JAMS*, XVII (1964), 369–70.

5. John Satterfield, "The Latin Church Music of Christopher Tye" (Ph.D. dissertation, The University of North Carolina, 1962). The dissertation is available in microfilm or Xerography as Order No. 63-3515 from University Microfilms, Ann Arbor, Michigan. A corrected version of its music, containing a new edition of the *"Euge Bone" Mass*, will be published by A-R Editions, Inc., in 1968–69.

Tye's work failed to reach any sixteenth-century collection of manuscripts on the Continent. It is understandable that his reformed church music, because of its English text, would not be useful abroad, and ironic that some of it would later circulate internationally with Latin text.[6] After the two Masses, items 1 and 2, the pieces rank alphabetically by incipit.

1. *"Euge Bone" Mass, a 6:* [7]
Bodleian MSS Mus. Sch. e. 376–81; [8] no. XVII in the indices, 17 in the part-books; 376: triplex, fols. 120^v–122^v; 377: medius, fols. 110^v–113^r; 378: first contratenor, fols. 130^v–132^v; 379: tenor, fols. 92^r–95^r; 380: bass, fols. 100^v–102^v; and 381: second contratenor, fols. 46^v–49^v.

2. *"Western Wind" Mass, a 4:*
British Museum Additional MSS 17802–5; no. 20 in the part-books; 17802: contratenor, fols. 35^v–45^v; 17803: triplex, fols. 34^r–43^v; [9] 17804: medius, fols. 34^r–44^v; and 17805: bass, fols. 33^r–41^v.[10]

3. *Ad te clamamus exsules, a 5:* [11]
Christ Church Mus. MSS 984–88; no. 14 in the part-books; 984:

---

6. For instance, *Rorate coeli* and *Si ambulem in medio* ("Polyphonic Motets," Nos. 63 and 64 [London: Cary & Co., 1931]). R. R. Terry, who edited the pieces, confesses that they are adaptations of Tye's *Actes of the Apostles*. Further, *Laudate nomen Domini, a 4,* in British Museum Additional MSS 31415, is an adaptation of Chapter IV in Tye's *Actes*. 31415 dates "after 1835," according to Augustus Hughes-Hughes, *Catalogue of the Manuscript Music in the British Museum* (London: printed by order of the trustees [of the British Museum], 1906), I, 352.

7. The *"Euge Bone" Mass* is in print; see n. 2 above.

8. Information about all the manuscripts follows the itemizing of Tye's Latin works.

9. The latter fol. is also numbered 45. For several fols. two numbers appear; I follow the choice of Hughes-Hughes, *Catalogue of the Manuscript Music in the British Museum*, I, 213.

10. Hughes-Hughes says Tye's Mass is "without name," but "Western Wind" is clearly in the parts. Gustave Reese is too optimistic in the implication that twenty complete motets and four complete Masses by Tye survive (cf. his *Music in the Renaissance*, p. 782).

11. The text is from the *Salve Regina*.

first tenor; 985: second tenor; 986: baritone; 987: first bass; and 988: second bass.

4. *Alleluia, a 4:* [12]
British Museum Additional MSS 17802–5; unnumbered in the part-books; 17802: contratenor, fol. 19ᵛ; 17803: triplex, fol. 17ʳ; 17804: medius, fol. 17ʳ; and 17805: bass, fol. 17ᵛ.

5. *Ave caput Christi, a 3:* [13]
Christ Church Mus. MS 45; all parts in the opening fols. 25ᵛ–26ʳ; superius: upside down, fols. 25ᵛ–26ʳ, where it must of course be read 26ʳ–25ᵛ; tenor: top up, bottom of fol. 25ᵛ; and bass: top up, bottom of fol. 26ʳ.

—. *Da illi, Domine:* see item 6b.

6a. *Domine Deus caelestis, a 3:*
British Museum MS R. M. 24. d. 2; no. 154 and probably including no. 155; [14] choir-book deployment of parts; altus: top of

---

12. Called *Alleluia (Per te, Dei Genitrix)* in *Grove's.*

13. Possibly a part of a longer work, the text of which may be seen in F. J. Mone (ed.), *Lateinische Hymnen des Mittelalters* (Freiburg im Breisgau: Herder'sche Verlagshandlung, 1853), I, 138. A contratenor part to an *Ave caput Christi, a 6,* no. 18 (but there are several series of numbers), is credited to Tye in Bodleian MS Mus. Sch. e. 423, pp. 257–61. A long rest at the beginning of 423's version leaves out all the text of the motet in the Christ Church MS and begins with the words *"perforata plaga tristis"* (*sic*). Clear motivic resemblances establish a close relationship between the Christ Church version and the Bodleian part, but naming the relationship may be impossible. Was the first section of 423's version *a 6* written for three voices only? Are they reproduced in 45? Or is 45 an arrangement or reduction of 423's first section that was actually for more voices? If the latter is the case, is the reduction Tye's?

14. Hilda Andrews listed *Domine Deus caelestis* in William Barclay Squire, *Catalogue of the King's Music Library* (London: printed by order of the trustees [of the British Museum], 1929), II, 215. The pieces were numbered at the time she worked, for she shows *Domine Deus caelestis* as in "R. M. 24. d. 2. (154.)." *In quo corrigit* she lists as in "R. M. 24. d. 2. (156.)." She could have missed the clear 155 that the numberer, whether scribe John Baldwin or a later hand, marked for *Da illi, Domine,* lying between *Domine Deus caelestis* and *In quo corrigit;* or she could have thought, as I do, that *Da illi, Domine,* a canon of two voices over a supporting bass, belongs with *Domine Deus caelestis* and is not a separate piece, the two being separated in each part only by a double bar line with a *fermata* on the preceding note, in other manuscripts the typical way of separating sections of text in one motet. Arkwright apparently did not know

fol. 151^v; tenor: bottom of fol. 151^v and top of fol. 152^r; and bass: bottom of fol. 152^r.

6b. *Da illi, Domine, a 3:*
British Museum MS R. M. 24. d. 2; no. 155 but probably intended to be the second section of no. 154; choir-book deployment of parts; for their locations see item 6a.

7. *Gloria, laus et honor, a 4:*
British Museum Additional MSS 17802–5; unnumbered in the part-books; 17802: contratenor, fols. 121^v–122^v; 17803: triplex, fols. 118^v–120^r; 17804: medius, fols. 121^v–122^v; and 17805: bass, fols. 115^r–116^v.

——. *In corde meo:* see item 9b.

8. *In pace, a 4:*
British Museum Additional MSS 17802–5; no. 39 in the part-books; 17802: contratenor, fols. 116^v–117^v; 17803: triplex, fols. 111^r–112^r; 17804: medius, fols. 114^v–115^r; and 17805: bass, fols. 107^v–108^r.

9a. *In quo corrigit, a 3:*
British Museum MS R. M. 24. d. 2; no. 156 and probably including no. 157; choir-book deployment of parts; altus: top of fol. 152^v; tenor: bottom of fol. 152^v; and bass: bottom of fol. 153^r.[15]

---

this manuscript when he wrote the catalogue for Tye, *Mass to Six Voices,* pp. 28 ff., but the Noble catalogue in *Grove's* may—the listing and indentation seem to say it does—consider *Domine Deus caelestis* and *Da illi, Domine* separate. A countertenor part to a *Domine Deus caelestis, a 6,* no. 19 (but there are several series of numbers), is credited to Tye in Bodleian MS Mus. Sch. e. 423, pp. 261–67. A long rest at the beginning of 423's version leaves out all the text of 24's. But after the rest 423 begins *"Da illi, Domine"* and states 24's tenor, though a fifth higher and written on the alto clef. 423 continues then with much more music in the part. The relationship between the two versions is again clear, but it cannot be named. See n. 13 above. 24's motet has only two of its three voices in canon; perhaps 423's version *a 6* had more.

15. The tenor is identical to a contratenor with the same text from a version *a 6* in Bodleian MS Mus. Sch. e. 423, pp. 220–22, where it is no. 29 (but there are several series of numbers). A rest in the manuscript following the *In quo corrigit* text leaves out *In corde meo,* which doubtless was sung by other parts. After the rest the part continues *"In labiis meis,"* which follows the *In corde meo* text in the psalm. Remarks toward the end of n. 13 are applicable here.

9b. *In corde meo, a 3:*
British Museum MS R. M. 24. d. 2; no. 157 but probably intended to be the second section of no. 156;[16] choir-book deployment of parts; for their locations see item 9a.

10. *Kyrie, a 4:* [17]
British Museum Additional MSS 17802–5; unnumbered in the part-books; 17802: contratenor, fols. 18^v–19^v; 17803: triplex, fols. 16^v–17^r; 17804: medius, fols. 16^v–17^r; and 17805: bass, fols. 16^v–17^r.

11. *Miserere mei, Deus, a 5:*
Bodleian MSS Mus. e. 1–5; no. i in the part-books; 1: altus, fols. 8^v–10^r; 2: first tenor, fols. 6^v–8^r; 3: second tenor, fols. 6^v–8^r; 4: first bass, fols. 5^v–7^r; and 5: second bass, fols. 6^v–8^r.[18]

Christ Church Mus. MSS 979–83; no. 27 in the part-books; 979: first tenor; 980: altus; 981: first bass; 982: no. 27 missing; [19] and 983: second bass.

Bodleian MS Mus. Sch. e. 423; no. 22 (but there are several series of numbers); first bass, pp. 123–27.

Peterhouse MSS 33–45; unnumbered in the part-books; 35: second tenor, fols. R3^r–R3^v; [20] 36: first bass, fols. 07^r–07^v; [21] and 37: second bass, fols. M3^r–M3^v; [22] none of the other parts in the sets making up 33–45 contain this piece.

---

16. Miss Andrews ignores the number, evidently considering *In corde meo* as a part of no. 156, *In quo corrigit*, which it follows immediately. See Squire, *Catalogue of the King's Music Library*, p. 215.

17. Called *Kyrie (Orbis factor)* in *Grove's*.

18. Bleedthrough makes Bodleian MS Mus. e. 3 the most difficult to decipher of all the manuscripts studied.

19. 982 begins with an extra part to no. 120, parts to nos. 62 and 68, then contains nos. in ordinal sequence from 93. With the exceptions of nos. 62 and 68, the portion of 982 through no. 92 is evidently lost.

20. The music of fol. R3^v is bound upside down in the manuscript.

21. The numbers are by Dom Anselm Hughes, *Catalogue of the Musical Manuscripts at Peterhouse, Cambridge* (Cambridge: Cambridge University Press, 1953), p. 41; actually the order is fol. 06, then a fol. with *Miserere* unnumbered, fol. P2, another unnumbered fol., then fol. P3. The music of 07^v is bound upside down.

22. The music of fol. M3^v is bound upside down.

Tenbury MS 1464; unnumbered in the part-book; second bass, fols. 37^v–39^r.[23]

12. *Omnes gentes plaudite, a 5:* [24]
Christ Church Mus. MSS 984–88; no. 15 in the part-books; 984: superius; 985: altus; 986: tenor; 987: first bass; and 988: second bass.

13. *Peccavimus cum patribus, a 7:*
Tenbury MSS 807–11; unnumbered in the part-books; 807: contratenor altus, fols. 21^r–22^r;[25] 808: first tenor, fols. 21^r– 22^r; 809: second tenor, fols. 21^r–22^r; 810: contratenor bassus, fols. 19^r, 20^r, bottom of 20^v; first bass, fols. 18^v, 19^v, top of 20^v; and 811: second bass, fols. 18^v–19^v.

Christ Church Mus. MSS 979–83; no. 120 in the part-books (but one part out of sequence in 982); 979: contratenor altus; 980: first tenor; 981: second tenor; 982: second bass with number inserted at beginning;[26] superius; and 983: first bass.

14. *Quia fecit, a 4:* [27]
Christ Church Mus. MS 45; all parts in the opening fols. 16^v– 17^r; tenor, top up, bottom of 16^v; altus, on its right side, top of 16^v; superius, upside down, top of 17^r; and bass, on its left side, bottom of 17^r.[28]

---

23. *Grove's* also lists *Miserere mei, Deus* as in Tenbury MS 1486. That bass part-book has a *Miserere* with different text and attributed to Robert White, no. 6, fols. 9^r–12^r; a *Miserere* with text unlike Tye's has John Sadler's name on the first page, no. 20, fols. 35^r–37^v. Edmund H. Fellowes, *Tudor Church Music Appendix with Supplementary Notes* (London: Oxford University Press, 1948), p. 6 (hereafter referred to as *TCM App.*), lists the latter as unidentified.

24. Except for the *"Euge Bone" Mass,* probably the only Tye Latin piece— prior to Satterfield, "The Latin Church Music of Christopher Tye"—to be printed complete; see H. B. Collins (ed.), Christopher Tye's *Omnes gentes plaudite manibus* ("Latin Church Music of the Polyphonic Schools," No. 72 [London: J. & W. Chester, Ltd., 1928]).

25. Edmund H. Fellowes, *The Catalogue of Manuscripts in St. Michael's College, Tenbury* (Paris: Editions de l'Oiseau Lyre, 1934), p. 169, lists *Peccavimus* at fol. 20; he seems to be in error.

26. See n. 19 above.

27. The text is from the *Magnificat.*

28. Percy Buck *et al.* (eds.), *Tudor Church Music* (London: Oxford University Press, 1923–29), lix (hereafter referred to as *TCM*), provides 45 with

Bodleian MS Mus. Sch. e. 423; no. 16 (but there are several series of numbers), pp. 250–53; a *Magnificat* part, that section of text beginning *"Quia fecit"* on p. 251, a duplicate of the altus of 45.

15. *Sub tuam protectionem, a 4:*
British Museum Additional MSS 17802–5; unnumbered in the part-books; 17802: contratenor, fols. 226^r–226^v; 17803: triplex, fols. 225^r–225^v; 17804: medius, fols. 216^v–217^v; and 17805: bass, fols. 205^v–206^v.

16. *Unde nostris, eia, fave votis, a 4:*
Christ Church Mus. MS 45; all parts in the opening fols. 19^v–20^r; tenor, top up, bottom of 19^v; superius on its right side, top of 19^v; altus, upside down, top of 20^r; and bass on its left side, bottom of 20^r.[29]

The manuscripts referred to in the catalogue above may be seen in the following locations:

---

a misnomer when it calls it a "part-book, in the technical sense of the word, with all the voice-parts written in different positions at the same opening, so that singers could face their several parts round one book." For the usual distinction between choir-book and part-book, see Willi Apel, *Harvard Dictionary of Music* (Cambridge, Mass.: Harvard University Press, 1944), pp. 139, 555. A choir-book with parts deployed as in 45 would have to be held flat on its back or placed on a table for singers to see it, and therefore it would be impractical for such religious services as I know. 45 was likely designed for home use; similar deployment of parts is mentioned in Reese, *Music in the Renaissance,* p. 836, and pictured in Georg Kinsky, *A History of Music in Pictures* (New York: Dover Publications, Inc., 1951), p. 101. On the possibility of 45's having been "arranged," see n. 13 above. Mr. Noble evidently made a mistake when he listed this *Quia fecit* as appearing in Tenbury MS 1469. Fellowes, *Catalogue . . . St. Michael's,* does not reach manuscript numbers as high as 1469. *TCM App.,* p. 9, seems to attribute the Tenbury version to Parsons. It appears in all part-books, 1469–71, on fol. 8^v; the cantus in 1469 is without complete text; the altus in 1470 is attributed to White, although the hand of the attribution is unlike the scribe's; the bass in 1471 seems likewise attributed to White, "seems" here because of illegibility. The text, complete in 1470 and 1471, is the same as Tye's, a short extract from the *Magnificat,* but the music in none of the Tenbury MSS is that of the Christ Church Mus. MS 45; the former is in imperfect time, the latter, perfect.

29. See n. 28 above.

Cambridge, University Library:

Peterhouse MSS 33–45; also known as the Caroline part-books, former and latter sets; [30] described in Dom Hughes, *Catalogue of the Musical Manuscripts at Peterhouse*, pp. x–xii.

London, British Museum:

British Museum MS R. M. 24. d. 2; described in Edward Lowinsky, "Early Scores in Manuscript," *JAMS*, XIII (1960), 155–56.

British Museum Additional MSS 17802–5; described in Hughes-Hughes, *Catalogue of the Manuscript Music in the British Museum*, I, 213, 271–72, and *TCM*, I, lviii.

Oxford, Bodleian Library:

Bodleian MSS Mus. e. 1–5; called Bodleian E 1–5 in *Grove's* and 29582–86 in Falconer Madan, *A Summary Catalogue of Western Manuscripts in the Bodleian Library at Oxford* (Oxford: Oxford University Press, 1905), V, 649–50, where they are described.

Bodleian MSS Mus. Sch. e. 376–81; called Bodleian E 376–81 in *Grove's,* the Forrest-Heyther (spelled Heather by Arkwright in Tye, *Mass to Six Voices, "Euge Bone,"* p. 4) Collection in Henry Davey, *History of English Music* (2nd ed.; London: J. Curwen & Sons Ltd., 1921), p. 89, and 26342–7 in Madan, *A Catalogue of Western Manuscripts*, V, 210–11, where they are described; Tye, *Mass to Six Voices*, pp. 3–4, also describes them.

Bodleian MS Mus. Sch. e. 423; called Bodleian E 423 in *Grove's* and 26558 in Madan, *A Catalogue of Western Manuscripts*, V, 236, where it is described.

---

30. Satterfield, "The Latin Church Music of Christopher Tye," p. 21, is out of date in the location of the Peterhouse manuscripts. Mr. E. J. Kenney, whose duties for Peterhouse College include those of librarian, told me in January, 1965, that the part-books were moved permanently to the University Library, Cambridge, because Hughes, *Catalogue of the Musical Manuscripts at Peterhouse*, resulted in a continuing series of requests for photographic reproductions. To fill each request, Mr. Kenney had to supervise the moving of the part-books from Peterhouse College to the University Library and back. He finally asked the University Library to keep them.

Oxford, Library of Christ Church College:

Christ Church Mus. MS 45; called also the Baldwin MSS in *TCM*, I, lix, where it is described.

Christ Church Mus. MSS 979–83; neither folios nor pages numbered; described in *TCM*, I, lix.

Christ Church Mus. MSS 984–88; neither folios nor pages numbered; described in *TCM*, I, lix.

Tenbury, Library of St. Michael's College:

Tenbury MSS 807–11; described in Fellowes, *Catalogue . . . St. Michael's,* pp. 168–69.

Tenbury MS 1464; described in *TCM App.*, p. 8.

Tenbury MSS 1469–71; called the Harmsworth Manuscripts and described in *TCM App.*, pp. 8–9.

Tenbury MS 1486; called the Braikenridge Manuscript and described in *TCM App.*, pp. 5–6.

OPERA IN FLORENCE:

1646–1731

Robert L. Weaver

GEORGE PEABODY COLLEGE FOR TEACHERS

Florentine opera after the first two decades of the seventeenth century has not yet been systematically studied. Venice, Bologna, Naples, Rome, and many other Italian cities, some of lesser importance than Florence, have their detailed histories, but Florence stands out oddly for the lack even of a theatrical chronicle. The studies and chronologies of Florentine opera that have been published have been limited to the productions at two theaters, the well-known *Teatro in via della Pergola* [1] and the less well-known theater of the Principe Ferdinando de' Medici at Pratolino. [2] The Pergola theater was open between 1657 and 1661, briefly again in 1688, after which it remained in disuetude until 1718 when it was reopened as a public theater. Performances at Pratolino began in 1679 and continued until 1710. The two publications concerning the Pratolino theater are limited to simple lists of the operas performed without further comment or analysis. Studies concerning the Pergola provide information more generously, but insofar as the seventeenth century history of the theater is treated, none has surpassed in value the first one

---

1. Alessandro Ademollo, *I primi fasti del teatro della Pergola* (Milano, 1885); Giuseppe Pavan, *Saggio di cronistoria teatrale . . . teatro degli Immobili* (Milano, 1901); Ugo Morini, *La Reale Accademia degli Immobili e il suo teatro La Pergola* (Firenze, 1905); Jarro (pseudonym of G. Piccini), *Storia anneddotica dei teatri fiorentini: I. Il teatro della Pergola* (Firenze, 1919).

2. Leo Puliti, *Cenni storici della vita del Serenissimo Ferdinando dei Medici* (Firenze, 1874); Renzo Lustig. "Per la cronistoria dell'antico teatro musicale. Il teatro della Villa Medicea di Pratolino," *RMI*, XXVI (1929), 2.

by Alessandro Ademollo. His study is, however, restricted not only to the one theater but in point of time to the first four years of the theater's operation.

There being no general account of Florentine productions of the seventeenth century, it is not surprising that the prevalent opinion is that the operas at the Pergola from 1657 to 1661 were isolated and without sequel and that, as Ambros wrote, "It seems as if with the death of Caccini and Peri [with the stated exception of Melani's *Il potestà*] native musical life of this city came to an end." [3] Little has been published since he wrote that would cause a revision of Ambros' assertion. It is hoped that the data presented herein will form sufficient basis for a reassessment of the role of Florence as a center of important operatic creativity during the seventeenth century.

Librettos or various records of 266 operas performed between 1646 and 1731 have been found. These performances took place in fourteen academic theaters, in three palaces or villas, and in unnamed theaters. The academic theaters were the Immobili (Pergola), the Infuocati (Cocomero), Casino Mediceo in Piazza San Marco, Centauro, Sorgenti, Casine Nuove, Cadenti, Improvisi, Oscuri, Efimeri, Inequali, Imperfetti, Nascenti, and Irresoluti.

The academicians of the Immobili in the four years of their principal activity (1657–61) produced six operas, including four comedies and two melodramas. The comedies will be found in the list of Florentine comedies appended to the present paper. The two melodramas were *L'Hipermestra* by Giovanni Andrea Moniglia and Francesco Cavalli in 1658 and *Ercole in Tebe* by Moniglia and Jacopo Melani in 1661. [4] Litigation over the estate of the protector, Cardinal Gian Carlo de' Medici, who had pro-

---

3. A. W. Ambros, *Geschichte der Musik,* ed. H. Leichtentritt (3rd ed.; Leipzig, 1909), IV, 813. Author's translation.

4. The libretto of *L'Hipermestra* was published in 1658 in Florence by St. di S.A.S. A copy is in the Biblioteca Nazionale Centrale di Firenze, *inter alia.* The libretto of *Ercole* was published by the Stamperia di S.A.S. in two editions in 1661, one of which has four plates and a *descrizione* by Alessandro Segni. Copies exist in the New York Public Library.

vided most of the funds for the construction of the theater, closed the theater following his death in 1661. At that moment the academicians were on the point of presenting a fifth comedy which was not then performed owing to the death of the protector. Later this comedy, *Amor vuol'inganno,* by Moniglia and Melani was performed by a *conversazione,* that is, an informal academy, in the gardens of the Marchese Corsini under a new title, *La vedova,* in 1680. The first of the five comedies, *Il potestà di Cològnole,* by the same poet and musician is justly the most renowned of the Florentine operas of the seventeenth century.

The most active theater until the reopening of the Pergola in 1718 as a commercial opera house, on the other hand, was that of the Accademia degli Infuocati in via Cocomero. This dramaturgical academy was founded in 1652. The theater had been previously built by the Accademia degli Immobili, but a group in the original academy, led by the Cardinal de' Medici, separated, constructed a new theater in via della Pergola, and took with them the name of the Immobili. Those who remained in via Cocomero adopted the new name of the Infuocati under the patronage of the Grand Duke Ferdinando II and later Cosimo III.

Records of the performances or actual librettos exist for 47 operas performed in the Teatro in via Cocomero between 1661 and 1731. Some of these operas were mounted, directed, paid for, and to some extent performed by the academicians (all important roles were performed by professional singers). Other operas were importations from Venice, Rome, or Bologna; however, even these importations retained some Florentine connection: that is, either the librettist or the composer was Tuscan. But from 1703 to 1731 the operas were more frequently importations, revivals, or works by the theater's own impresario. The change doubtless reflects a shift from academic to commercial performances in the theater.

There is reason to suspect, however, that the Cocomero may have been used on occasion as a public theater even before 1703. Over 75 librettos or records of performances before 1718 give no clues about the theater in which they were performed. Some operas were importations without Florentine connections. Some were possibly performed by itinerant professional companies: the 1670 libretto for Jacopo Melani's setting of Filippo Acciajuoli's *Il Girello,* performed first in Rome in 1669, is signed by *I comici del Girello.* There were seven performances of the opera within six years throughout Italy. These two facts suggest that the *comici,* a term commonly used to describe actors of the *commedia dell' arte* to distinguish them from *musici* or *recitanti,* were a touring company. The actual existence of a public theater is confirmed by a report of the papal nuncio to Florence, Lorenzo Trotto, dated May 3, 1667, in which he speaks of presentations of *Egisto dramma musicale in questo publico teatro.*[5] Faustini's and Cavalli's *Egisto* was, like *Il Girello,* so frequently performed that it would seem also to be the work of a touring company. Since it is known definitely that the Pergola was closed because of litigation, the Cocomero is the obvious choice for the public theater. Evidence in support of the supposition is provided by an unusually loquacious libretto of 1703, *Griselda,*[6] which in the *argomento* identifies the theater to be that of the Accademia degli Infuocati, that is, the Cocomero, yet which acknowledges only the librettist, Zeno, the composer, Albinoni, and the *recitanti.* The omission of any accolade of the noble cavaliers who made the performance possible or lent their talents and fortunes to the opera's realization, in spite of the libretto's generally free flow of information, indicates that *Griselda* does not belong properly to academic opera. If, indeed, the Cocomero was used as a public theater, the total number of operas performed there may be as high as 125 from 1646 to 1731.

Three other academies are recorded as having mounted at least two operas. The Conversazione del Centauro published a libretto for a performance in 1684 [7] and is among those listed by the Settimani Diaries as having performed an opera for the wed-

5. Rome, Archivio Vaticano, *Nunziatura di Firenze,* Vol. 50, pp. 75, 76 ff.
6. Florence, Biblioteca Nazionale Centrale.
7. See No. 16 in the appended list.

ding festivities of 1688.[8] The Sorgenti produced operas in 1657, 1661,[9] and in 1688, the last again cited by Settimani.

Of greater importance than the Centauro and Sorgenti is the Accademia or the Conversazione del Casino Mediceo in Piazza San Marco, whose patronage of opera has been hitherto unnoticed. The Casino Mediceo was the residence of the Cardinal Francesco Maria de' Medici, the younger brother of Cosimo III. Presumably he was the patron of the academy. Maylender, the historian of Italian academies, reports nothing of this academy.[10] The academicians mounted at least seven operas between 1678 and 1695.[11] Two librettos declare themselves to be birthday presentations (Francesco's birthday fell on November 12) in the years 1681 and 1682, suggesting that it may have been the habit of the academicians to honor the Cardinal with an annual operatic performance.[12]

The operas listed above represent numerically no massive productivity. The most thorough research will never, I am sure, discover in Florence performances enough to compete with Venice or to displace Rome. Furthermore, a large number of the Florentine productions were actually first performed in Venice, Rome, or Bologna. Mixed among the importations, nevertheless, are native operas that constitute Florence's unique and

---

8. Puliti, *Ferdinando dei Medici,* p. 38 n. 12.

9. SCIPIONE IN CARTAGINE (Firenze, Bonardi, 1657). Libretto cited by Isadore Carini, *L'Arcadia dal 1680 al 1890* (Roma, 1891), I, 559. Text by Moniglia. Composer unknown. LA DORI OVVERO LA SCHIAVA FEDELE. Text by A. Apolloni. Music by Antonio Cesti. See Alfred Loewenberg, *Annals of Opera 1597–1940* (Cambridge, 1943), pp. 20 ff.

10. Michele Maylender, *Storia delle Accademie d'Italia,* 5 vols. (Bologna, 1926–30).

11. LA REGINA FLORIDEA (Vangelisti, 1678), libretto at the Conservatorio "Luigi Cherubini" by Gius. Giacomini; ADALINDA (Vangelisti, 1679), anonymous libretto in the Bibl. Estense; IL SIDONIO OVERO IL RARO ESEMPIO DI COSTANZA E FEDE (Vangelisti, 1680), libretto in the Bibl. Marucelliana by Gius. Giacomini; QUINTO LUCREZIO PROSCRITTO (Vangelisti, 1681), libretto in the Bibl. Marucelliana by G. A. Moniglia, music (lost) by Lorenzo Cattani; IL CONTE DI CUTRO (see No. 14 in the appended list); GNEO MARZIO CORIOLANO (Vangelisti, n.d. but 25 v 1686), libretto in British Museum by G. A. Moniglia, music (lost) by Lorenzo Cattani; IL CONTE D'ALTAMURA (see No. 24 in the appended list).

12. Nos. 3 and 4 of Note 11.

generally unrecognized contribution to seventeenth century opera
—comic opera. Of the 266 recorded performances between 1646
and 1731, 41 are comic.. Twenty of the 41 are repetitions of
works previously performed in Florence,[13] and four are written
for first performances elsewhere, albeit in the case of two by
Tuscan librettists at least.[14] Altogether, then, 17 comic operas
are written for first performances in Florence or at Pratolino.

Of these 17 comic operas, three are written for Pratolino,[15]
which, though it would be classified as a private villa of the
Medici, must have actually been a more or less informal academy, for Principe Ferdinando supervised the performances as an
amateur director in the same manner as the noble superintendents
of the earlier comedies at the Pergola.[16] Ten comedies are written for particular academies: five for the Immobili, the last remaining unperformed until 1680; [17] two for the Casino Mediceo; [18] and one each for the Infuocati, Casine Nuove, and the
Cadenti.[19] Two more are undoubtedly intended for performances
by academies although the librettos give no indication of it. In
any case, the second performances of both comic operas take
place in academic circles, the first being performed by the Infuo-

---

13. Nos. 6, 8, 9, 17–19, 26–30, 32, and 33 of the appended list.

14. Nos. 7, 10, 16, and 23. Nos. 10 and 23 are by Acciajuoli and Villifranchi,
respectively, both Tuscans.

15. Nos. 15, 22, and 25.

16. Typical wording of citations as they appear in a court diary contained
within the *Diario Capponi* 273 (Florence, Biblioteca Nazionale), which is otherwise a random collection of chronologies, is as follows: A dì 16 d° (August,
1687) Il Ser. P. Ferd (inando de' Medici) ando a Pratolino villegiare p(er)
fare la commedia in musica. (f. 237) A dì d° (26 August, 1687) Il S. P. Ferd.
fece fare la p(rima) commedia in musica. (f. 237') Il dì 20 (January, 1688)
Torno il Ser. P. Ferd. da Pratolino avendovi fatto molte volte sua commedia
in musica et altri feste. (f. 239) Such notices during the three years of the
diary (1686–88) indicate that Ferdinando went every August and Carnival to
Pratolino. Ten to fifteen days later the Medici family, that is, Ferdinando's
mother, the Grand Duchess Vittoria della Rovere; his uncle, the Cardinal Francesco Maria de' Medici; and his brother and sister, the Grand Prince Gian
Gastone and the Grand Princess Anna Maria Ludovica, all journeyed to Pratolino to see the comedy which Ferdinando and his academicians had prepared.
Evidently the Grand Duke Cosimo III stayed at home.

17. Nos. 1, 2, 3, 4, and 13.

18. Nos. 14 and 24.

19. Nos. 11, 20, and 21, respectively.

cati and the second at Pratolino.[20] Finally, two comic operas are written for performances at the Pergola and Cocomero theaters after they have been converted into regularly functioning public theaters on lease from the academies.[21]

These operas are stamped with the character of the academy. They display to a greater or lesser degree the trappings of classical imitations, such as *travestimenti* and *cognizioni* whereby everyone turns out to be someone else. Stereotyped texts, such as the monologue of the clever servant, or even a specific motive (such as the pot of gold in *Il potestà*), are taken from the Latin comic playwrights. Academic also is the use of dialects ostensibly for philological study as well as for humor: Moniglia appended etymological glossaries to his comedies which borrow style and mannerisms from the *Vocabulario della Crusca,* the scholarly and academic dictionary of the seventeenth and eighteenth century. The influence of high-minded gentlemen is shown, too, in the limited degree to which mordant satire is used. The characterizations of stock figures are softened or eliminated. Understandably enough, the pedant is quite rare. Finally, the conditions under which the academies produced operas are reflected in the restraint to be found in the staging and the general resources in comparison with the courtly or commercial melodramas of the mid-century. From descriptions it can be surmised that the greatest display was reserved for the ballets and intermedii in which the members of the academy themselves danced.

The librettos also owe a great deal to the *commedia dell 'arte:* the character-types, the *parte ridicoli* and *serie,* the *vecchi,* the *innamorati,* are to be found embroiled in the standard plot of young love thwarted by the avariciousness or senile libido of parents or guardians. The characters are identified with the middle classes or with country nobility, and locations are suitably removed from Florence, sometimes in Tuscany, sometimes in Naples or Sicily. The more severe stock characters such as Captain Spavento, Doctor Graziano (rare), the *Magnifico,* and the *Gobbo* (stuttering hunchback) are present in the early comedies,

---

20. Nos. 5 and 12 are the first performances; nos. 9 and 18, the repetitions.
21. Nos. 31 and 34.

but the characterizations grow more refined and generalized even to the point of extinction by the end of the century.

Apollonio in his *Storia del teatro italiano* has observed of spoken drama in general that in Florence and particularly in her academies a classical spirit was nurtured even during the grandest flowering of the Baroque.[22] The statement is especially appropriate to these native Tuscan comic operas.

A few of these comic librettos enjoyed revivals at the beginning of the eighteenth century. There was a revival of *Il potestà* in 1717 and another in 1727, and one each of two by Villifranchi: *L'ipocondriaco* in 1718 and *La serva favorita* in 1727.[23] In addition, one anonymous libretto, *La vanità delusa,* performed in 1731, was a close imitation of Moniglia's *Il conte di Cutro.* Outside of Florence, the same poet's *La serva nobile* was anonymously rewritten for a performance in Rome in 1721.[24] A stronger link with the eighteenth century is through Bologna. *Il potestà* had been performed in Bologna in 1673.[25] It was resurrected in 1730 with a new setting by Giuseppe Maria Buini, who also composed a new setting for Villifranchi's *L'ipocondriaco* in 1717, probably the same setting used in Florence the following year. The influence of these two librettos is easily seen in Buini's own original librettos that followed.[26]

Scores for only one Florentine academic comic opera have as yet been uncovered, namely, for *Il potestà.* The music for *Il Girello* has been preserved in several copies, but it is of a somewhat different character, being a burlesque, and it was not writ-

---

22. Mario Apollonio, *Storia del teatro italiano* (Firenze, 1946), II, 29 ff.

23. Subsequent study has revealed a greater vogue for these revivals than previously suspected (*cf.* note p. 17). The following are not included in list of comic operas as the end of this article: *Tacere et amare,* 1717; *Il finto chimico,* 1720; *Il conte di Cutro,* 1721; *La serva nobile,* 1720 and 1731; *Lo speziale di villa,* 1730 and 1731. All were performed at the Cocomero. The librettos are in Bologna, CMBM.

24. LA SERVA NOBILE (Roma, Eredi del Corbelletti, 1721). Copy in the British Museum. The composer is not identified.

25. Corrado Ricci, *I teatri di Bologna nei secoli XVII–XVIII* (Bologna, 1888), p. 434.

26. Edward J. Dent, "Giuseppe Maria Buini," *SIMG,* XIII (1911–12), 329 ff. Also F. Vatielli, "Operisti-librettisti dei secoli XVII e XVIII," *RMI,* XLIII (1939), 608.

ten originally for a Florentine performance, although by native Florentines. Alessandro Stradella's score for *Il Trespolo tutore* is in the Estense Library in Modena, but Florence can hardly claim more than a direct influence upon it. The dearth of scores is most regrettable, but as the historical role of Florence in the creation of the genre of comic opera becomes more generally recognized, we may hope that additional scores will be unearthed so that the musical as well as the literary growth of the genre can be reconstructed.

COMIC OPERAS PERFORMED IN FLORENCE AND
PRATOLINO, 1657–1731
Abbreviations:

AV: Biblioteca Apostolica Vaticana, Rome; BM: British Museum, London; CLC: Biblioteca del Conservatorio "Luigi Cherubini," Florence; CMBM: Civico Museo Bibliografico Musicale (formerly the Liceo Musicale "Giambattista Martini") di Bologna; CN: Biblioteca del Conservatorio di Napoli; CRM: Bibliothèque du Conservatoire Royal de Musique de Bruxelles; EST: Biblioteca Estense, Modena; HU: Harvard University Library, Cambridge, Mass.; LC: Library of Congress, Washington, D.C.; MAR: Biblioteca Marucelliana, Florence; ML: Biblioteca Medicea-Laurenziana, Florence; NCF: Biblioteca Nazionale Centrale di Firenze; NP: Bibliothèque Nationale de Paris; SC: Biblioteca di S. Cecilia, Rome; VE: Biblioteca Nazionale Centrale Vittorio Emanuele II, Rome.

Information concerning each opera follows this order: date (Roman numerals indicate the month), theater, title. 1. Librettist (publisher—all are located in Florence and the dates of publication are the same as the entry unless otherwise stated). Libraries possessing copies of the libretto. 2. Composer. Libraries possessing scores. If any item is replaced by three periods (. . .), that information is unknown or the item has not been located.

1. 1657, 7.ii. Pergola. IL POTESTÀ DI COLÒGNOLE.
   1. Giovanni Maria Moniglia (Bonardi). NCF. 2. Jacopo Melani. AV, CLC. Eitner, *QL*, cites one score in Berlin.
2. 1658, 20.ii. Pergola. IL PAZZO PER FORZA.

1. Moniglia (Bonardi). NCF. 2 Melani. . . .
3. 1659, Carnival. Pergola. IL VECCHIO BALORDO.
   1. Moniglia (. . .). MSS in NCF, ML. 2. Melani. . . .
4. 1660, 31.i. Pergola. LA SERVA NOBILE.
   1. Moniglia (Stamperia nuova all'Insegna della Stella).
   BM, NCF, SC. 2. Domenico Anglesi. . . .
5. 1661, . . . LE NOZZE IN SOGNO.
   1. Pietro Susini (Insegna della Stella). NCF. 2. . . .
6. 1661, Autumn. Cocomero. IL POTESTÀ DI
   COLÒGNOLE.
   1. Moniglia (Rontini). BM. 2. Melani. As above.
7. 1662, . . . AMOR VUOL GIOVENTÙ.
   1. Ludovico Cortesi (Insegna della Stella). VE. 2. . . .
8. 1664, . . . AMOR VUOL GIOVENTÙ.
   1. Cortesi (Florence and Bologna, Gio. Battista Ferroni).
   NP. 2. . . . May not be published for a particular performance.
9. 1665, . . . Cocomero. LE NOZZE IN SOGNO.
   1. Susini (Insegna della Stella). VE. 2. . . .
10. 1670, . . . IL GIRELLO.
    1. Filippo Acciajuoli (Stamperia di S. A. S.). CMBM.
    2. Melani. AV, BM, CN, EST.
11. 1674, 7.i. Cocomero. TACERE ET AMARE.
    1. Moniglia (Vangelisti e Matini). CMBM, CRM, NCF.
    2. Melani. . . .
12. 1680, . . . IL FINTO CHIMICO.
    1. Attributed in NCF catalogue to Giovanni Cosimo Villifranchi (Vangelisti). NCF. 2. . . .
13. 1680, . . . Garden of Marchese Bartolomeo Corsini.
    LA VEDOVA.
    1. Moniglia. Original libretto unknown. Reprint in Moniglia, *Poesie dramatiche* (St. di S. A. S., 1689), III, 280.
    2. Melani. . . .
14. 1682, 12. xi. Casino Mediceo. IL CONTE DI CUTRO.
    1. Moniglia (Vangelisti, 1682 [*sic*]. The dedication is signed 1683.) CRM. 2. Lorenzo Cattani. . . .
15. 1683, . . . Pratolino. LO SPEZIALE DI VILLA.
    1. Villifranchi (Vangelisti). CRM, MAR. 2. . . .

16. 1684, . . . Conversazione del Centauro. LA DONNA ANCORA E FEDELE.
    1. Domenico Filippo Contini (Vangelisti, 1634 [*sic*]). MAR. 2. Possibly Bernardo Pasquini. . . .
17. 1684, . . . Pratolino. LO SPEZIALE DI VILLA.
    1. Villifranchi (Vangelisti). NCF. 2. . . .
18. 1686, . . . Pratolino. IL FINTO CHIMICO.
    1. Villifranchi (Vangelisti). CRM, LC. 2. . . .
19. 1687, . . . Pratolino. IL PAZZO PER FORZA.
    1. Moniglia (Vangelisti). NCF. 2. Giovanni Maria Pagliardi. . . .
20. 1688, x. Conversazione delle Casine nuove. BERTOLINA REGINA D'ARCADIA.
    1. Girolamo Guicciardini. Mentioned in the Settimanni Diaries (Florence, Archivio Mediceo) and the Diario del Pastoso (Florence, Biblioteca Riccardiana).
21. 1688, x. Teatro dei Cadenti. LE GLORIOSE DISAVENTURE DI ODOARDO FIGLIO DEL RE DI SICILIA. 1. . . . Mentioned in the Settimanni and Pastoso Diaries. 2. . . .
22. 1689, . . . Pratolino. LA SERVA FAVORITA.
    1. Villifranchi (St. di S. A. S.). CRM, HU. 2. . . .
23. 1692, . . . Pratolino. IL TRESPOLO TUTORE.
    1. Villifranchi. . . . 2. . . .
24. 1695, . . . Casino Mediceo di San Marco. IL CONTE D'ALTAMURA, OVVERO IL VECCHIO GELOSO.
    1. Domencio Tornaquinci (Rontini). NCF. 2. . . .
25. 1695, . . . Pratolino. L'IPOCONDRIACO.
    1. Villifranchi (St. di S. A. S.). HU, LC. 2. . . .
26. 1697, . . . IL GIRELLO.
    1. Filippo Acciajuoli (Vangelisti). CMBM. 2. Possibly Melani. Cf. no. 10.
27. 1717, Carnival. Cocomero. IL POTESTÀ DI COLÒGNOLE.
    1. Moniglia (condensed: Albizzini). NCF. 2. Possibly Giuseppe Maria Buini. . . .
28. 1718, Summer (?). Cocomero. L'IPOCONDRIACO.
    1. Villifranchi. No libretto located: cited by Clément,

Dictionnaire des Opéras (Paris, 1905), p. 585. 2. Buini. . . .

29. 1719, . . . Cocomero. LO SPEZIALE DI VILLA.
   1. Villifranchi (Verdi). NCF. 2. . . .

30. 1723, . . . IL FINTO CHIMICO.
   1. Villifranchi (Albizzini). NCF. 2. . . .

31. 1725, Carnival. Pergola. UN VECCHIO INNAMORATO.
   1. . . . Libretto not located. Cited by Morini, *Teatro La Pergola,* p. 41. 2. Giuseppe Orlandini. May be an intermedio.

32. 1727, . . . Cocomero. IL POTESTÀ DI COLÒGNOLE.
   1. Moniglia (condensed: Paperini). NCF. 2. Possibly Buini. . . .

33. 1727, Carnival. Cocomero. LA SERVA FAVORITA.
   1. Villifranchi (Paperini). CMBM, NCF. 2. Giovanni Chinzer. . . .

34. 1731, Autumn. Cocomero. LA VANITÀ DELUSA.
   1. . . . (Giuseppe Pagani e Melchiorre Alberighi). LC.
   2. Giovanni Chinzer.

AUTHOR'S NOTE: Since writing this article several years ago, I have become acquainted with the publications of Mario Fabbri on the subject of, or related to, the history of opera in Florence, notably, among many, the splendid article on Florence in the *Enciclopedia dello spettacolo* (Roma, 1958), which comes closer to being a complete survey and to revealing the vigor and originality of the Florentines of the seventeenth century than any previous publication. Indeed, his article serves to emphasize the need for an accurate and complete chronology and for analytical studies of Florentine opera. I am currently preparing a chronology to the year 1750 with full bibliographical annotation and citations of comments contained in diaries and books of etiquette. Obviously the chronology will alter some of the statistics contained in the present article. The substance, however, will not be affected.

SIXTEENTH-CENTURY MUSICIANS

IN MATTHESON'S *EHRENPFORTE*

Karl Gustav Fellerer
UNIVERSITÄT KÖLN
Translated by Lilian P. Pruett

The picture of the past changes from generation to generation, and the evaluation of individual personalities changes with the picture. Frequently, music literature of the seventeenth and eighteenth centuries places in the foreground musicians who are forgotten in succeeding times; the verdict of contemporaries is often different from that of history.

In each period, however, it is significant to note which elements of the past continue to remain alive, which musicians of past centuries are known, and how the period deals with artforms of the past. In part this involves an uninterrupted transmission of past art, in part a conscious return to musical documents of the past. Nineteenth-century historiography attempted to delve into the music of past centuries. Counterpoint theories of the eighteenth century continue the traditions established in sixteenth-century "strict style" and refer to examples of classical polyphony. The contrapuntal theories of Giuseppe Paolucci,[1] Giambattista Martini,[2] Johann Joseph Fux,[3] among others, are

---

1. *Arte pratica di contrappunto dimostrata con esempi di varj autori.* Venezia, Tomo I, 1766, Tomo II, III, 1772. The work contains compositions by Asola, Agostini, Benevoli, Lassus, Marcello, Morales, Palestrina, Porta, Rota, Vittoria, Zarlino.

2. *Esemplare ossia saggio fondamentale pratico di contrappunto sopra il canto fermo.* Bologna, Tomo I, 1774, Tomo II, 1776. Contained are works by Agostini, Animuccia, Barbieri, Benevoli, Cifra, Falconio, Gabussi, Gesualdo, Marcello, Marenzio, Monteverdi, Morales, Ortiz, Palestrina, Parmeggiano, Pasquale, Porta, Rota, Turini, Vittoria, Willaert, Zarlino.

3. *Gradus ad Parnassum, sive Manductio ad compositionem musicae regularem* (Viennae, 1725).

built upon analytical investigations of works from the sixteenth century, those of later times, and of contemporary works. Concomitant with this we find a rising interest in the composers themselves. Attempts are made to represent the lives and works of the sixteenth-century masters, attempts which are often, to be sure, based on questionable source material, on uncertain traditions, and frequently enriched by imaginative additions and suppositions. It is significant for the time, however, as to which sixteenth-century musicians are known to and dealt with by music writers of the eighteenth century.

Johann Mattheson, in his *Ehrenpforte,*[4] gives honors to the following as being among the "most capable maestri di cappella, composers, music scholars, and musicians": Martin ARNOLD, Sethus CALVISIUS, Michael COLET, Pankraz CRUEGER, Claude GOUDIMEL, Otto Siegried HARNISCH, Orlandus LASSUS, Angelus POLITIANUS, Andreas RASELIUS, Jan Pieter SWEELINCK, Jodok WILLICH. Thus, he lists only a small circle of musicians of the sixteenth century. It appears to be quite a random grouping; Italian composers, for example, are not included. The conception of the historical significance of musicians and theorists of the sixteenth century is lacking in Mattheson. He could, therefore, accept these very divergent figures in a common grouping. In his preface to the *Ehrenpforte* Mattheson stresses that ". . . very little was taken from printed sources, mainly only such matters pertaining to a few persons whose reputations rest on their writings on music. On the other hand, the greatest contribution stems from personal reports and from authentic manuscripts: for this reason the descriptions contained in our *Ehrenpforte* are all the more valid" (p. XI). Mattheson's choice of sixteenth-century musicians is explained by his reliance on somewhat fortuitous sources as well as by his striving to serve his contemporaries and to place the center of gravity in contemporary music activity. He is concerned not with a complete listing, but rather with a personal evaluation. In his

---

4. *Grundlage einer Ehrenpforte woran der tüchtigsten Capellmeister, Componisten, Musikgelehrten, Tonkünstler etc. Leben, Werke, Verdienste, etc. erscheinen sollen. Zum fernern Ausbau angegeben von Mattheson* (Hamburg, 1740). New edition by M. Schneider (Berlin, 1910).

words: "One can recognize most clearly in which significant respects our effort differs from an actual dictionary by comparing the former with the latter" (p. XXVI).

When Mattheson published his *Ehrenpforte* in 1740, Johann Gottfried Walther's *Musicalisches Lexicon* (Leipzig, 1732) was already available. The latter work cites, besides the subject listings, ". . . musicians who excelled through theory and practice in old as well as newer times, albeit in different nations, and what has become known by them or what they have left in writings" (title page). As a principal source Walther ("Vorbericht") names Sebastien de BROSSARD who, however, ". . . lists only the names of musicians and theorists [of which there are over 900] without reporting who they were and what they wrote" (the *Dictionnaire de musique,* Amsterdam, n.d., after the first edition, Paris, 1703). Furthermore, for practical music Walther refers to the *Indice di tutte le opere di musica* of Paul PARSTORFFER (Munich, 1653) and to the catalogues of the Amsterdam publisher ROGER and his son-in-law CÈNE, as well as to communications by Joh. Christoph SCHMITT, Joh. Christian BOEHMEN, Joh. Christoph RICHTER, Joh. David HEINICHEN, Franz Xaver MURSCHHAUSER, and Wolfgang Caspar PRINTZ'S *Historische Beschreibung der edelen Sing- und Kling-Kunst* (Dresden, 1690). Printz's eleventh chapter, entitled "Of musicians who won especial praise and fame above others in the sixteenth century after the birth of Christ," represents Walther's most important source for descriptions of sixteenth-century musicians. The individual articles of Walther's lexicon cite numerous other sources. Besides general literature which mentions individual composers, he relies above all on single works taken from catalogues of books and general bibliographies. Owing to Walther's considerable knowledge of literature, he was able to list numerous musicians of the sixteenth century. The extent of his inclusions follows the extent of his knowledge, regardless of the importance of the composers.

An idea of the musico-historical significance of the masters is as nonexistent in Walther as in Mattheson. Josquin is described as a pupil of Ockeghem and as chapelmaster of Louis XII of France, and Glearean's evaluation of the "great ingenii" is ac-

cepted. The epitaph is discussed in detail, following Printz and
Franc. SWERTIUS (*Athenae belgicae,* Antwerp, 1628). In con-
nection with Palestrina, Walther mentions his hymns of 1589
and later editions of the Masses (1610 and 1639), after A.
LIBERATI (*Lettera scritta . . . In riposta ad una del Sig. Ovidio
Persapegi,* Rome, 1685), G. M. BONONCINI (*Musico prattico,*
I, Bologna, 1688), A. PISA (*Battuta della musica dichiarata,*
Rome, 1611), J. SUAREZ (*Praenestes antiquae,* Rome, 1655),
and continues the myth of the "princeps musicae" to whom we
owe the saving of church music. Mattheson's *Göttingischer
Ephorus* (Hamburg, 1727) is cited. The following remark is
noteworthy: "Simultaneously singing voices are called after his
name *alla Palaestrina,* otherwise known as *a cappella.*" Lassus
receives more detailed biographical treatment, and reference is
made to Gesner and Boissard, who list twenty works by Lassus,
as well as to Draudius and Mattheson's *Critica musica* (Hamburg, 1722), p. 2. Joh. Jakob BOISSARD includes Lassus
among the numerous musicians from the Middle Ages on up to
his time in his *Bibliotheca chalcographica illustrium virorum*
(1591), as do Isaac BULLART in his *Les Vies et les Eloges
historique des hommes illustrés* (Paris, 1682, not mentioned by
Walther), Paulus FEHER in his *Theatrum virorum eruditione
clarorum* (Nürnberg, 1688), or Melchior ADAM in his *Vitae
Pilosophorum germanorum* (Frankfurt, 1705). Besides the
Leipzig. allgemeines historisches Lexikon of Joh. Franz BUD-
DEUS (Leipzig, 1709 ff.), Walther mentions as sources (E.?)
Reusner's epitaph in Otto AICHER's *Theatrum funebre* (Salz-
burg, 1675), as well as Conrad GESNER's *Bibliotheca univer-
salis* (Tigvri, 1545), and Georg DRAUDIUS's *Bibliotheca clas-
sica* (Frankfurt, 1611). Anecdotes and undocumented traditions
form the bases of these reports which do, indeed, transmit the
names of Lassus and Palestrina, but contain conceptions of
neither their work nor their historical importance. In German
music literature Lassus is placed before Palestrina. Since S.
QUICKELBERG's early assessment of Lassus in H. PANTA-
LEON'S *Prosopographia heroum atque illustrium virorum totius
Germaniae* (Basel, 1565–66), biographical notices absorbed
certain inaccuracies, though preserving the memory of Lassus.

Besides sources already named, Lassus finds mention also in A. DUVERDIER's *Bibliothèque* (Lyon, 1585), N. REUSNER's *Icones* (Regensburg, 1587), L. GUICCIARDINI's *Descrittione de tutti i paesi bassi* (Antwerp, 1567), de LOCRIUS's *Chronicon* (Arras, 1616), Th. LANSIUS's *Consultatio* (Tübingen, 1620), H. FABER's *Compendium* (Jena, 1636), Ph. BRASSEUR's *Sydera illustrium Nannoniae scriptorum* (Mons, 1637), L. MORERI's *Dictionnaire historique* (Lyon, 1674), A. WERCKMEISTER's *Musicae mathematicae Hodegus* (Frankfurt, 1686), J. L. LECERF's *Comparaison* (Brussels, 1704), among others.[5] His works,[6] however, received little notice following the remarks of A. GUMPELTZHAIMER in his *Compendium musicae* (Augsburg, 1591), J. BURMEISTER in his *Musica poetica* (Rostock, 1606), M. BERINGER in his *Musica* (Nürnberg, 1610), M. PRAETORIUS in his *Syntagma musicum* (Wolfenbüttel, 1621), and Chr. CALDENBACH in his *Dissertatio musica* (Tübingen, 1664), among others. Editions of individual works by Lassus in the seventeenth century came to a halt with Ballard's edition of the *Missa Jager* (Paris, 1687).

As with Lassus, the seventeenth century dealt also with Palestrina; however, besides biographical notices and anecdotes, his works received greater attention.[7] His art became the foundation of musical and contrapuntal precepts in Italy and was therefore evaluated as exemplary in music theory of the time, even in the face of monodic and thoroughbass practices. Already L. ZACCONI, in his *Prattica di musica* (Venice, 1592, 1622), comes to terms with the individuality of Palestrina's art, and D. P. CERONE, in *El Melopeo y Maestro* (Naples, 1613), and JOAO IV of Portugal in his *Risposte* (Rome, 1655) attempt to come to an understanding of Palestrina's works through detailed analyses. A. BERARDI in his *Arcani musicali* (Bologna, 1690) derives thirteen contrapuntal principles from the work of Palestrina; this is to mention only a few of the numerous music-

---

5. A review of Lassus' changing historical position is given by W. Boetticher, *Orlando di Lasso und seine Zeit*, I (Kassel, 1958).

6. Cf. *ibid.*, 729 ff.

7. K. G. Fellerer, *Palestrina* (2nd ed.: Düsseldorf, 1960).

theoretical writings in the seventeenth century which deal with Palestrina.

Palestrina's style remained alive in the *stile antico,* albeit changed through time-conditioned peculiarities, as the "stile alla Palaestrina" stressed by J. G. Walther.[8] This practical application of Palestrina's art brought increased interest in its musico-theoretical treatment. In the eighteenth century G. PAOLUCCI's *Arte pratica di Contrapunto* (Venice, 1765–72) and G. B. MARTINI's *Saggio fondamentale pratica di Contrapunto* (Bologna, 1774) present us with the great summary of classical polyphony with respect to compositional techniques. They draw upon not only examples of Palestrina and Lassus, but on many sixteenth-century contemporaries as well. J. J. FUX had treated of the Palestrina style already in 1725 in his *Gradus ad Parnassum,*[9] and had thereby given a new foundation to German music theory and compositional science. In his *Ehrenpforte* Mattheson honors with mention neither Palestrina nor Fux, and deals with Lassus only briefly on the basis of remarks by PRAETORIUS, J. A. THUANUS, and REUSNER; in the *Critica musica* (Hamburg, 1725), II, p. 104,[10] he waxes enthusiastic about Lassus's *Magnum opus musicum.* The numerous prints of Palestrina and Lassus which are still listed in the literature of the sixteenth and seventeenth centuries remained unknown to him. Of the polyphony of the sixteenth century and of its music-historical role he had no notion. Similarly, in German music literature of the

---

8. K. G. Fellerer, *Der Palestrinastil und seine Bedeutung in der vokalen Kirchenmusik der achzehnten Jahrhunderts* (Augsburg, 1929).

9. In dialogue (in the *Praefatio ad lectorem*) Fux juxtaposes Palestrina (represented as Aloysius) and himself (Josephus) as teacher and student: "Postrema ad faciliorem captum, utque veritas magis elucesceret, secundam partem dialogice tractandam assumpsi, ubi per Aloysium, Magistrum, clarissimum illud Musicae lumen Praenestinum, vel ut alii volunt, Praenestinum intelligo, cui totum, quidquid in hoc genere scientiae in me est, in acceptis refero, cuiusque memoriam, dum vivam, maximo pietatis officio proseque nunquam desinam. Josephi autem nomine Discipulum Musicae artis addiscendae cupidum compello."

10. *Critica musica d. i. Grundrichtige Untersuch- und Beurtheilung vieler Theils vorgefassten, Theils einfältigen Meinungen, Argumenten und Einwürffe, so in alten und neuen, gedruckten und ungedruckten Musicalischen Schrifften zu finden* (Hamburg, 1722–25).

eighteenth century up to Forkel, understanding of classical polyphony continued to remain slight.

With the Italians, however, occupation in the eighteenth century with the "school style" of classical polyphony kept alive interest in the art of the sixteenth century, not the least in connection with the church musical requirements of an *a cappella* style. In south German areas there arose a new, though faulty, understanding of classical polyphony through J. J. Fux, based on the art of Palestrina and other Italians.

Mattheson deemed the cantor Martin ARNOLD (1537–1605) worthy of a longer entry in the *Ehrenpforte* than Lassus, rating alongside the former another cantor, Michael COLET (1545–1616). Of Sethus CALVISIUS (1556–1615), whose quartal theories he discussed in *Das forschende Orchester* (Hamburg, 1721), Mattheson gives only trivial news, nothing establishing his historical significance; likewise for Andreas RASELIUS (1563–1602) and Otto Siegfried HARNISCH (*ca.* 1568–1623). J. P. SWEELINCK (1562–1621) is treated in somewhat greater detail (wherein an undocumented student-teacher relationship with Zarlino is assumed), and of his "keyboard things" Mattheson comments that they are written ". . . in a manner then very popular and now nearly unknown" (p. 331–32). Mattheson's *Ehrenpforte* is oriented towards the music of his time and in this light such a verdict is understandable.[11] Of Claude GOUDIMEL (1514–72) as well he brings together only unrelated bits of information from older literature without discussing his works. Such random selection, determined often by local significance rather than by historical importance, is applied to music theorists as well. GLAREAN,[12] ZACCONI,[13] and other theorists important to the development of sixteenth-century music theory are missing. On the other hand, Mattheson rescues from obscurity the physician Jodok WILLICH (1501–52), who

---

11. Perhaps a continuation of the work announced in the title to the *Ehrenpforte* would have included further musicians of the sixteenth century. Such a continuation did not, however, appear.

12. *Dodecachordon* (Basel, 1547).

13. *Prattica di musica utile te necessaria si al Compositore per comporre i Canti suoi regolatamente, si anco al Cantore per assicurarsi in tutte le cose cantabili, divisa in quattro libro* (Venetia, 1592).

founded a *collegium musicum* in Frankfurt/Oder, the Florentine Angelo POLITIANUS (1454–94), who posed some questions pertaining to music in his *Miscellanea XX* (Lyon, 1550), and the schoolmaster Pankraz CRUEGER (died 1614), who devoted special attention to music in his school in Lübeck.

In the many writings of Mattheson a richer factual knowledge of the sixteenth century is revealed, a knowledge, however, which did not provide him with criteria for evaluating the significance of the era's musicians. Thus, the *Ehrenpforte* offers a scanty selection of sixteenth-century musicians and an even scantier survey of their work. Though important to its time, the *Ehrenpforte* drew a picture of the sixteenth century which was false and unreal. Unhappily, these erroneous notions retained currency in the numerous treatises of the eighteenth century which are based on Mattheson, whereas in musical practice, J. S. Bach [14] turned his interests towards the classical polyphony of Italy.

---

14. K. G. Fellerer, "J. S. Bachs Bearbeitung der *Missa sine nomine* von Palestrina," *Bach-Jahrbuch* XXIV (Leipzig, 1927), 303; G. von Dadelsen, "Eine unbekannte Messen-Bearbeitung Bachs," in *Festschrift K. G. Fellerer,* ed. H. Hüschen (Regensburg, 1962), 88.

PABLO NASARRE'S *ESCUELA MUSICA:*

A REAPPRAISAL

Almonte C. Howell, Jr.
UNIVERSITY OF GEORGIA

If scholars were asked to name the most monumental music theory works of the Renaissance and Baroque eras, works that by their size and scope cover the whole spectrum of musical thought of their respective cultures, most lists would include Zarlino's *Istituzioni,* Praetorius' *Syntagma musicum,* Bermudo's *Declaracion de instrumentos,* and Mersenne's *Harmonie universelle,* to name some of the more prominent. Few if any would include the *Escuela musica* of Fray Pablo Nasarre. Yet between this neglected work and those named above there are many striking points of comparison that should justify Nasarre's being better known to the world of musical scholarship.

The known facts of Nasarre's biography are few, and some of those most widely cited are from questionable sources. We do know that he was blind from birth, and that he was born in the province of Aragon some time around the middle of the seventeenth century. The date 1664 is universally given for his birth, but it is highly doubtful on several counts. First, its apparent earliest source is the *Calendario musical* published in 1859 in Barcelona by Mariano Soriano Fuertes under the pseudonym of "Roberto," a source also responsible for the spurious date sometimes given for Morales' birth.[1] Second, he would have been only

---

1. Robert Stevenson, *Spanish Cathedral Music in the Golden Age* (Berkeley, 1961), p. 7 and footnote 26. Saldoni's *Diccionario Biográfico-Bibliográfico de Efemérides de Músicos españoles,* (4 vols.; Madrid, 1868–81), is often cited as the earliest source of the Nasarre birthdate, but Saldoni attributes it to the *Calendario* and disclaims all responsibility for it himself.

seventeen years old when, in 1681, permission was granted to publish his first rather ambitious theory work, *Fragmentos musicos*. Third, he speaks of *Escuela musica* in the foreword to Volume I in 1724 as the fruit of 50 years' labor, but it is hardly conceivable that he began it at the age of ten. The year 1654 would seem to be about as late a date as we can reasonably assume for his birth, allowing his 50 years' labor to have begun around the age of twenty, and to have included, of course, the publication of *Fragmentos musicos*. The other facts of his biography, some originating from title pages and dedications, others from the old dictionaries, are less open to question. He was a pupil of Pablo Bruna, the celebrated blind organist of Daroca; he entered the Real Convento de San Francisco in Zaragoza at twenty-two as organist, remaining there until his death in 1730; and Martinez de la Roca, famous organist of the cathedral of Toledo, was among his pupils. We hear of him as siding with the conservatives in one of the most celebrated musical quarrels of eighteenth-century Spain, the controversy aroused by a certain daring dissonance in the *Missa Scala Aretina* of Francisco Valls, though he left no writings on the question.[2]

His theory publications are *Fragmentos musicos,* first published in Zaragoza in 1683 with a much amplified edition published in Madrid in 1700, and the *Escuela musica, segun la practica moderna,* published in two volumes in Zaragoza in 1723–24. This enormous work is of folio size, with slightly over 500 pages in each volume. Curiously enough, Volume II appeared first, in 1723, and Volume I appeared the following year from a different printer of the same city.

In addition, some fragments remain of Nasarre's activity as a composer. Frequently cited in reference works is the villancico of 1686, *Arde en incendio de Amor,* found in a manuscript of seventeenth- and eighteenth-century villancicos in the Biblioteca Central of Barcelona.[3] Three toccatas for organ also exist in a

2. Nasarre's role is mentioned in Felipe Pedrell's *Catàlech de la Biblioteca Musical de la Diputacio de Barcelona* (Barcelona, 1908–9), I, 64–87 *passim*. For a condensed presentation of the controversy, see Jose Subirá, *Historia de la Música española e hispanoamericana* (Barcelona, 1953), pp. 552–54.

3. Pedrell, *Catàlech,* II, 25.

late seventeenth-century organ manuscript in this library, cata-
logued as M 1011. Saldoni cites Nasarre as the composer of
numerous organ versets and church compositions for voices and
continuo, on the authority of one Sr. Perez, who claimed to have
seen the vocal pieces.[4]

Nasarre has come down to us with an unfortunate reputation.
Those who know of him at all probably remember him by the
caustic *bon mot* of Eximeno, that he was *organista de nacimiento
y ciego de profesión* (organist by birth and a blind man by profession). Although even Rameau and Tartini come under fire in
Eximeno's battle against the persistence of Pythagoreanism—
the attempt to rationalize a mathematical basis for all aspects
of music—the worst offenders on this score among the moderns
were Cerone and Nasarre, with their archaic concern for celestial
harmonies, proportions, and the influence of the heavenly bodies.
Not content with the effect of his two better-known Italian
treatises,[5] Eximeno chose these two writers for special attack in
a massive polemic novel in Spanish, *Don Lazarillo Vizcardi,*
circulated in manuscript by its author but posthumously printed
in 1872–73 in Madrid under the editorship of Barbieri. It is a
kind of musical *Don Quixote,* in which the obsessed knight is
replaced by a crazed church organist, and the ancient books of
chivalry by Cerone's *El Melopeo y Maestro* and Nasarre's *Escuela musica.* The organist becomes *loco* from the too-assiduous
reading of these works, teaches his followers how to set up a
horoscope based on the eight modes, and catches a fever from
going out on a cold night to hear the harmony of the spheres.

Most of the later treatments of Nasarre have continued to
reflect Eximeno's evaluation of him. Menendez y Pelayo discusses
Escuela musica in his monumental *Historia de las ideas estéticas
en España* of the 1880's, a work which naturally would dwell
more on the Eximeno controversy than on the technical features
of *Escuela musica,* though Menendez y Pelayo does speak favor-

---

4. Saldoni, *Diccionario,* II, 94–97.
5. *Dell' origine e delle regole della musica* (Rome, 1774), and *Dubbio . . .
sopra il Saggio fondamentale pratico di contrapunto del Reverendissimo Padre
Maestro Giambattista Martini* (Rome, 1775). Spanish translations of both appeared in Madrid in the 1790's.

ably of Nasarre's presentation of the Spanish musical tradition. Pedrell analyzes *Escuela musica* in his unfinished *Los musicos españoles antiguos y modernos en sus libros o escritos sobre la música* (Barcelona, 1888), but his chauvinistic hatred of Cerone and his partisanship of the ideas of Eximeno partially blind him to the merits of Nasarre's work. Mitjana's treatment in his 1914 article on Spanish music in the Lavignac *Encyclopédie de la musique* is cribbed largely from Menendez y Pelayo. Subirá's discussion in *Historia de la música española* (Barcelona-Madrid, 1953), follows Pedrell's, and if anything, is even more hostile. He dwells mainly on the disastrous effect brought about by Nasarre in keeping alive the Cerone influence. Recent music encyclopedias, if they mention Nasarre at all, cite him in terms of Eximeno's views.

On what bases can one propose a revaluation and perhaps a revival of the reputation of *Escuela musica*? Upon examining the treatise, one soon realizes that it is not an eighteenth-century document at all in the usual implication of the term. Representing a final expansion and consummation of a work already launched as far back as 1681, emanating from the shelter of the monastery in a country that had fallen steadily behind the rest of Europe in both economic and musical development and was still clinging to the traditions and glories of its musical Golden Age, *Escuela musica* is a last monumental presentation of that tradition. As one becomes familiar with Bermudo, Santa Maria, Montanos, Lorente, and the other recorders of the tradition, one becomes increasingly aware of the value of Nasarre as a last illuminator of those same lines of thought.

Nasarre was, of course, aware of the musical changes of his time. In his role of protector of the ancient art and the native Spanish tradition, he gives us many insights on the points of difference between the old and the new, the Spanish and the foreign. Where current developments seem well within the Spanish tradition, such as the progress of organ music up to his day, he expresses full approval. And in his lively picture of the duties and positions of the church musicians of his society he is thoroughly timely, though undoubtedly describing practices that had changed little from earlier epochs.

With regard to the reliability of Nasarre's treatment of the musical tradition he represented, one need have little doubt. The voluminous eulogies prefixed to his books by some of the principal musicians and churchmen of the day indicate how universally his word was accepted by his contemporaries. Citations of Nasarre as an indubitable authority continue in the Spanish treatises dealing with sacred music through the rest of the century, and even a musician so far evolved from the traditions of Nasarre as Padre Soler mentions him with unquestioning respect in his own *Llave de la modulacion* (Madrid, 1762). Apparently no writer ventures to take issue with his work until Eximeno. The very authority held by Nasarre's writings makes him an obvious target for Eximeno's ridicule, a censure that represents rebellion against a whole tradition.

Each of the two volumes of *Escuela musica* is divided into four books, and each book contains twenty chapters. Those who have criticized the work for being full of confusion have certainly not taken into consideration its painstaking organization, for each book deals quite consistently with the topic of its title, and within each book there is likewise a careful plan of organization, indicated by the chapter headings.

The sources drawn upon for *Escuela musica* are not listed in one place, but analysis of them is simplified by the copious marginal citations that run throughout the two volumes, usually accompanied by direct quotations from the originals. Although Nasarre was apparently restricted to the Latin and Spanish languages, he displays a remarkable array of sources, ranging from the Greek philosophers (in Latin translation) through the medieval church fathers down to the theologians, philosophers, and music theorists of the seventeenth century. Over 90 different authors are cited. Aristotle by far leads the way, with over 100 such citations. Commentators upon Aristotle and encyclopedic organizers of knowledge in the Aristotelian manner are also well represented, from those of early times (Alexander of Aphrodisias, Ustratius, Simplicius, Ammonius, Joannes Grammaticus) down to those of later centuries (Averroes, Bartholomaeus Anglicus, Albertus Magnus, Alexander Alensis, Franz Titelmans, Lorenzo Beyerlinck). For questions of theology and liturgy, he turned most frequently to Thomas Aquinas and Guillaume Durand. His favorite music theorist was his own countryman Salinas, the most learned of the Spanish theorists, with 30 citations. Among theorists writing in the Spanish language, Bermudo takes first place, with 15 citations. For all the attempts to lump Nasarre together with Cerone, he only cites *El Melopeo y Maestro* some 11 times, and then sometimes to differ with it. Other peninsular theorists whose works he quotes several times include Martin de Azpilcueta, Montanos, Tapio Numantino (the plagiarizer of Bermudo [6]), Lorente, and Joseph de Torres. Non-Spanish writers on music among his favorites are Boethius and Gregorio Fabro (Gregor Faber), who lead the way with 12 quotations each, followed by Franchino Gaforio with 11. Also cited are Cassiodorus, Guido of Arezzo, Marchettus of Padua, Tinctoris, Kircher, and Zarlino, among others. In the light of this impressive array of authorities, it is difficult to understand why Pedrell and others refer to him as chiefly an empiricist.

In his "Prologue to the Reader" of Vol. I, Nasarre seems to earn himself the title of reactionary, if one were to read no further. One of the chief reasons for the book, he tells us, is to combat the abuses of dissonance of recent years, particularly "in music for one solo voice, accompanied by species of dissonance . . . outside the rules which art has at its disposal." [7] His conservatism, as he shows here and demonstrates throughout the book, is not merely opposition to change and progress; it is partly an attempt to protect the Spanish tradition, and to keep it in its own individual path, so productive of past glories.

Book I is entitled "The Harmonic Sound, its Divisions, and its Effects." This book, the most theoretical, traditional, and filled with the speculations and superstitions of the ancients, has also no doubt been the most strongly responsible for Nasarre's un-

---

6. This plagiarism has been revealed independently in Robert Stevenson, *Juan Bermudo* (The Hague, 1961), pp. 6–7; and Francisco José León Tello, *Estudios de Historia de la Teoría Musical* (Madrid, 1962), pp. 313–35, where a detailed analysis of it is given.

7. I, c1 v.: "Esta corruptela se halla por comun en Musica de una voz sola, poniendo los acompañamientos de ella en especies disonantes en algunos periodos, fuera de las reglas que el Arte tiene dispuestas para su uso."

fortunate reputation. Much of it comes directly from Greek thought, especially Aristotle, and much also from Boethius, with an unquestioning acceptance of outmoded viewpoints surprising so late as the eighteenth century. Yet as a document of musical thought in Spain in the Baroque Era, it is of great interest, for no doubt it reflects accurately the ideas acceptable to the Inquisition-ridden church, and subscribed to by the great majority of practitioners of sacred music. Similar ideas are found in the lesser theory books and practical instructors of this time and later, and not until the provocative writings of Padre Soler, Eximeno, and others in the latter half of the century do we begin to see new postulates of musical thought.

He begins Book I with the conventional eulogies of music, and a more personal complaint that so many professors of the other sciences regard it so little despite the honor in which it was held by wise men through the ages. Chapter II contains a mixture of legend and distorted history concerning the invention of music and the etymology of the word itself. In speaking of the main divisions of music, he follows the hoary Boethian classification into *musica mundana, humana,* and *de instrumentis,* the latter further subdivided into *instrumentos naturales* (all vocal music), *orgánicos* (wind instruments), and *de cuerda* (stringed instruments). The following chapter, devoted to *musica mundana,* deals with celestial proportions. That for *musica humana* demonstrates harmonic proportions within the human being, including the mixture of elements and humors, and the proportional relationships among the parts of the body. For *musica de instrumentos* no separate chapter is needed, since this is the concern of the remainder of the treatise.

Chapters VI–X of Book I treat the nature of sound (quite accurately described as vibrations produced by bodies and transmitted through air), the difference between high and low pitches (high sounds move less air, but move it more rapidly—not too far afield from the modern wave theory), the causes of imperfections in instrumental sounds, the differences between natural and artificial sounds, and the nature of echoes. In the amusing chapter (IX) on natural sounds, he attempts to notate some of the bird calls and sounds of chickens. Chapters XI-XIII deal with the human voices, classifying the various ranges of the boy, the adult male, the adult female, and the eunuch. Several items supply information on choral practices: first, that the contralto, tenor, and bass parts were all taken by adult males; and second, that although the usual practice is to accompany, no sound is considered more delectable than that of voices *a cappella*.

The remaining five chapters of Book I discuss the effects of music, and doubtless contributed largely to Nasarre's reputation for muddleheadedness. Their topics range from the use of music in the cure of specific diseases to the importance of purity in church music. Of antiquarian interest is a full discussion in Chapters XVIII and XIX of the eight modes, the planet or heavenly body connected with each, and some plainsong examples illustrating each, a presentation which is one of the last but one of the most complete in an illustrious series found in Spanish treatises from Ramis through Bermudo, Cerone, and dozens of lesser writers. As an example, we might summarize his discussion of Mode II, Hypodorian: this mode is associated with the moon, contains the affections of sadness, lamenting, and inconstancy, and is exemplified by the Gradual, Offertory, and Sequence *Dies Irae* of the Mass for the Dead.

Book II is Nasarre's contribution to that most beloved topic of Spanish writers on music from the earliest dawn of Spanish theory—plainsong. Some of the first printed treatises of Spain were devoted exclusively to it; during the eighteenth century the number of plainsong instruction books continued to multiply, and through the history of Spanish theory the major treatises always gave it a substantial portion of space.

To those acquainted with the treatment of plainsong through the course of Spanish musical writings, the uniformity and consistency of that treatment are striking. The same organization, classifications, and terminology are employed from the earliest writings in Spanish down through the eighteenth century. Nasarre's treatment in *Escuela musica* is full, authoritative, and absolutely faithful to these traditions, so that it might be taken as representative of this corpus of theory as a whole. The respect in which it was held is indicated by its frequent citation by later writers of chant instructors.

Nasarre devotes Chapters I through XV to the theoretical bases and terminology of chant, termed *canto llano* in Spanish. This section is of great value not only for completeness but also for the clarity of the definitions it gives of Spanish plainsong terminology. We are shown the traditional gamut, with the notes identified by letters, by solmization syllables, and by Greek names; we are introduced to the Guidonian Hand, still very much alive in eighteenth century Spanish music instruction; and we are presented with the *voces* (the syllables), the *deducciones* (the hexachords), and the *propriedades* (the three varieties of hexachord). In the discussion of modes are shown the seven octave-species or *diapasones,* out of which eight are derived through their division in terms of *diapente* (fifth) and *diatesaron* (fourth); the plagals (*discipulos*) place the diatesaron below, the authentics (*maestros*) place it above the *diapente*. Within the modes, melodies are classified as having *perfeccion* (those that exactly fit the ambitus), *imperfeccion* (those that use less than the full diapason), and *plusquam perfeccion* (those that exceed the diapason). *Tonos mixtos* are those that utilize the full range of the combined authentic and plagal ambitus, *tonos conmixtos* those that bring in cadences foreign to the normal modal limits, and *tonos irregulares* those whose *finales* are not part of the regular modal system.[8] With regard to accidentals, we find Nasarre ranged on the side of the practical-minded theorists such as Santa Maria and Lorente in favor of the use of a B-flat signature with modes 5 and 6, as opposed to the more theoretical-minded Bermudo. We learn also that F-sharp can occur in plainsong for the correction of a tritone, though Nasarre considers B-flat preferable in this function when possible.

Chapters XVI through XVIII, discussing the types of chant in the various liturgical services, contain much of interest to the student of the organ and its connection with the liturgy. For example, in Chapter XVI he discusses the use of organ in alternation with the choir for the Kyrie but not for the other chants of the ordinary; this throws light on the frequency of occurrence of

---

8. The origin of these melodic classifications is discussed in Klaus Wolfgang Niemöller, "Zur Tonus-Lehre der italienischen Musiktheorie des ausgehenden Mittelalters," *Kirchenmusikalisches Jahrbuch,* 40 (1956), 23–32.

Kyrie versets in Spanish organ liturgy, but the comparative rarity of complete organ Masses. He also explains another phenomenon of Spanish Kyrie usage that illuminates, for example, the Cabezón versets for the Kyrie in each of the eight modes: a Spanish practice, he reports, is to select a Kyrie not according to its degree of solemnity, but rather according to its mode, which should fit that of the preceding Introit.

Chapter XIX deals with another traditional type of Spanish chant, that sung in mensural notation with mixed long and short values and regular meters. Such mensural chant, termed *canto figurado* by some theorists, was used for most of the office hymns, the sequences, and some of the chants of the ordinary. The most celebrated example is the traditional Spanish *Pange lingua* in triple meter, an engaging and surprisingly modern tune that was an overwhelming favorite for organ settings from Cabezón through the organ literature of the eighteenth century.

Book III is devoted to what the Spanish term *Canto de organo,* a term that has nothing to do with the organ, but applies to mensural music in general. Synonyms for it, given in Chapter I, are *canto ritmico, canto metrico,* and *canto mensural.* This is one of the two most informative books in the treatise, and the very conservatism of the work and of Spanish church music in Nasarre's time endows it with its greatest value to the scholar, for it continues to be a reliable guide to practices that extend back to the Golden Age of Spanish church music. Constant reference is made to the classics of Spanish theory such as Salinas and Bermudo, in many cases illuminating points that are somewhat ambiguous in these. Of course one must be aware of statements that apply only to later music, but Nasarre himself frequently clarifies the differences between ancient and modern practice.

The first major topic, covered in Chapters IV-X, is the subject of time values, meters, and that traditional Spanish unit of measurement, the *compas.*[9] The closest equivalent to *compas* in our terminology is the bar, and in eighteenth-century Spanish music the *compas* is almost invariably marked with the barline. But the concept of *compas* considerably antedates the concept of bar,

---

9. Modern spelling requires an accent: *compás.* In all citations of terms from Nasarre's work we are retaining his orthography.

going back to the earliest Spanish writers on music in the late
fifteenth century, and *compas* is related more to a standard rate
of beating than to the idea of a metrical unit. For example, while
some of the faster ternary meters have a ternary *compas,* some
of the slower ones are made up of groupings of three *compases,*
each of which is binary. In general it can be said (of the traditional meters, at least, and not the newer ones introduced from
Italy) that the *compas* consists of one semibreve unless the time
signature bears a slash, and in that case, of one breve. Viewed
another way, one might say that the Spanish *compas* seems to be
the measurement of the distance from one strong beat to the
next.[10]

Nasarre's description in Chapter IV of the manner of beating
the *compas* is at least as ancient in Spanish theory as the treatise
of Duran, *Sumula de canto de organo* of 1498. The *compas* is
divided into two movements of the hand, one descending, the
other ascending; the first, or downbeat is called the *dar* ("to give
forth"), the second or upbeat the *alzar* ("to raise" or "to lift").
There are two kinds of *compas, igual* (binary, with *dar* and *alzar*
of the same duration), and *desigual* (ternary, with one motion
twice the duration of the other). Nowhere in traditional Spanish
theory is there any clear indication of an actual three beats to the
compas. The normal *compas desigual* will have two units on the
dar to one on the *alzar;* but Nasarre alone among the theorists
indicates certain kinds of pieces in which the *alzar* will be
the doubled beat (Chapters IX and X).

Nasarre introduces us to the four traditional meters of Spanish
sacred music, and apparently the ones still most commonly used
in his day. Two are binary, two are ternary, and within each pair
one is the augmented form of the other. Of the two binary
meters, dealt with in Chapter V, one is *compas mayor,* also

---

10. The relation of the term *compas* to the earlier concept, tactus, and the
later concept, bar, would make a challenging study in itself. Part of the challenge lies in the fact that the same word *compas* was retained as the earlier
function gave way to the later. Theory writing in Spanish, as far as I am aware,
did not employ the word *tacto.* In French, on the other hand, *tacte* and *compas*
seem to have been used synonymously in speaking of the tactus. With Nasarre's
writing we seem to have a sort of halfway point between the ancient and modern meanings of *compas.*

called *compas entero* to indicate that it is thought of as the complete *compas* of traditional music. It contains one breve to the *compas* and is indicated by the half circle with a slash: ₵ . The other is known as *compas menor* or *compasillo* and contains (like modern 4/4) one semibreve to the *compas*. It is marked with the half circle: C . The functions and relationships of these two meters need further clarification for the study of performance practices.[11] In the organ music, one finds both signatures, sometimes changing from one to the other in the course of a piece. The Spanish theorists seem to differ among themselves as to the actual relationships: Bermudo speaks of *compasillo* (or *compasete* as he terms it) as being the faster, but as Nasarre quite correctly points out, *compas mayor* really produces faster music because it brings in twice as many notes to the *compas*. But after all, he reminds the reader, the arbitrary setting of the tempo or rate of beating is what will ultimately determine the speed of the music, proving that, at least in his time, the pulse was not given at a fixed, standard rate.

Among the two ternary meters or *compases desiguales,* dealt with in Chapters VI and VII, *proporcion mayor* is marked with 3 ₵ or $\frac{3}{2}$ ₵, and it contains one breve divided into three semibreves, six minims, etc. *Proporcion menor* is expressed by $\frac{3}{2}$ C and $\frac{3}{2}$ (or sometimes C), and it contains one semibreve divided into three minims, six semiminims, etc. The term *proporcion* and the use of three over two indicate the continued recognition of the proportional significance of these, as containing three units in place of two in the corresponding binary meters. Nasarre states that the *proporcion menor* is more appropriate for secular music than sacred, especially in rhythms that dot the first minim.

Nasarre treats in passing various other meters less in use. Interesting is his coverage in Chapter VII of that with the signature of the full circle, the ternary of the ancients, which he calls

---

11. An illuminating discussion of the matter in terms of an earlier period is seen in Charles Jacobs, *Tempo Notation in Renaissance Spain* (Brooklyn: Institute of Medieval Music, 1964).

ternario menor. It is taken in *compas igual,* for in it the breve is the ternary value, but the semibreve is the unit of the *compas,* so that it requires a grouping of three *compases* to produce the ternary effect. This meter appears from time to time in Spanish organ music, often without the ternary signature, as for example in the Cabezón *Pange lingua* variations, deceiving the performer at first glance into thinking it a binary work, until he discovers the ternary grouping into which its bars naturally fall. Chapter IX, treating various proportions such as *dupla, tripla, sesquialtera,* and others, brings in time signatures and barrings of more modern aspect, such as 6/4 and 12/8. Though they are conceived in older proportional terms, musically they differ little from their modern usage.

The other topic treated exhaustively in Book III is that of the modes or tones of *canto de organo* (Chapters XIV–XVII). The treatment is so detailed, and the subject so worthy of a separate study, that we shall content ourselves here with a few general observations. First, as for the words *modo* and *tono,* their synonymous use by most of the European theorists goes back to Boethius himself, who saw no essential difference between them. Bermudo follows him in this, and of the important Spanish theorists, only Salinas distinguishes between them, equating *tonus* with the idea of keys or transposition scales, and *modus* with the octave-species, or different arrangements of steps and half steps within the octave. In Chapter XIV Nasarre acknowledges this distinction by Salinas, but seems content to follow the majority of Spanish writers in using the word *tono* with both meanings. Indeed, if the distinction made by Salinas is valid, the term *tono* is more accurate, since the purely modal differences are becoming increasingly effaced, and the *tonos* are more and more functioning merely as transposition scales.

A second point in which Nasarre follows virtually the entire corpus of Spanish theory is his fidelity to the idea of eight modes and no more. Perhaps the long shadow of the Church of Spain was partially responsible for this. He does cite the four additional ones from Cerone's description, but considers these unnecessary, since in practice C major is usually assigned to the fifth tone, and A minor to the third.

A third point to note is Nasarre's limitation to the accidentals in practical use in his time. This is still the era of mean-tone tuning, which means that only five accidentals were available on keyboard instruments—B-flat, E-flat, F-sharp, C-sharp, and G-sharp. Almost his only mention of the existence of equal temperament is in the discussion of the "Spanish guitar," [12] which unlike other instruments, divides the whole step "geometrically" into two equal half steps; but he does not propose that this system be followed by the other instruments. For the harp and the harpsichord re-tuning is easy, so that one can play any key, and in Chapters XVIII and XIX he shows how the eight tones can be transposed to keys up to five sharps or flats for these instruments. But this is only when the instruments have been re-tuned to change the semitones in line with mean-tone tuning, as for example re-tuning B-flat into A-sharp, or F-sharp into G-flat.

Nasarre recognizes in Chapter XIV that the issue of diapason or octave-species becomes a little cloudy in dealing with polyphonic music. He points out that in each mode the trebles and tenors have one type of ambitus, the contraltos and basses another. In general, he says, for authentic modes the ambitus of the trebles and tenors will be in "harmonic" construction (the fifth below, the fourth above), and that of the contraltos and basses in "arithmetic" (the fourth below, and the fifth above). The contrary will be true in the plagal modes.

The main bulk of Nasarre's discussion of the *tonos de canto de organo* is the practical business of describing the common usage of the time, including the finales, mediations or dominants, octave-species, and key signatures. This material is presented in several different series: in Chapter XV we have the normal tones of sung polyphony and the normal tones for the organ in accompanying and alternating with the choir, in Chapter XVI the *tonos accidentales* (that is, transposed) for voices, and in Chapter XVII the *tonos accidentales* for organ. Among the organ tones distinction is made between those for the psalms, with their special structural problems, and those for the nonpsalmodic chants and polyphonic compositions. Even among the common

---

12. I, 316 and again 462.

tones, those for organ differ in some cases from the sung ones because of the common practice of notating for the voices at one pitch level and transposing the actual sound to another. For example, Tone V is generally notated as an F scale for the voices, but transposed down a fourth in performance; the organ key therefore is C.

Nasarre concludes Book III with three chapters discussing the use of instruments in accompanying. He deals at length with the harp and its notation, pointing out that this instrument is almost as widely used in Spanish churches as the organ. Its greatest value lies in its flexibility of tuning. In Chapters XIX and XX he treats accompanying on the keyboard. He shows us the traditional Spanish keyboard tablature, but points out that it is now virtually obsolete, as indeed the contemporaneous manuscripts of organ music prove. For a much more thorough coverage of keyboard accompanying, he refers the reader to the popular and widespread treatise on that subject by Joseph de Torres.[13]

Book IV is another of great interest to the musicologist, for it discusses the instruments of the era, with particular attention to keyboard instruments. The general topic of the book is proportions, and his rather unusual approach to instruments is by way of the proportions among their parts, addressed especially to instrument makers as a guide to scientific principles of construction.

The opening chapters of the book concern proportions and mathematical principles in general. The instructive value of this section is still great for today's readers, and one will seldom see, whether in ancient or modern writing, any more lucid and well-illustrated presentation of the mathematical concepts so constantly referred to in early music theory. Outstanding are Chapters IV and V, the first dealing with the five genera of proportions (Multiplex, Superparticular, Superpartiens, Multiplex superparticular, and Multiplex superpartiens), and the sec-

---

13. *Reglas generales de acompañar, en organo, clavicordio, y harpa . .* (Madrid, 1702). Nasarre was doubtless glad of the opportunity to repay a debt of gratitude to Torres, principal organist of the Royal Chapel and printer of music, for having published the 1700 edition of *Fragmentos musicos* along with laudatory statements of his own concerning Nasarre.

ond with the three kinds of proportional series (Arithmetic, Geometric, and Harmonic).

Before turning to instruments, Nasarre discusses the mathematical aspects of two of the topics treated in the previous book, the modes and the time values. The material on time values in Chapters VIII, IX, and XII, despite a mathematical orientation, throws more light on performance practices and the differences between Spanish and Italian usage than did the treatment of the same matter in the previous book. Nasarre points out in Chapter XII that a greater number of time signatures and a greater flexibility of the rate of beating produce a far greater variety of musical tempos in modern music than were available to the musicians of the past. But sudden and extreme changes of tempo, he says, are a foreign importation, due particularly to Italian taste. The Spanish tradition and the natural inclination of Spanish taste is to accelerate gradually and with carefully marked proportions.

The last seven chapters of Book IV are devoted to instruments. Chapter XIV approaches the subject from a somewhat abstract standpoint by discussing the proportional aspects of the shapes and forms of instruments. In Chapter XV Nasarre gives descriptions of the main types and tunings of stringed instruments. Included are the harp, with the fullest discussion of all, the six- and seven-course vihuelas, and the five-course vihuela, called the *guitarra española*. Among the bowed stringed instruments are the *violinc*, the *violone* (here meaning violoncello), the *vihuela de arco* (viola da gamba), the *lira* (probably the lyra da braccio, referred to by Nasarre as practically obsolete in his time), and that strange one-stringed instrument, the *tromba marina*.

Chapter XVI treats of the stringed keyboard instruments. Although the *manocordio*,[14] *clavicordio,* and other such instruments are mentioned frequently in Bermudo and other Spanish theorists, Nasarre is one of the few to discuss them technically enough to make clear what term applies to what instrument. We discover quite unequivocally here that the Spanish term *clavi-*

---

14. The spelling used by Nasarre, though one may more commonly find *monacordio* and *monicordio*. On the other hand *monocordio* refers to the monochord.

cordio refers to the harpsichord, while the clavichord proper is called the *manocordio*. The *manocordio,* we learn, is essential to the beginning study of the organ. In addition to these two more common instruments, he devotes a lengthy discussion to the *claviorgano* an instrument with both strings and organ pipes, either mechanism able to sound separately or both together. Chapter XVII concerns the wind instruments. Both here and in the previous book he stresses their continued use in church music for doubling the voices, a regular feature of Spanish cathedrals and royal chapels. Such was the function of the *ministriles,* as the old cathedral accounts call the wind-instrument players. The instruments mentioned most prominently are the *flautas, chirimías* (shawms or oboes), *baxones* (bassoons), *cornetas* (the instrument with finger holes and cup mouthpiece), *trompetas,* and *sacabuches* (trombones). Nasarre holds that *sacabuches* form a better bass to the oboes than do the bassoons because they have a clearer tone quality.

The remaining three chapters are devoted to the organ, and apparently constitute the most complete discussion of it in any Spanish work before the nineteenth century—in fact virtually the only pre-nineteenth-century treatment that goes into technical detail. Chapter XVIII discusses the tonal make-up of the Spanish organ. Pitch levels of pipes are given in a measure characteristic of early Spanish stoplists, the *palmo,*[15] of approximately eight inches. Twenty-six *palmos* is our 16′ pitch level, 13 our 8′ or normal unison pitch, 6½ our 4′ level. The measurements for the fifth and twelfth are 9 and 4½ *palmos* respectively. Nasarre classifies organs into four categories: those based on 16′ pitch for the largest cathedrals and churches; those based on 8′ for the moderate-sized churches; the little 4′ organs for the smallest churches; and finally the *portatiles,* also based on 4′ pitch. He lists the constitution of the chorus of principals (called *flautados*) for a large church organ: included are the principal, octave, twelfth, fifteenth, nineteenth, twenty-second, and twenty-sixth. He also gives the composition of the main mixtures, the heavy one called the *lleno,* and the lighter one termed the *cimbala.* He

---

15. Sometimes *palma.*

discusses the factors affecting the tone quality of pipes, such as scale, shape of mouth, shape of body, and material of which the pipe is made. We are shown why tin makes a better pipe tone than lead: after all, is not tin under the influence of Jupiter while lead is governed by Saturn? A section is devoted to the reed pipes, with descriptions of such distinctively Spanish reeds as the *clarin* (exterior trumpet), and the *trompeta real* ("royal trumpet," a softer interior trumpet). Chapter XIX is of more interest to the organ builder than to the general musician. It contains an exhaustive discussion of the internal construction of the instrument, its proportions and pipe scales,[16] and the construction materials. The final chapter deals with organ tuning. Of particular interest is a passage on setting the temperament preparatory to tuning the instrument, using the middle octaves of the 8' *flautado*. It is a good presentation of the practical method of setting up a keyboard for mean-tone tuning. In summary, the temperament involves proceeding by slightly narrowed fifths and pure major thirds. Most of the notes are derived through a circle of slightly flattened fifths, but B, F-sharp, C-sharp, and G-sharp are established as pure major thirds.

The first volume of *Escuela musica,* though much of it is of a highly practical nature and based on observation of contemporary practices, has been chiefly descriptive. The imparting of skills, especially composition, is the main concern of the second volume. It duplicates Volume I in some topics, such as modes and metres, but the emphasis now is upon their role in composing.

The first book of Volume II deals with progressions, intervals, and dissonance treatment. Its topics include progressions (*movimientos*) in general, the consonances, to each of which he devotes a separate chapter, the dissonances, and the various acceptable ways of treating the latter in composition. Occasional pieces of incidental information provide insight on performance practices of Nasarre's time. For instance Chapter IV, on the unison, affords us the rather surprising information that the practice of

---

16. Dr. James Wyly (Elmhurst College, Elmhurst, Illinois), whose knowledge of Spanish organs is exhaustive, tells me that Nasarre's proportional figures, especially for pipe scales, are not always dependable.

using several singers to a part—choral singing in other words—
is rare in Spain for polyphonic music, and is mainly restricted to
plainsong. On the other hand the practice is common in Italy,
where those who have heard it find it very agreeable. It occurs
mainly in Spanish polyphonic music when an eight-voiced composition is reduced at some section to four voices. So unusual is
choral singing for Spanish ears that he finds it necessary to give
a theoretical justification for the use of consecutive unisons thus
resulting, since these are otherwise forbidden in counterpoint.
Nassare's treatment of the imperfect consonances in Chapters
XI–XIV shows how mean-tone tuning must be taken into consideration in composition: thirds and sixths occur in various
sizes, and at times G-sharp must be used to supply the missing
A-flat, or E-flat must substitute for D-sharp; but these effects are
very harsh, especially when used in the interval of the sixth.
Nasarre says little concerning the treatment of dissonance that
would not have been fully approved by Palestrina or Victoria.
His general conservatism here may perhaps be symbolized by his
statements condemning the freely-introduced interval of the
minor seventh (Chapter XVIII), even in the dominant chord,
though he admits that many musicians justify such use now with
the claim that it "sounds good."

Chapters XIX and XX, which close Book I, expound in a
very interesting fashion upon an idea present in some of the
earlier Spanish theorists, but nowhere treated so fully as here,
that of *supposicion*. According to this concept, dissonances are
justified by "supposing" the consonances for which they are sub-
stituted. In suspension dissonances the consonance is supposed
in place of the dissonance that actually sounds. All sorts of *glosas*
or ornamental figures are justified by supposing the legitimate
note that they displace. This interesting viewpoint provides a
counter argument to those who claim, like Sachs, that the purity
of the Palestrina style is a "disastrous illusion" [17] because of the
practice of diminution that prevailed in actual performance. If
one may believe Nasarre, in properly executed diminution the
listener will still experience or imagine the correct note, that is,

---

17. *Our Musical Heritage* (2nd ed.; New York, 1955), pp. 153–54.

the note that has been displaced by the diminution. *Supposicion* has an important bearing on musical meters: many passages that seem to violate the rules of dissonance treatment are justified if one supposes the meter different from what it appears in its notated form. As a telling example, Nasarre presents in Chapter XIX a passage notated in *compasillo* (C, semibreve to the *compas*) with apparently incorrectly treated suspension dissonances; but when one perceives that it is actually *ternario* (O, each three *compases* equalling one perfect breve) it becomes entirely correct, as he demonstrates by re-notating it in the latter meter.

Book II deals with counterpoint over a cantus firmus. It includes an elaborate series of progressive exercises, one of the sources of Eximeno's censure, though actually a traditional and perfectly natural approach to the pedagogy of counterpoint. The progressions include the familiar species: proceeding from larger note values to smaller and mixed values, from one voice with cantus firmus (termed *contrapunto suelto,* "single counterpoint") up to four or more voices with cantus firmus (termed *contrapunto a concierto,* "concerted counterpoint"), and from a plain-song cantus firmus in long values to a free cantus firmus in mixed values. In general, Nasarre is closer to the Renaissance than to the Baroque in the strictness he requires in the treatment of dissonance and sonority. He is aware of this strictness, and ascribes it to the Spanish taste. "In foreign nations such as Italy, France, and others," he says, "they do not consider it necessary to place each voice on the consonance appropriate to it, to make it sound best . . . but in Spain there is no doubt that music is the more beautiful for being the more bound by the rules. I write according to the practice in our nation. . . ." [18] Mentioned in Chapter XIX is the Italian preference for four parts augmented by the unison doublings of several voices to the part, as against the Spanish preference for thick textures of 6, 8, or more parts.

A secondary value of Book II is its further illumination of

---

18. II, 246: "En Naciones estrañas, como son Italia, Francia, y otros, no se haze cuenta con poner cada voz en la consonancia que le toca, que pues suena bien . . . pero en España no ay duda en que le musica es mas primorosa, por trabajarse mas ceñida à las reglas. Yo escrivo segun se practica en nuestra Nacion. . . ."

metrical problems through practical examples of the meters. Not only are counterpoint exercises given in all the main meters used in Spanish *canto de organo,* but it also is shown how these meters fit each other in various combinations. The contrapuntal examples cast further light on the relative tempos of the metrical signs, since dissonance treatment is partly a function of the tempo. For example, a tempo that permits dissonance on passing minims will naturally be faster than one that requires all minims not in suspension to be consonant.

Book III deals with free composition, that is, composition without cantus firmus, termed *composicion suelta.* Nasarre begins with four-voiced free counterpoint, and discusses the use of imitative forms. In Chapter III the terms *paso, fuga,* and *canon* are given; in Spanish terminology of the eighteenth century *paso* seems to be the equivalent of fugue, while *fuga* applies to strict canon. *Canon* designates the type of canon in which two or more parts are derived from one by the use of printed signs. A fourth term, *intento,* is less clearly defined, but probably applies to a point of imitation, as well as to the subject being imitated. These terms are of interest to the student of Spanish Baroque organ music, since they occur as generic titles in the literature of the instrument. *Paso* and *intento* may possibly be eighteenth-century substitutes for the classic term *tiento.*

Chapters VI–XII contain a systematic discussion of types of composition common to that time, from one-voiced works through works for eight or more voices. One-voiced compositions, treated in Chapter VI, include both plainsong and non-liturgical solo works with accompaniment. We learn here that although Latin texts predominate in the Spanish church, the vernacular was permitted for two major festivals, Christmas and Corpus Christi. Secular solo works in Spanish are generally called *tonos,* Nasarre indicates, although he prefers the term *cantilena.*

Nasarre divides the study of two-part composition in Chapter VII into works for two voices, works for two instruments, and works for voice with instrument. *Simphonia* is his term for a purely instrumental piece, and the term *sonata* does not seem to appear at all in the *Escuela.* Discussion of three-voiced works in

Chapter VIII forces him to recognize the popularity of the trio instrumental scoring of the Italians, though the Spanish themselves employ it far less. He points out the Italian use of dissonances, violent changes of pace, and figured embellishments, all of which provide excitement but lack the purity of the Spanish style. He suggests that perhaps the most beautiful music of all might result from the blend of Italian variety with Spanish perfection of sonority.

The treatment in Chapter IX of composition in four voices leads to a discussion of Spanish instrumental music, which prefers this texture. In organ music, two standard arrangements of the four voices occur: (1) for *composiciones llenas* (uniform registration throughout a single keyboard) the voices are generally divided two and two between the hands; (2) pieces in *medio registro* (the upper and lower halves of the same keyboard in different registrations) more often distribute the voices three and one, giving the highly embellished solo voice to one hand and the three accompanying voices to the other. Acquaintance with the original manuscripts of seventeenth- and early eighteenth-century Spanish organ works—the works of Aguilera or Cabanilles, for example—bears out the accuracy of his description. Furthermore, four-voiced texture tends to be rather inflexibly maintained because of the general practice of notating organ music in four-stave open score.

Purely instrumental music seldom exceeds four voices, but a variety of types of vocal compositions is seen in the larger textures, described in Chapters X–XII. Included are works with additional canonic voices, works for divided choir, and works for concerted bodies of voices and instruments. The remainder of the book concerns what the composer needs to know about meters and moods or "ayres" of music, about the application of the eight modes to composition, and about accidentals, particularly in cadences. The conservatism of the style Nasarre advocates, and his resistance to the innovations of the Italians are in constant evidence. Traditional Spanish meters, for instance, he considers more fit for the solemn atmosphere of church than such Italian signatures as 2/4 or 3/8, which are more suited to light secular music. Or he echoes the two-century-old warnings of

Bermudo against the violation of the purity of the modes, and utters a diatribe against the Italian abuse of accidentals, a practice "insufferable to the artistic ear." [19] In the concluding chapter of Book III, Nasarre sums up six principles for the composition of good music: (1) choose with care the mode to be used, and follow its natural limitations, modulating from it only with caution and for a justifiable expressive reason; (2) follow the scientific laws of composition; (3) retain perfect sonority in the concord of sounds; (4) stick to the natural limitations of the voices or instruments for which one is writing; (5) distinguish between the sacred Latin and secular "vulgar" styles; and (6) follow the sense and meaning of the text.

The fourth and concluding book of Volume II is entitled "The *Glosa* and other matters necessary to composers." It is really two books in one, the first ten chapters being devoted to the *glosa* or embellishment, and the remaining ten to the *otras advertenceis*, including such matters as the duties of various classes of musicians, the teaching and playing of organ, and preparation for competitive examinations in music.

The opening chapter states Nasarre's theory of the purpose and place of the *glosa* in music. Following Aristotle's division of music into the "Moral" (the following of laws), the "Affective" (the producing of the passions), and the "Abstractive" (the delighting of the spirit), *glosas* are utilized for the latter two of these functions. Nevertheless, a distinction among *glosas* themselves divide them between the "scientific" and the "natural," the former regulated by rules of composition, the latter used intuitively more to please the senses than the reason. The natural or instinctive type would generally be that improvised in performance, the scientific type that utilized in composition. The true essence of the *glosa* is *supposicion,* the "supposing" of a single note that is replaced by two or more notes of smaller value (cf. above). Through this means the *glosa* can be analyzed and made to follow the natural laws of composition.

The chapters that follow present the classification of types of *glosa* and the laws of correct and incorrect treatment. Of most

---

19. II, 370.

interest is Chapter X, which gives additional insight on performance practices, and national differences between Spanish and
Italian usage. The Spanish, we learn, prefer *glosas* in instrumental music to those in vocal, and feel that diminution suits
the needs and nature of instruments more than of voices. Glosas
in vocal music interfere with the text, which the Spanish treat
with more respect than do the Italians. A compromise of great
effectiveness is for the voice to sing its part unembellished, with
glosas used in the accompanying parts. Nevertheless, Nasarre
does discuss vocal *glosas* and presents a valuable musical illustration of a vocal passage first unornamented and then with
glosas.

The last ten chapters of Book IV are of interest today for information on performance practices, on teaching methods, and on
the duties and sociological positions of the church musicians of
Nasarre's time.

Chapter XI deals with the obligations of chapel masters and
other maestros who teach music. *Maestro de capilla,* the most
honored office in the field of music, carries three chief duties:
composing, teaching, and conducting. Among instrumentalists,
the organist is by far the most essential in church music, because
although other instruments may accompany voices, only the
organ may play alone during the service.

The duties of the teacher of choral singing and composing
comprise Chapter XII. Nasarre recommends eight or nine as the
best age for starting the vocal training of children. They should
be grounded in solmization, the aural perception of intervals, and
note values. Later they will learn to improvise *glosas* in performance, and to improvise counterpoint over given melodies.
Essential in training the child in correct elements of music is to
explain the reasons for all the rules.

Chapter XIII gives further advice for those wishing to teach
composition. A section is devoted to short methods for those who
would learn to compose purely for pastime. By this method it
can be taught in less than a year.

Chapter XIV deals with conducting practices. Four requirements for good conducting are (1) to be a good practical composer; (2) to have a good ear; (3) to be dextrous in indicating

time; and (4) to use careful rehearsal and preparative methods. In Nasarre's discussion of the first two points, we are made aware of some problems that faced the conductor of that time but that we are spared today. The most demanding of these, perhaps, was the necessity of learning to follow simultaneously separate parts not arranged in score. The conductor must have these so well under control that he can correct faulty entrances instantly by singing the part accurately himself. Point (3) involves such matters as the correct interpretation of time signatures, especially when they change during the course of the composition, requiring a slower or faster beat. He emphasizes the importance of the two motions of *dar* and *alzar* (downbeat and upbeat for each *compas*), and the practice of using two only, one the double of the other, in triple meters.

Chapters XV through XIX are devoted to the teaching and playing of organ. According to the author, this art deserves more attention than the matters previously treated because few churches can afford *capillas,* but many more compensate for the elaborate polyphony of voices and instruments by using organ in alternation with plainsong. Nasarre treats in detail such fundamentals as the position of body and hands, the importance of good rhythm and legato, and the age, native endowment, and intelligence requisite for undertaking the study of the organ.

Chapter XVII deals with the execution of organ music. A discussion of fingering leads to his only treatment of Spanish embellishments, and apparently the only detailed discussion of it after the sixteenth and early seventeenth century presentations of Santa Maria, Bermudo, Correa de Arauxo, and others. The earlier terms *redoble* and *quiebro* are supplanted by new ones— *trino* for the trill, and *aleado* for the mordent. The *trino* is so called because it requires three fingers, although it has a minimum of five notes. Nasarre's *trino* seems to begin always with a turn starting on the main note, followed by a trill between main note and upper neighbor:

In the stringed keyboard instruments with their dying tone, trills are used by necessity, and should be kept through the whole value of the note. On the organ they are used only for their pleasing qualities, and may cease after half the value of the note. For the right hand the third finger is best for the main note, for the left hand the second finger. The beats of the trill should be at the same rate throughout. It is interesting to note that Nasarre's *trino* corresponds exactly with the *redoble* described by Santa Maria [20] over a century and a half earlier, a clear indication of the uniformity of the Spanish keyboard tradition. The *aleado* of Nasarre is the familiar mordent consisting of three notes: the main note, the one below, and a return to the main note. These should be executed by the second and third fingers in either hand. He cautions that mordents not interrupt the *compas*, and that they not be used in fast passage work because of their tendency to spoil the clarity. Overuse of mordents marks the amateur. The latter part of the chapter contains an interesting discussion of ancient versus modern organ music. Here Nasarre hardly shows himself to be a reactionary. He outlines the improvement in organs in the last century, and the greater advancement of the music thereby. These improvements have included the divided keyboard and the greater variety of registers and tone colors. Improvements in playing technique include the use of the divided register with solo against three voices, the even greater demands of two solo voices in one register against two accompanying voices in the other, and the increase in the agility and complexity of *glosas*. Because of the advancement in *glosa* technique and the more brilliant registers of the modern organ, accompanying voices often have as much activity as solo ones, which are distinguished from their accompaniment only in the use of reed color. Conservatives—not including himself among their number —speak of the old music as best because it was "of greater gravity and beauty." [21] Here he disagrees. The gravity and beauty are increased by today's greater advancement in technique, and especially by increased use of imitation, even in accompanying voices. No doubt representative composers of the style-periods he has in mind would include Cabezón and Soto among the

---

20. Fray Tomás de Santa María, *Libro llamado Arte de tañer Fantasia* (Valladolid, 1565), fol. 46 v. ff. An English edition by the author and Earle Hultberg is in preparation.

21. II, 474: "mas grave y de mas primor."

ancients,[22] Cabanilles, Aguilera de Heredia, and Bruna among the moderns, for the points of difference he has described are very clear in comparing the music of these two generations.

Chapter XVIII explains why an organist should be thoroughly grounded in music theory and composition: he must understand how to remain in the mode while improvising in alternation with plain song, how to improvise with such variety as to hold the interest of the listeners, how to conduct in place of the *maestro de capilla* when necessary, and how to examine candidates for musical posts, and he must possess sound judgment in the evaluation of organs. The discussion of improvisation contains a full statement of Nasarre's ideals of what organ music should be. (It must be emphasized here that the written music that has come down to us is only a sparse record of the kinds of pieces that were improvised continually by master organists.)

> For one who plays the organ every day, variety in the music is a great advantage for the purpose of giving pleasure; he who is a composer can vary his music greatly, inventing new ideas every day; now playing divided keyboard pieces for right and left hands, now playing a single voice with ornamented accompaniment, now using imitation, sometimes with two treble voices, other times with two bass voices, utilizing registrations appropriate to the musical ideas. Likewise he can play unified keyboard pieces with much variety in the musical ideas as well as in the moods, bringing in a subject in a point of imitation, playing with it a while, and interweaving other subjects with it; so that in addition to being the way of giving pleasure through musical variety, it displays considerable dexterity, to the extent that great musical intelligence will be attributed to the organist who knows how to pursue a point of imitation skillfully on the instrument.[23]

---

22. The fact that the music of Cabezón and his generation was still known and used in early eighteenth-century Spain is proved by the important four-volume organ manuscript in the Biblioteca nacional de Madrid, *Flores de musica,* compiled 1706–9 by Fray Antonio Martín y Coll. See Anglés and Subirá, *Catálogo musical de la Biblioteca nacional de Madrid,* I (Barcelona, 1946,) 295–309. Although composers in the collection are not identified in the original, Dr. Wyly and I have noted the presence, apparently. hitherto unrecognized, of pieces from Cabezón's *Obras* of 1587 alongside the many pieces of later schools. Anglés identifies a few by Auguilera and Cabanilles.

23. II, 477: ". . . el que pulsa el Organo todos los dias, es muy conveniente el que varie de musica si ha de dar gusto; y el que es Compositor, puede varier mucho, inventando cada dia nuevas ideas; yà tocando partido de mano derecha, de mano izquierda, yà suelto, con los acompañamientos glossados, yà con imitaciones, unas vezes dos Tiples, otros dos Baxos, acomodando los registros que fueren mas al caso, segun las ideas. Tambien tocando en lleno con muchas

The nineteenth chapter contains a number of specific duties of the organist. Solo playing and playing in alternation with the choir are of course the principal ones, and he speaks with admiration not only of the fugal improvisations of the great Spanish virtuosos, but also of the imitations and embellishments they play over plainsong melodies, especially over the traditional Spanish *Pange lingua*. Particularly essential in the daily service is improvisation over the psalm tone melodies in alternation with the choir, but the organist must be careful in retaining the finalis to help the singers enter properly in their versets. Nasarre also discusses some of the problems of accompanying, both from the bass part and (for solo songs) from the treble melody. The chapter continues with a discussion of specialized teaching problems that faced the organist. After treating some of the techniques of teaching the blind, he gives a quaint discussion of the proper attitude of the organist who must teach young girls preparing for convent life. Such teaching is burdensome "because of the inconstancy of the sex, the tender age, and the smallness of the hand. . . . But all these are circumstances for the greater mortification of the teacher in the exercise of patience; and that alone that obliges him to undergo these circumstances is the holy end that the pupils shall succeed in being brides of Christ, praising Him here on earth in order that they may do so afterward for eternity in the chorus of virgins." [24]

Nasarre concludes *Escuela musica* with a chapter on the competitive examinations for musical posts in the churches. He covers the positions of music directors (*maestros*), organists, singers, harpists, and wind instrument players, the latter two classes

---

diferencias, assi en las ideas, como en los ayres, yà entrando un passo, sirviendole de thema, sobre el qual pueda tocar algun tiempo, enlazando otros intentos sobre èl; que à mas de ser modo que deleyta por la variedad de musica, es muy primoroso, y tanto, que se atribuye la inteligencia de la musica à un organista que sepa entrar, y seguir un passo con propriedad en el instrumento."

24. II, 483: ". . . por la inconstancia de el sexo, la poca edad, y la mano pequeña. . . . Todas estas son circunstancias para mayor mortificacion de un Maestro, por el exercicio de paciencia: y solo le puede obligar à passar por ello el fin santo de que lleguen à lograr el ser Esposas de Christo, alabandole acà en la tierra, para que lo puedan hazer despues por una eternidad en el Coro de las Virgines."

widely used in the cathedrals. Three classes of positions are available to organists: (1) cathedrals and richly endowed chapels; (2) collegiate and parochial churches without *capilla* but with a benefice for an organist; and (3) places with a salary for the sacristan or teacher of children that also carries with it the obligation of playing the organ. The first class of position—cathedral or *capilla* organist—requires all the ability of the chapelmaster himself, since the organist will often have to substitute for him. The candidate must be able to play solo music on both single and divided keyboard, should be able to improvise four-voiced imitations on a given theme, should be able to transpose both for accompanying and alternating in *tonos accidentales,* and should be able to accompany chorus, solo voices, and transposing wind instruments. Class (2), the parish organist, should also be able to improvise with variety, both in free style and over a plainsong cantus firmus. For the third class, of course, the organ examination will be much less demanding, since the candidate will have also to be judged for his fitness in the other duties of the post. He should, however, be able to play Mass and occasional Vesper services.

Thus Nasarre's voluminous treatise, which began with the music of the spheres, finishes with practical observations upon workaday problems. It is hoped that the reader has been given some indication of the quantity and quality of material to be found in *Escuela Musica.* It cannot be expected, of course, that a work so behind the time in which it was published, and coming at a time and place so out of the main stream of music history as Spain of the late seventeenth and early eighteenth centuries, can assume a position in the history of theory comparable to that of Praetorius' *Syntagma musicum* or Mersenne's *Harmonie universelle.* But it will have been a useful service to remove a little of the stigma cast upon the work by Eximeno and others, and to point it out as a valuable source of information relative to the Spanish musical milieu of the Renaissance and Baroque eras.

NICOLAS BERNIER (1665–1734):

A BIBLIOGRAPHIC STUDY

Philip Nelson
HARPUR COLLEGE, STATE UNIVERSITY OF NEW YORK, BINGHAMTON

Until recently the musical life in France from Lully to Rameau was regarded as one which occupied itself almost entirely with the cultivation of instrumental music and opera. Present-day studies, most recently those on Marc-Antoine Charpentier (1634–1704),[1] Michel-Richard Delalande (1657–1726),[2] and André Campra (1660–1744),[3] have brought to light a hitherto little known sacred vocal and choral repertoire which was cultivated with distinction.

One of the composers prominent during this period whose output did not include opera or purely instrumental music was Nicolas Bernier, born at Mantes-La-Jolie (Seine-et-Oise), on either the fifth or sixth day of June, 1665,[4] and died in Paris on 6 June, 1734.[5] Relatively little is known about the composer's

---

1. Clarence H. Barber, "The Liturgical Music of Marc-Antoine Charpentier" (unpublished Ph.D. dissertation, Harvard University, 1955).

2. Marcelle Benoit, *et al., Michel-Richard Delalande,* under the direction of Nobert Dufourcq (Paris: Editions A. et J. Picard, 1957); and James Richards, "The 'Grand Motet' of the Late Baroque in France as Exemplified by Michel-Richard de Lalande and a Selected Group of his Contemporaries" (unpublished Ph.D. dissertation, University of Southern California, 1950).

3. Maurice Barthélémy, *André Campra* (Paris: Editions A. et J. Picard, 1957).

4. Mantes Archives, "Paroisse Saint-Maclou #4, Baptêmes, Mariages, Sépultures, Décembre 1651 à 1669."

5. Paris, Archives Nationales: Z² 3126, 1734, 6 juillet, *Procès verbal d'apposition do scellés chez Mr Bernier, maître de la Musique de la Chapelle du Roy;* and Z² 3126, 1734, 12 juillet, *Inventaire après le décès de Monsieur Nicolas Bernier, Mr de Musique de la Chapelle du Roi.*

life prior to his appointment as *Maître de Musique* at the Sainte-Chapelle in 1704,[6] except that he was an unsuccessful candidate for the position of *Maître de Musique* at the cathedral in Rouen in 1693,[7] and that he was appointed to similar positions at Notre-Dame de Chartres from 1694 to 1698 and at l'Eglise Saint-Germain l'Auxerrois in Paris from 1698 to 1704.[8] For the next twenty-two years Bernier served at the Sainte-Chapelle, and in 1723 he was also appointed *sous-maître* at the Chapelle du Roi at Versailles [9]—a post he held until his death.

Owing to the lack of any prior inventory concerning Bernier's musical output, an effort has been made to locate and classify all of his extant works. Accordingly, this article is devoted to a bibliographic study of Bernier's works.

No single library possesses all the extant works from Bernier's pen. The Bibliothèque Nationale, Bibliothèque du Conservatoire, and Bibliothèque de la Ville de Lyon each contains certain unique items.

Bernier's known output encompasses the following genres: *Grands Motets, Petits Motets, Leçons de Ténèbres, Cantates,* and *Airs Divers.* Only in his fifth book of *cantates, Les Nuits de Sceaux,* do we find any strictly instrumental music.[10] The pedagogical treatise, *Principes de Composition de Mr Bernier,* has also come down to us.

Reports of a *Te Deum* and a Mass by Bernier are found in the journals of the eighteenth century,[11] but the music itself apparently has not survived. The present writer was unable to locate any trace of these compositions during his search through the libraries of France, Western Europe, and America.

---

6. Arch. Nat. LL 610, fol. 44 r°, *Registres de la Sainte-Chapelle,* 5 avril 1704.

7. Collette et Bourdon, *Histoire de la Maîtrise de Rouen* (Rouen: Imprimerie Espérance Cogniard, 1892), Part II, p. 125.

8. L'abbé Clerval, *L'ancienne Maîtrise de Notre-Dame de Chartres* (Chartres: Librairie R. Selleret, 1899), pp. 87–88.

9. *Le Mercure* (Novembre, 1722), II, 193.

10. *Les Nuits de Sceaux,* Instrumental dances, pp. 25–53.

11. See for example: *Mercure Galant* (avril, 1704), p. 291; *Le Mercure* (septembre, 1721), p. 199; *Mercure de France* (septembre, II, 1729), p. 2224; and *Mercure de France* (octobre, 1729), p. 2383.

MANUSCRIPT SOURCES

We know that when Bernier died he left thirty-six motets in manuscript "pour l'usage de la Chapelle du Roy." [12] Presumably, these were *grands motets*. Today only eleven *grands motets* are extant, all of which are in manuscript.[13] Although none of these is signed or dated, a comparison between the writing in Bernier's holograph testament [14] (the only authentic example of Bernier's writing known to the present author) and that of the *grands motets* reveals that only four [15] may be considered as possible autographs, and even here it is impossible to state the copyist's identity positively.

The *Leçons de Ténèbres* found only at Lyon [16] were very probably copied by the priest Jean-Baptiste Gouffet, organist at St. Bonaventure.[17]

The *Principes de Composition de M. Bernier* exists in a manuscript source.[18]

Although numerous manuscript copies of the *petits motets, cantates,* and *airs divers* are held in various public and private libraries, none of these presents any material not found in the printed editions.

The authorship of four *petits motets,* one *cantate,* and four

---

12. Arch. Nat. Z² 3126, 1734, 12 juillet. *Inventaire après le décès de Monsieur Nicolas Bernier, Mʳ de Musique de la Chapelle du Roy.*

13. Nine are located in the Bibliothèque du Conservatoire (H. 469, H. 470, H. 471, H. 472, H. 473, H. 474, H. 476, H. 477, Rés. F. 312) and two are found in the Bibliothèque de la Ville de Lyon (133.717 and 129.978).

14. Arch. Nat. Paris: Minutier Central, XXIX, 419, Depost de Testament, 6 juillet 1734.

15. Bibl. Cons. Paris H. 469, *Benedic anima mea;* H. 474, *Misere mei;* H. 476, *Lauda anima mea;* H. 477, *Venite exultemus.*

16. Bibliothèque de la Ville de Lyon (133.971).

17. I am indebted to Monsieur Henry Joly, Conservateur en Chef, for this information.

18. Bibl. Natl. Paris Rés. Vmb ms2. This treatise is obviously based on long pedagogical experience; it leads the student step by step through the principles of composition, providing numerous musical illustrations which sustain the text. In it Bernier stands revealed as a teacher who understood the student's needs and met them in a thoroughly practical manner. The interested reader should consult: Nicolas Bernier, *Principles of Composition,* trans. and ed. Philip F. Nelson (New York: Institute of Mediaeval Music, 1964).

airs divers previously ascribed to Bernier is doubted by the present writer. These compositions are listed at the conclusion of the Table of Works.

PRINTED SOURCES

The three volumes of the *petits motets* dated 1703, 1713, and 1741 contain 26, 15, and 4 motets respectively.[19] The Parisian printer Foucault was responsible for the editions of 1703 and 1713,[20] while the posthumous edition of 1741 was brought out by François de la Croix.[21] It is interesting to note that on 3 mars, 1724, a *Privilège Général* for twelve years was granted the Parisian printer, Christophe Ballard, "pour les *chants des offices de différents Saints nouveaus* composez en plein chant par sieur Bernier, maître de la musique de nostre chapelle et de nostre Sainte Chapelle à Paris." [22] I have been unable to locate any copy of this work, either in manuscript or printed form.

Of Bernier's seven volumes of *cantates,* each of the first four books (not dated and without the name of the composer on the title page) contains six *cantates* and bears the *Privilège du Roy* of 1703. The fifth book of *cantates, Les Nuits de Sceaux,* which is dedicated to the Duchesse du Maine, carried the *Privilège* of 1715 and consists of two *divertissements* with instrumental dances. Books six and seven contain six *cantates* each and their title pages, although not indicating Bernier's name, do carry the engraving dates of 1718 and 1723 respectively. Foucault printed the first six books of *cantates,* while the seventh was published

---

19. See Works of Nicolas Bernier at the conclusion of this article.

20. All the printed editions of Bernier's works, both *petits motets* and *cantates,* bear a *Privilège du Roy* for fifteen years, which may be considered the equivalent of today's copyright. For further information concerning the history of the *Privilège,* see: Michel Brenet, "La librairie musicale en France de 1653 à 1790, d'après les Registres de Privilèges," *Sammelbände der internationalen Musikgesellshaft,* VIII (1906–7), 401–66.

21. Bernier in his testament says: "Je lègue et donne au susdit Sieur de la Croix touttes les planches gravées de mon premier et de mon second oeuvre de motets, et les planches du troisième que j'avois commencé qui n'ont pas esté estampées, et l'argent provenant de la vente desd. motets, qu'il aura reçu lors de mon déceds."

22. Bibl. Natl. Paris ms. fr. 21952.

"Chez le Sr Boivin." In addition, the *cantate, Les Nymphes de Diane,* printed by Foucault and bearing the *Privilège du Roy* of 1703, has come down to us.[23]

Although the dates given above are those of the earliest editions, title pages showing rising purchase prices give evidence of reimpressions.[24]

After Bernier's death and in accordance with his testament the plates of his *cantates* were bequeathed to Madame Pélagie Marais, his goddaughter.[25] Evidence that she did, in fact, reprint at least four of the seven books of Bernier's *cantates* is found at the Bibliothèque du Conservatoire.[26] Madame Van Hove's *Privilège du Roy* is dated "2 mai 1739"[27] with the publication of the

23. Bibl. Cons. Paris X59 (1–2), found at end of 1er and 2e livres; L. 3332(2), bound with *Les Nuits de Sceaux.*

24. Foucault's 1703 edition of the Premier livre (Bibl. Natl. Vm^{7}214) gives the price as *5 10^t en blanc,* whereas his later edition, not dated but carrying the *Privilège* of 1703 (Bibl. Natl. Vm^{7}222) indicated *10* as the purchase price. The following notice is found on p. 96: "L'auteur a esté obligé d'augmenter, de dix Sols, le prix du présent livres de Cantates, à cause de la dépense qu'il a fait, tant pour faire regravér à neuf plusieurs planches usées, que pour faire retoucher la plus part des autres dont les réglures et les notes estoient à demi effacées."

25. Bernier's testament states: "Je lègue et donne à Madame Pélagie Marais ma filleule, Epouse de Mr Van Hove député du commerce de Lisle en Flandres, touttes les planches de mes cantates françaises qui sont chez Ballard imprimeur, dont il y en a quelques unes chez Monsieur de la Croix, maistre de musique du Roy en la Sainte-Chapelle, qui a eu la bonté d'en débiter les estampes, et l'argent qui pouroit estre entre les mains dudit Sieur de la Croix provenant de la vente desdites cantates lors de mon déceds."

26. *Premier livre*: D1019, Title page bears signature of Marais Van Hove; D10368, Title page bears signature of Marais Van Hove.

Second livre: L. 3484, Contains both *Premier* and *Second livres.* Signature of Marais Van Hove appears on title page of *Second livre.*

Troisième livre: D1021, Title page bears signature of Marais Van Hove.

Quatrième livre: D1022, Title page bears signature of Marais Van Hove.

27. Bibl. Cons. D10368. After the title page there appears the following: "Extrait du Privilège du Roy" "Par Grâce et Privilège du Roy donné à Paris le 30e Jour d'Avril Mil Sept cens trente neuf. Signé Sainson."

"Il est permis à Margueritte Pélagie MARAIS épouse du Sieur Roger Vanhowe de faire Graver et Imprimer les Cantates Françoises et autres Musique de la composition du Sieur BERNIER tant Vocales qu'instrumentales à une ou plusieurs parties, de les vendre et débiter au Public et ce durant le tems et espace de Douze années consécutives; Et très expresses deffences sont faittes à

first and second books taking place in 1740 [28] and books three and four appearing in 1745.[29]

The *airs divers* are almost wholly contained in the eight *recueils* of the *Nouvelles Poésies*.[30] It is interesting to note that Bernier's music is used far less often in these eight *recueils* than that of his contemporaries Lully, Clérambault, and Campra.

In summary, the list of works by Nicolas Bernier located and verified includes: forty-five *petits motets,* eleven *grands motets,* nine *leçons de ténèbres,* seven books of secular cantatas (plus *Les Nymphes de Diane*), and a few *airs divers.* Below follows a table listing by category those works we have identified either through examination or literary reference.

WORKS OF NICOLAS BERNIER

I. Music.
    A. Mass setting(s)   (Known by literary reference only. Score(s) unlocated.)
    B. *Grands Motets*   (All are in manuscript; #2–10 at Bibliothèque du Conservatoire; #11–12 at Bibliothèque de la Ville de Lyon.)
        1. Te Deum (Known by literary reference only. Score unlocated.)
        2. Benedic Anima Mea
        3. Laudate Dominus Quoniam

---

tous Imprimeurs, Libraires, Graveurs, et autre personnes d'Imprimer et Graver les dittes pièces de Musique, d'en vendre, contrefaire, mesme en extraire aucune chose, à peine de six Mille Livres d'Amende, et de tous dépens, dommages et intérêts, comme il est plus amplement porté du dit Privilège.

"Registré sur le Xᵉ Registre de la Chambre Royalle et sindicalle des Libraires et Imprimeurs N° 216, Fol. 195, à Paris, le 2 May Mil sept cens trente neuf. Signé LANGLOIS sindic."

28. Bibl. Cons. L3484.
29. Bibl. Cons. D. 1021, 1022.
30. Bibl. Natl. Vm¹1578 *Nouvelles Poésies, Spirituelles et Morales*
       1600 *Sur Les Plus Beaux Airs de la Musique Françoise et Italienne avec une Basse Continue.*

4. Beatus Vir
5. Confitebor Tibi Domine
6. Deus Noster Refugium
7. Miserere Mei
8. Lauda Anima Mea Dominum
9. Venite Exultemus
10. Lauda Jerusalem
11. Cum Invocarem
12. Cantate Domino

C. *Petits Motets*

1. Première Oeuvre, 1703
   Contains: 16 motets   *a1*
              7 motets   *a2*
              3 motets   *a3*

2. Seconde oeuvre, 1713
   Contains: 11 motets   *a1*
              3 motets   *a2*
              1 motet   *a3*

3. Troisième oeuvre, 1741
   Collection of four motets (3 *a1*, 1 *a3*) by Bernier and fifteen by François de la Croix.

D. *Leçons de Ténèbres*   (Manuscript. Found only at Bibliothèque de la Ville de Lyon.)

1. Only one complete "set" of *leçons* located.
   3 lessons for First Day
   3 lessons for Second Day
   3 lessons for Third Day

E. *Cantates*

1. Premier livre, 1703
   Six *cantates:*   all *a1*

2. Second livre, 1703
   Six *cantates:*   5 *a1*
                 1 *a2*

3. Troisième livre, 1703
   Six *cantates:*   5 *a1*
                 1 *a2*

    4. Quatrième livre, 1703
      Six *cantates:* 5 *a1*
                 1 *a2*

    5. Cinquième livre, *Les Nuits de Sceaux,* 1715
      Premier et Second Divertissement

    6. Sixième livre, 1718
      Six *cantates:* all *a1*

    7. Septième livre, 1723
      Six *cantates:* all *a1*

    8. *Les Nymphes de Diane*
      Cantate a2

F. *Airs Divers*

    1. *Nouvelles Poésies* (8 *recueils*), 1730–37
      Bernier represented in all but the sixth *recueil*

    2. *Nouveau Recueil de Chansons Choisies,* 1736
      "Chasse l'ennui qui te possède"

    3. *Recueil d'Airs Sérieux et à Boire,* 1706
      "On ne peut s'empêcher d'aimer"

II. Writings

  A. Pedagogical Treatise

    1. *Principes de Composition de Mr Bernier*
    This manuscript treatise found only at the Bibliothèque Nationale.

III. Works of Doubtful Authorship

  A. *Polyphème*—Paris, Bibliothèque du Conservatoire X133A.
  Manuscript; not dated. "Partition de Cantate de Basse sans accompagnement." Although this Cantate (pp. 1–11) bears Bernier's name, I have not located it in any other collection.

  B. *Polyphème*—Paris, Bibliothèque du Conservatoire X133C.
  Manuscript; not dated. "Partition de Cantate de Basse avec accompagnement." No composer's name given, but examination reveals it is same composition as X133A.

C. *Receuille* [*sic*] *d'Airs Choisies*—Paris, Bibliothèque du Conservatoire Rés. 1957.
Manuscript; not dated. Bernier credited with three duos and one air. No correspondence between these and printed works located.

D. *Sicut Cervus*—Paris, Bibliothèque Nationale Vm^1-1175bis.
Seventeenth century manuscript. Attributed to Bernier by Ecorcheville. No other example of this motet located.

E. *Salve Regina*—Paris, Bibliothèque Nationale Vm^1-1175a,b,c.
Manuscript copy by Sebastian de Brossard dated 1696. Brossard's manuscript bears this inscription: "Salve Regina. Incerto autore. Je le crois de Mr Bernier." There are three books: vox cantant (a), organo (b), basso viola (c). This setting of the Salve Regina text is not the same as that found in his Première oeuvre, 1703 (pp. 139–45).

F. *Resonate*—Paris, Bibliothèque Nationale Vm^{1}1687.
Manuscript copy dated 1713. Attributed to Bernier by Ecorcheville. No other example of this motet located.

G. *Quis Habitat*—Paris, Bibliothèque Nationale Vm^{1}1688
Manuscript copy; not dated. Attributed to Bernier by Ecorcheville. No other example of this motet located.

THE PARADOX OF

EIGHTEENTH-CENTURY MUSIC

J. A. Westrup
OXFORD UNIVERSITY

The function of words is to impart information, to sustain argument, and to excite emotion. Too often, however, they are used as a substitute for thinking. We are familiar enough with this in the world of politics and rarely pay any serious attention to what is said. But the fault is not peculiar to politicians: it is found also among historians and critics, and as we are often inclined to accept what they say, from natural laziness or from a predisposition to agree, we often end up in a fog even denser than the one in which they have wrapped themselves. It might be added that philosophers, in attempting to define their terms, are sometimes apt to produce the very obscurity which they set out to remove. In current criticism the word "ambivalent" is a good example of a word which is rapidly losing whatever sense it originally had. In the history of music there is a similar carelessness, and inevitably a similar obscurity. Certain terms, often arbitrarily invented by a single individual, acquire a vogue which makes them indispensable fodder for indolent students. Anyone who has had to read examination papers in music will know the monotonous regularity with which these terms are served up, without any evidence that the candidate knows what they mean or has asked himself whether they are valid. This is only natural, since the books which he studies so avidly, and sometimes reproduces textually in his answers, often suffer from exactly the same glibness.

Here are a mere handful of the terms which are currently in

use: Baroque, *Aufklärung* or Enlightenment, *Empfindsamkeit,*
style galant and *Sturm und Drang.* According to Burney, Hasse
had a poor opinion of Francesco Durante: he described him as
"not only dry, but *baroque,* that is, coarse and uncouth." This
was in 1772. "Baroque," like "Gothic," was then a term of abuse.
It was the art historians who made it respectable and fashionable,
but it was not until the 1920's that it was adopted by musicians.
It has now replaced entirely Riemann's description of the seventeenth and early eighteenth centuries as the "basso continuo
period." That was not a very good description, since it defined
the period by technique rather than by style; but it is doubtful
whether "baroque" is much better. Insofar as it suggests to our
minds a particularly elaborate form of church architecture, it is
definitely misleading. If we were to submit to this association of
ideas we should expect all so-called baroque music to be splendid
in its resources and extravagant in its presentation. But this is not
true. The resources of baroque music are generally modest and
its presentation is frequently restrained. Undoubtedly melodic
decoration plays an important part, and so does ornamentation.
But decoration does not necessarily imply extravagance, and the
very authors of the period who give instruction in ornamentation
are the first to warn performers against overdoing it. Perhaps
this can be illustrated best by taking an example from Handel—
the Largo which precedes the finale of the twelfth of his *Concerti*
grossi, Op. 6, published in 1740.

Our reactions to this piece will probably vary; but I imagine
most people would agree that it does not correspond to any of
the popular associations of the word "baroque." It is not extravagant in detail, it is not tortured in expression. To put it more
bluntly, it is not in any sense a period piece: as an expression
of emotion it would be equally valid in the twentieth century.
What strikes us here is that this is the work of an individual. It
would be paying Handel an extravagant compliment to say that
all of his music is as good as this. Like every other composer, he
was sometimes content to keep the wheels in motion and rely on
his infallible technique to see him through. But if this were all
that is to be found in his music, we should not revere him as a
great master. This awareness of personal expression is some-

thing that strikes us in all baroque music, and perhaps most vividly in the music of the early seventeenth century. The achievements of the first opera composers were not directed at stunning the ear with exuberance but at using music to express the drama on the stage—and by the simplest possible means, by the beauty of the human voice. This music is the very reverse of what is generally understood by orderly construction; and here we come up against another misconception of baroque music in general—that it aims at regularity and formal perfection. This belief leads people into the grievous error of supposing that you always know what Handel is going to do, whereas his moves are nearly always unforeseen and frequently surprise us by doing what is unexpected. This can be true even of so industrious a manufacturer of music as Vivaldi, who is said to have been described by Dallapiccola as "the composer not of six hundred concertos but of one concerto written six hundred times over." Take for example the well-known D minor concerto from the collection known as "L'estro armonico," which Bach admired sufficiently to arrange as an organ solo. "L'estro armonico" means something like "musical inspiration"—a revealing title for a collection published in 1712. The slow movement of this concerto is in that lazy, rocking rhythm known as *siciliano,* and the individual melodic phrases are clichés which could be found in the music of dozens of composers of the same period. The rhythm is conventional, the details both of melody and of harmony are unoriginal. We might expect as a result that the movement would be cut to a standard formula, satisfying in its logic but lacking any capacity to stir our emotions. The facts are quite different. Out of these raw materials Vivaldi has fashioned a movement which despises any idea of fitting into a preconceived framework: on the contrary the music seems to wander where it wills.

We find the same thing in opera. Casual students of the period are apt to believe that a baroque opera consists of a relentless series of *da capo* arias interspersed with recitative which is musically negligible. It is true that eighteenth-century critics argued that the *da capo* aria could make nonsense of the text. Algarotti, writing in 1755, declared that the repetition of the first part of an aria was "repugnant to the natural process of our speech and passions." Undoubtedly there were composers whose desire to satisfy the demand for fine singing led them to write in such haste that they became insensitive to the words. But this sort of carelessness was by no means general; nor does the use of a formal scheme imply formality. The first movement of Mozart's G minor symphony is in sonata form; but no one would dream of describing it as rigid. The operatic aria of the early eighteenth century was essentially a soliloquy, whether it was addressed to another person or not. It was no more undramatic than Hamlet's "To be or not to be," and it was capable of endless variety. If we fail to realize this, it may be because the art of singing these pieces has been almost entirely lost. It is also as well to remember that there was more to an opera than *da capo* arias and conversational recitative. The most dramatic scenes, foreshadowing the *gran scena* of Verdi's day, were in recitative with the co-operation of the orchestra. Here everything is unpredictable. There is no continuous melody, no background scheme of harmony. The composer is free of all limitations and for that reason has a greater responsibility. He has to translate into music the tension that we witness on the stage. Handel's "Alcina," first performed in 1735, is about an enchantress who turns her discarded lovers into animals. Mrs. Pendarves, a devoted friend of Handel's, attended a rehearsal of this work. "Tis so fine," she wrote to her mother, "I have not words to describe it," and added: "Whilst Mr. Handel was playing his part, I could not help thinking him a necromancer in the midst of his own enchantments." The opinion may seem fanciful, but it is not so wide of the mark. Perhaps she was thinking particularly of the scene where Alcina, deserted by Ruggiero, summons her familiar spirits to help her. To say that the scene is in recitative gives no hint of its power: we need to hear the music.

We have dealt so far with two opposite misconceptions of "baroque music": the assumption that it provides a parallel to baroque architecture, and the belief, based on insufficient knowledge, that it is necessarily characterized by orderly construction. There is a further possible misinterpretation which might be considered. It might have been expected that in throwing off the old and adventuring into new territory the music of this period would have shown a greater awareness of the resources of harmony, a new exploitation of chordal relationships. The contrary is true. It was the late sixteenth-century composers who broke through the frontiers of traditional harmony and used chromaticism to wring pathos out of the texts they set or to create similar associations in instrumental music. Something of this lingered on in the seventeenth century. When Purcell's fantasias for viols first became generally known in the present century they were regarded by some people as being curiously modern in tone and were even described as "in advance of their time." This was a mistaken opinion, because no form of artistic expression can be in advance of its time: it is one of the elements that give the time its character. Furthermore, this wandering from key to key, rather like the progressions in some of Frescobaldi's toccatas, was not modern at all in 1680, when Purcell wrote his fantasias; it was old-fashioned. The new music of the time was based on a firmly diatonic foundation, as Purcell himself proved when he got into his stride. This does not mean that chromaticism was abandoned, but it became harnessed to a key system. It was only in recitative with orchestra that composers felt free to throw their bonnets over the windmill. The contrast was all the more noticeable because of their adherence elsewhere to a balanced harmonic structure.

We are faced with an inescapable conclusion. What is called "baroque music" has so many facets and presents so many exceptions to any rule that the adjective cannot be accepted as in any sense an adequate description of it. It might be argued that this is equally true of other similar labels, but the comparison is not exact. If we speak of medieval music, we are using the term to indicate a period of time, and the fact that we do not all agree about the limits of the period does not render the description invalid. From another point of view it is not unacceptable to speak of the Romantic period, because composers of this period were conscious of being Romantics—conscious, in fact, to the point of being self-conscious. Several of them wrote at length on the subject. Eighteenth-century writers on music wrote at even greater length, but their aims were rather different. Furthermore, those who were most voluble were by no means outstanding composers. Mizler, in a brief supplement to C. P. E. Bach's life of John Sebastian, wrote: "Our lately departed Bach did not . . . occupy himself with deep theoretical speculations on music, but was all the stronger in the practice of the art." The same might have been said, with equal truth, about other eminent composers of the time.

Eighteenth-century writers on music could hardly escape the influence of contemporary philosophy. Kant defined *Aufklärung* as the opposite of sloppy thinking. It meant having the courage to think for oneself. Enlightenment meant the exercise of reason. This was obviously a challenge to the church, but it did not prevent composers from writing Masses, whatever they may have thought in private. Indeed, it is difficult to see how reason alone could be a satisfactory guide to the composition of any music, though writers tried hard to bring it into line with other forms of creative activity. Charles Avison, organist in Newcastle on Tyne, who published "An Essay on Musical Expression" in 1753, begins a comparison between music and painting by saying that "they are both founded in Geometry, and have Proportion for their Subject." Similarly, Mizler, who founded a Sozietät der musicalischen Wissenschaften, maintained that a knowledge of mathematics was indispensable to even the greatest composer. Hawkins, in the "Preliminary Discourse" to his "History" (1776), takes the typically "enlightened" view, if one may call it that, that "setting aside the harmony of colouring, and the delineation of beautiful forms, the pleasure we receive from [painting], great as it is, consists in the truth of the representation." In other words painting, as he says, is "an imitative art." There was nothing new in this doctrine, any more than there was in the association between music and mathematics. It goes back to the Greek principle of *mimesis* or imitation. Whether reason can enter into such an operation is very doubtful. Reason will not help the painter to produce a good copy of what he sees; for that he needs a good eye and a steady hand. There is a further difficulty: reason is directed to the pursuit of truth, whereas mere representation cannot tell you the truth about anything.

Hawkins evidently felt that there was no exact parallel between painting and music. "In music," he says, "there is little beyond itself to which we need, or indeed can, refer to heighten its charms." At the same time he maintains that the principles of harmony "are general and universal," and its proportions are similar to those found in the sphere, the cube, and the cone. But the observation of these proportions makes no appeal to our imagination; it is only reason that is gratified. "In short," he concludes, "there are few things in nature which music is capable of imitating, and those are of a kind so uninteresting, that we may venture to pronounce, that as its principles are founded in geometrical truth, and seem to result from some general and universal law of nature, so its excellence is intrinsic, absolute, and inherent, and, in short, resolvable only into His will, who has ordered all things in number, weight, and measure." This is all very fine up to a point. Most of us would agree that the imitation of nature in music is generally childish and unprofitable, though quite a number of composers have been tempted from time to time to practice it. But when Hawkins goes on to say that we enjoy music because it has its foundation in nature—by which he means natural laws—and because reason recognizes what the sense approves, we feel called upon to protest. It is perfectly true to say that music has its own logic; it would hardly be intelligible if it did not. But the logical processes of composition have nothing to do with reason as understood by philosophers. Music, in fact, is an irrational art. This was clearly understood by Rameau, because he was a composer first and theorist second. Music, he maintained, does not live by rules alone. "Even if the rules known were beyond criticism, what are rules that enslave genius? It is for imagination to give orders." "One can judge music," he says, "only through the medium of hearing: reason has authority only inasmuch as it agrees with the ear." And there is one other opinion which might be taken to heart by teachers at the present day: "Fugue is an ornament in music whose only principle is good taste."

These are not the doctrines of the Enlightenment, and it is hardly surprising that they were not generally accepted. The average writer was willing to agree with Hawkins that it is not the function of music to represent the sights and sounds of nature. But it must represent something. The answer is that it represents emotions, or as was sometimes said, it paints the passions. This again is a harking back to Greek doctrine, though Plato's discussion of the subject is weakened by moral considerations. German writers of the eighteenth century use the word *Affekten* for the passions or emotional states, corresponding roughly to the "humours" of medieval medicine. Mattheson, one of the most voluminous of early eighteenth-century writers, actually describes his chapter on the passions as an *Affekten-Lehre,* a doctrine of the passions. The basis of this doctrine was that music, whether vocal or instrumental, must be founded on emotion, and that there was a great variety of emotions. So far from banishing reason from the composition of music the *Affekten-Lehre* prescribed it, since only by the exercise of reason could the composer distinguish between the passions and find the right way to represent them. Reason would also help him to avoid extravagance. As Mattheson said, "it is not enough simply to express the more violent passions by means of a crude uproar." This reminds us of Mozart's remark that "passions, whether violent or not, must never be expressed in such a way as to excite disgust."

The doctrine of "topics" and "figures," both borrowed from rhetoric, is obviously allied to the *Affekten-Lehre,* but it is more concerned with the actual technique of composition—with choosing what to say and with having at your command a number of different ways of saying it. That such figures were widely used will be obvious even to those who know only a handful of works by late baroque composers. But clichés, to describe them in the lowest possible terms, are not peculiar to baroque music; without them the music of any period would present such an unfamiliar aspect that it would hardly be intelligible except to initiates. It must be remembered that the writers whom I have been discussing were primarily authors of didactic works. They were not in the first place concerned with analyzing the music of their time: their object was much more to help inexperienced composers to discover the fullest means of expression and above all to achieve what must be a virtue in any music—consistency. Unfortunately the *Affekten-Lehre* has been elevated by many subsequent writers to a position where it appears to be a universal principle governing the practice of all early eighteenth-century composers. On the face of it this is improbable, since composers do not necessarily do what they are told. As Geoffrey Clive puts it in his book "The Romantic Enlightenment," "whatever ideal of self-realization is dominant for a particular age, there will always be individuals who see their salvation in deviating from it and seeking heaven somewhere else." It is not true, for instance, that all baroque arias maintain a specific affection throughout; there are plenty of examples to the contrary. As for the method of representing emotion, it is obvious that there cannot be one single way of representing a particular emotion, and equally that the same form of expression may do duty for quite a number of different emotions. We can easily test this for ourselves by examining the opening of the aria "Piangerò la sorte mia" sung by Cleopatra in Handel's "Giulio Cesare." What is happening here? Is it a love-song? Certainly not in the accepted sense. Cleopatra believes that Caesar has been killed and is pouring out her heart in passionate lamentation. If the modern interpretation of the *Affekten-Lehre* is to be taken literally, we ought to know from the very first bars what her emotions are, but quite obviously we do not.

The belief that early eighteenth-century composers employed a sort of stock vocabulary of musical expression has had a vicious effect on criticism and has led many students to accept a fallacy as truth. It is true that Johann Kuhnau, Bach's predecessor at Leipzig, analyzed in detail the musical symbols appropriate to a setting of the first psalm; but this does not justify us in assuming that music of this period in general, and Bach's in particular, is riddled with symbolism. Kuhnau's object was to show that a consideration of this question could be a help to a composer. We can see clearly that any theory of universal symbolism breaks down completely when we have to deal with cases where composers have borrowed music from themselves. Handel's "Messiah" affords some notorious and striking examples. On July 3, 1741, he wrote a duet for two sopranos to an Italian text expressing the utmost distrust of love and beauty: love is blind and beauty is cruel—they are both deceitful gods. Seven weeks later he began the composition of "Messiah" and used the first part of this duet as material for the chorus "For unto us a child is born."

No amount of special pleading will convince anyone that the music is equally suitable to both texts. There is something particularly incongruous in hearing the melodic line of "Troppo siete menzognere" fitted to the words "And the government shall be upon his shoulders."

It may be argued that Handel is a special case. If that is so, let us turn to Bach, who was an inveterate adapter of material no longer required. On December 8, 1733, he performed what he called a *dramma per musica* in celebration of the birthday of the Queen of Poland—the King of Poland was also Elector of Saxony. The score, incidentally, was finished the day before; but these last-minute rushes were not uncommon in the eighteenth century. As might be expected, the text bristles with fulsome compliments to the royal lady, contributed by various gods and goddesses. The fifth movement is an alto aria in B minor, sung by Pallas Athene, with oboe d'amore obbligato. The goddess calls on the Muses to abandon their old songs and simply rejoice in the happy day. The fact that the aria is in a minor key is no more surprising than the fact that Cleopatra's lament in Handel's "Giulio Cesare" is in the major. Eighteenth-century composers were not troubled by the modern superstition that the major key suggests cheerfulness and the minor grief; nor indeed were later composers—Schubert is an admirable example. Bach's aria becomes more and more florid as it proceeds, and demands considerable virtuosity both from the singer and from the oboist. The reason for this is that Pallas is urging the Muses to fill their breasts with joy; the music takes its cue from the words and blossoms into an almost intoxicating exuberance.

Once this festal work had been performed there was no further use for it. Hence when Bach was writing the Christmas Oratorio a year later this was one of several sources from which he could borrow. Our aria turns up in the second of the six cantatas which make up the oratorio. This time it is for tenor in E minor, and the obbligato is for flute. The words are an injunction to the shepherds to haste to the manger to see the child Jesus. There is no connection between the texts of the two versions except that in both cases an individual is addressing a group, and in both cases the word *Freude* occurs. The Muses are told: "Füllt mit

Freude eure Brust," and the shepherds: "Geht, die Freude heisst zu schön." This is the point at which the coloratura begins. Before long the soloist in the first version is warbling happily on the second syllable of *erfreut*. In the second version the runs are given to the first syllable of *labet*—part of the sentence "labet Herz und Sinnen." It is obvious that we have not got here so marked a discrepancy as in the case of Handel's "For unto us a child is born." At the same time the mood of the two versions is not identical. Both are concerned with joy, but the Christmas Oratorio introduces a new element in the shape of the injunction to the shepherds to hasten: there is nothing corresponding to this in the first version. If, as we are so often told, music and text are so intimately linked in early eighteenth-century music, and if Bach's art is threaded through and through with symbolism, how is it that the same music can do double duty? And this is not an isolated example.

It is not wholly possible to separate *Empfindsamkeit* from the music we have been discussing. There is one obvious reason for this. *Empfindsamkeit* means "sensibility," or "sensitiveness," as we should probably say at the present day; and this is clearly a quality that we cannot confine to a single period. There is plenty of music by Marenzio in the sixteenth century or Purcell in the seventeenth which is sensitive to a high degree; and there is also a good deal in Bach's music that equally deserves the epithet. But *Empfindsamkeit* can also mean sentimentality, and that is a quality that we do not find in Bach or indeed in Handel. When Burney visited Carl Philipp Emanuel Bach at Hamburg he had the pleasure of hearing the composer play the clavichord. "In the pathetic and slow movements," he tells us, "whenever he had a long note to express, he absolutely contrived to produce, from his instrument, a cry of sorrow and complaint, such as can only be effected upon the clavichord, and perhaps by himself." The account continues: "After dinner, which was elegantly served, and chearfully eaten, I prevailed upon him to sit down again to a clavichord, and he played, with little intermission, till near eleven o'clock at night. During this time, he grew so animated and *possessed,* that he not only played, but looked like one inspired. His eyes were fixed, his under lip fell, and drops of effervescence distilled from his countenance." Here is *Emp-findsamkeit* with a vengeance. We might almost be in the Romantic period, when Liszt fainted at the keyboard and Madame Malibran, having heard Beethoven's C minor symphony for the first time, was seized with convulsions and had to be carried out of the room. Writers sometimes refer to an *empfindsamer Stil;* but it was not so much a style as a form of expression. It is significant that the rapture which Burney witnessed occurred during performance on a keyboard instrument. Here, as in Chopin's piano music, there was opportunity for a subtle art of association. This extended actually to the point of including recitative in keyboard music, a practice which is found in C. P. E. Bach's work and was still alive in Beethoven's time. Strictly speaking, instrumental recitative is meaningless, since the accents of recitative are derived from words. But familiarity with sung recitative can create so strong an association that the keyboard seems to speak to us, even though there are no words to tell us what it is saying; and the same thing can be done with other instruments. It is clear that the inclusion of recitative broke down any ordered symmetry of instrumental music. But a self-conscious art of expression does not necessarily imply extravagance. The guiding principle was good taste—a principle which it is easier to accept than to define. It is worth noting that C. P. E. Bach himself protested against the harmonic extravagance to be found in sung recitative in what he calls the recent past—"vor nicht gar langer Zeit."

Empfindsamkeit, in this specialized sense, can hardly be called a movement. It was rather a phase, which evaporated in the work of Haydn and Mozart. Both of these composers had a great admiration for C. P. E. Bach, but they were reared in a different climate and they both had too sure a sense of style to be led astray by caprice. Expression for them was something more vital than a temporary indulgence in sentiment, as indeed it had been for J. S. Bach, and it could be employed within the framework of any style—even the *style galant.* The *style galant* definitely was a style, based on the courtly artificiality of the French aristocracy and transplanted into Germany, where every petty princeling liked to imagine himself as a duplicate of the French king.

It was not quite so important as its name might suggest. We can see it in a clearer light if we translate *style* as "fashion" and *galant* as "smart." It would be wrong to assume that composers in the early part of the eighteenth century were contemptuous of fashion: Bach's Brandenburg concertos are extremely fashionable music. But the *style galant* of the mid-eighteenth century seems, at any rate to us, to be more brittle, less substantial. It may be that we are wrong; it may be that the music of the Mannheim composers was as solidly based as Bach's. If we do err in our judgment it is because these prancing rhythms, these finicky twiddles seem to make their appeal too much on the surface. That they appealed to aristocratic employers of the time is obvious enough. This was a fashion that could give pleasure without exciting thought. It was entertaining and at the same time polite; and if insistence on it became wearisome there was always the possibility of introducing the rhythms and even the melodic idioms of the peasantry, so that the prince could imagine that after all he was not living in gilded isolation but could share the tastes of his grooms and dairymaids.

Mozart, brought up in the atmosphere of courts from his early days, was too prudent to ignore the fashion when it came to writing music for entertainment. In his earlier years particularly he had his ear very firmly to the ground. But he was too much an individualist to be content with mere fashion. His emancipation from it was virtually complete once he had to struggle along on his own feet in Vienna. The accents of the *style galant* linger on here and there, but they are absorbed into an idiom which looks at larger horizons. Even when his music is on a small scale Mozart defies any attempt to put him in this or that pigeon-hole. What is happening when Barbarina in 'Figaro' is searching for the pin? Is it the exercise of reason that we are listening to, is it sentimentality, is it mere *galanterie?* The answer is that it is none of these things: it is humanity speaking through Mozart.

We come finally to *Sturm und Drang*—a term which has been applied to music more loosely, perhaps, and more carelessly than any other. Modern writers even speak of Haydn's *Sturm und Drang* period, as though he had been secretly taking drugs over a number of years. "Sturm und Drang" was the title of a play by

Friedrich Maximilian von Klinger produced in 1776. It gave its name to a whole school of violent and revolutionary drama which may be regarded as a reaction against the more polite and sophisticated tendencies of the time. The connection of this movement, however, with music is tenuous, particularly in the case of Haydn, who had virtually no interest in literature and at the time was pursuing his craft more or less in isolation at Esterház. As he said himself, he was cut off from the world and forced to be original. The irruption of violent and dramatic forms of expression into music comes not from the spoken drama but from opera, where there were particular opportunities for it in recitative accompanied by the orchestra. C. P. E. Bach was as receptive to this kind of dramatic expression as he was to *Empfindsamkeit:* in fact one might say that these are two opposite sides of the same medal. It has been remarked that Haydn was particularly prone to this sort of dramatization in the early seventies; but there is no evidence whatever that this was due to any influence other than the music of his contemporaries. In fact, it is evident that his stormy music, if one may call it that, was the result of a psychological development of which we know nothing. The opening of his symphony No. 44—the so-called *Trauer* symphony— is a good example of his manner at this time and reminds us, if we need reminding, that no artist is single-minded. The jolly Haydn of legend is not entirely a fiction, since he wrote any amount of music which bubbles over with innocent gaiety; but it is only a part of the complete picture. The same is true of Mozart, in whom profound melancholy and a sense of somber anxiety exist side by side with unaffected happiness. The G minor symphony is more than an assemblage of contrasts; it is the portrait of a human being.

The moral of all this is that art can be analyzed but cannot be expected to conform to precepts. It is significant that much of our discussion has been concerned with German music. The reason is simple. It was above all the Germans, with their passion for philosophizing, who sought to define the music of their time, and in doing so laid dangerous traps for historians of the present day. Throughout the eighteenth century the Italians poured out a stream of operas, both serious and gay, which obstinately refuse to fall into any ready-made category. If we are trying to build up a true picture of the paradox of eighteenth-century music we might do worse than take Kant's advice and start thinking for ourselves. "History," in the words of Geoffrey Clive, whom I quoted earlier, "presents us with a world full of confusion and conflict which, from the time of Aristotle, philosophers, theologians, and then scientists have been prone to ignore or deprive of true import." And he adds: "Historians . . . if they are good historians . . . will deal just as scrupulously with the bizarre, the unexpected, the seemingly senseless, and the accidents and betrayals."

HANS WAECHTLIN 1508

THE HAND OF GOD:

A NATURAL HISTORY OF

THE CANTATAS OF J. S. BACH

William Klenz
HARPUR COLLEGE, STATE UNIVERSITY OF NEW YORK, BINGHAMTON

Our technological age, preoccupied with the "scientifically" demonstrable—has shown small patience with and believes it has escaped the necessity for the most important of human occupations (it was once called Humanism): the making of myths, images and symbols by which man understands the world and the cosmos. Even in music, an art dedicated solely to this end, we are of late very diffident about admitting the presence of anything beyond the sound-entity in what we are apt to proclaim, with obvious, but inexplicable satisfaction as "pure music." This is all very well; we can create "pure music" for our own time if we wish—purify it right out of existence, as some of us seem in a fair way to do—another age will judge us harshly enough. However, we have learned that the imagic, mythic element is blood and bone of any art that is not sheer mountebankery, and is, perhaps, the more powerful for not being recognized. It ill becomes us to inherit and visit the genteel poverty of our diffident philosophical and esthetic compulsions upon other, richer periods, at least, not in the name of veracity. Recent experience has taught us how much the recovery of the actual sonorities of Baroque music means to its comprehension. It should be platitudinous to observe that the recovery and recognition of the symbolic language on which it is based is of an importance at least equal to the reconstruction of its sensual surface, formal and incidental conventions.

As his increasingly complex environment becomes oppressive

or incomprehensible, those to whom man turns for counsel and therapy find themselves compelled to learn and heed a symbolic language once thought completely buried and obscured by human "progress." [1] The systematic exponents of this language call themselves psychoanalysts—Freudian or Jungian or whatever. Its natural agents, who have it as their mother tongue and speak it with no accent, are artists, and sometimes (when they are honest), men of religion. But even thus enfranchised, they are not immune to the effects of changes in spiritual climate, and, like immigrant children, hasten to forget the old language to be ready with the new.

The disingenuous ignorance ("I know what I like" or "it's famous, it must be good"), which marks the current lay attitude to the arts is the other half of insecurity. The specialist creates his antithesis, the charlatan, and the rarefication of the atmosphere around technological achievements and the values embodied in the arts contribute to the spiritual *malaise* of our time. Deprived of direct, Protean, contact with substance and symbol, we approach even the most spiritual of our artistic properties as entertainment, advertising, or trophies. We are "collectors," as witness the endless mechanical proliferation and consequent attenuation of "safe," "famous," "approved" art works and their juxtaposition to the most incongruous surroundings and undignified treatment.[2]

Obviously we dare not accord these things their full symbolic values (any more than we dare allow domestic electronic devices to actually duplicate the full resonance of a symphony orchestra); they shame us or overwhelm us. From having lost touch with the direct fertilizing contact with symbolic language of sound and movement, we have arrived at the impossible position of denying its existence in an art of which it is the very substance —an art whose existence is otherwise inexplicable.

The "basic" music of the West, the "corpus . . . of Gregorian music . . . the most complete artistic treasure bequeathed to us

---

1. E. Fromm, *The Forgotten Language* (New York, 1951).

2. The recent visits of the *Mona Lisa* (average viewing time, police surveilled, "keep it moving, please," thirty seconds) and of Michelangelo's *Pietà* at a notoriously commercial World Fair are cases in point.

by antiquity," [3] by its apparent functional, declamatory simplicity and severity, would seem to preclude symbolic projection, but, in fact, has been developed to present symbolism of all kinds. The customary threefold hierarchy of the Kyrie and the occasional hierarchical assignment of pitch and melodic elements in *Gloria Patri et Filio, et Spirito Sancto* [4] are clear examples. Another is the Communion for the third Sunday in Quadragesima: *Passer invenit sibi domum et turtur nidum.* [5]

The neume, being a graphic representation of the vocal movement which is itself descriptive, also comes to convey a visual suggestion, so that the two images reinforce each other. The much denigrated *Augenmusik* has sources very close to the origins of notation—the neume begins by illustrating the sound of the word and ends up resembling the thing described. In the final sentence, *beati qui habitant in domo Dei,* how graphically (and, in the cursive neumes of the Hartker MS even more vividly) are the arches, roofs, and towers of the House of the Lord conveyed by the neume sequence, cephalicus, podatus, porrectus, clivis, climacus on the word *domo*! In the liturgical drama *Quem Quaeritis,* [6] with what force the movement of the rolling away of the stone from the Tomb is set forth on the word *revolvet*! Thus, the means of musical representation extend from the purely aural (echoic) to the purely visual (true *Augenmusik*) and the general usage also contains the element of dynamic suggestion of motion and an ideological symbolism, these being based on some form of numerology (consonance, dissonance, rhythm, etc.). The totality of these means and their use as musical pictorialism may be roughly described as "madrigalism."

As in so much else, J. S. Bach stands pre-eminent as a practitioner of musical representation and madrigalism, unsurpassed in vigor of image and resource. His reputation as an abstract,

---

3. Winifred Douglas, *Church Music in History and Practice* (London, 1962).
4. E.g., Respond *Obtulerunt* Festa Feb. 2, *Graduale Romanum* (1948 ed.), p. 431.
5. Here, *et turtur* (turtle dove) is sung to three liquescent neumes (Epiphonus) in succession, creating an aural image or suggestion of the bird.
6. A. Schering, *Geschichte der Musik in Beispielen* (Leipzig, 1933), No. 8.

cerebral, formalistic artist is only the evidence of the breakdown of communication, the decline of the common symbolic language he and his epoch spoke. By historical position and natural inclination, his enormous preoccupation with musical symbolism was inevitable. He was heir to a long tradition of humanistic madrigalism brought to German Protestant music by Heinrich Schütz and his pupils. He was born and passed his formative years in a century that was obsessed with symbolism in art and literature. It was the era of the graphic emblem book and the final alchemical treatises, combinations of pictorial and literary "conceit" in which, by an imagic alchemy, idea was transmuted to symbol and sign to concept.[7] These, along with decorated devotional works make up a significant part of the output of the great German school [8] of engravers and woodblock cutters at whose head stands the great figure of Albrecht Dürer whose works are like those of Schütz and Bach, permeated with traditional symbolism. The taste and talent for graphic representation ran in the Bach family. Karl Geiringer describes and gives an illustration of the decorated cover of a Birthday Cantata by Bach's uncle, Georg Christoph.[9] It employs precisely the symbolic vocabulary of the emblem books: a cloud-cuffed hand bearing a trefoil, a triangle (sistrum) with three rings and a padlock with three hasps representing the solidarity of the three brothers Georg Christoph, Johann Christoph, and Ambrosius, Bach's father.

Also, several of the Bach descendants, linear and lateral, were painters and artists. J. S. Bach II, Bach's grandson, son of K. P. E. Bach, was a gifted painter who also studied engraving [10] with Stock in Leipzig, whose studio was in the very house of J. G. Immanuel Breitkopf, the founder of the firm which was to engrave and print the Gesellschaft edition! Others of the family who have left art works are Nikolaus Ephraim, Gottlieb Fr.,

---

7. Mario Praz, *Studies in Seventeenth Century Imagery* (London, 1939).
8. Of which the splendid pages of the Bach-Gesellschaft edition are themselves no unworthy examples.
9. Karl Geiringer, *The Bach Family* (New York, 1954), pp. 49, 64.
10. *Ibid.,* p. 471.

Samuel Anton, Johann Phillip, and Paul Bach.[11] Terry [12] lists among Bach's books a *Biblia illustrata* of Abraham Calovius, as well as the *Itinerarium Sacrae Scripturae* (1579, 1718) of Heinrich Bunting and *Opere* (1544) of Flavius Josephus which he says "declare Bach's search for vivid and authentic pictures of Bible scenes and characters." The titles of others are redolent of the literary conceit and symbolism (e.g., "Evangelischer Augapfel"; "Güldener Apfel in silbern Schal"; "Richtschnur der Christi Göttliche Liebes-Flamme") that we find in the Cantata libretti. The librettists who supplied the texts for Bach's church works were, of course, also steeped in emblematic literary symbolism which, along with classified rhetorical and syntactical devices, was their stock-in-trade. The composer was expected to have a command of the system of rhetorical figures developed from the heritage of Augustine and Quintilianus [13] propagated by German Humanists, both Catholic and Protestant, and a central part of liberal education. This is clear from the number of books published on the subject,[14] and from the fact that such a work as Johann Walther's *Musikalisches Lexicon* (1732) includes definitions of rhetorical figures as a matter of course. Indeed, from what we can see of Bach's personality at this distance, he might easily have been the author of, and would have willingly subscribed to the lines of Castiglione's *Cortegiano:* "if the words used by a writer bear with them a little, I will not say difficulty, but recondite wit . . . they give somewhat greater authority to the writing, and cause the reader to be more wary and attentive and to ponder more, and, to delight in the ingenuity and learning of the writer." [15] Nor is it without significance that Bach, in his letter to the Leipzig Town Council of August 23, 1730, refers to concerted church music as *Figural Music*. Thus, it should not be cause for doubtful or patronizing surprise to find Bach's work

---

11. *Ibid.*, pp. 108, 445–49.

12. Charles Sanford Terry, *Bach* (Rev. ed.; London, 1933), p. 276.

13. Glen Haydon, "On the Problem of Expression in Baroque Music," *JAMS,* III (1950), 113–19.

14. Arnold Schmitz, *Die Bildlichkeit der wortgebundenen Musik Johann Sebastian Bachs* (Mainz, 1950).

15. Quoted by M. Praz, *Studies in Seventeenth Century Imagery*, p. 14.

infused with every kind of symbolic or imagic treatment. On the contrary, it would be a wonder if it were not.[16] Nor should descriptive, pictorial, and symbolic treatment be sought in a restrictive sense, but rather in the most inclusive sense, just as Bach's librettists intended us to read their texts. These display in many instances, whatever they may be as literature, very highly developed use of symbolic imagery. Poetic elements, images, and emblems which strike us as merely decorative are often of profound or recondite meaning of which the authors and Bach were completely aware. These meanings are based upon those inherited from classical antiquity through medieval alchemy and Renaissance humanism, and have been made a general study, investigated and clarified for therapeutic purposes by many recent writers including C. G. Jung and his followers, I. Jacobi and Erich Neumann.[17] Frequently, the confrontation of the symbols found in J. S. Bach and their interpretations in these works reveals an imagic *poesis* of startling intensity.

Of purely visual symbols, the great Cross which blazes forth on the page of the first recitative of the St. Matthew Passion is well recognized. It is, in reality, the complete symbol of the Crucifixion, being three crosses in one. The whole pattern represents the central Cross; the initial diminished third changing-tone figure is one ancillary and the ascending sixth and descending fourth of the cadence forms the other. Jung's interpretation of the cross symbolism in general is vast and complex—much too far-reaching to enter upon here. However, its use by Bach and significance in this place should require no further comment or justification.

In Cantata 206, *Schleicht spielende Wellen*, a birthday can-

---

16. A Schmitz, *Die Bildlichkeit*, p. 51, "in der wortgebundenen Musik Bachs gibt es kaum einen Tonsatz der keine Figur enthielte."

17. C. G. Jung, Collected Works, Vol. 9, part 1, *The Archetypes and the Collective Unconscious* (ACU); Vol. 12, *Psychology and Alchemy* (PA); Vol. 3, *Symbols of Transformation* (ST) (New York, 1960); I. Jacobi, *Complex, Archetype, Symbol* (CAS) (New York, 1959); E. Neumann, *The Origins and History of Consciousness* (OHC) (New York, 1954); N. Eliade, *Myths, Dreams and Mysteries* (New York, 1960).

tata for August IV of Saxony and Poland, an aria is addressed to his consort, the Hapsburg Archduchess Maria Josepha.[18] It contains the text (probably by Picander) "du stammst von den Lorbeerzweigen drum muss deiner Eheband auch dem fruchtbar'n Lorbeern gleichen" (thou stemm'st from the laurel twig, thus should your conjugal bond resemble the fruitful laurel tree). Bach (BG 20, 2, p. 45) sets the word "Band" (bond) as a whole note (do we see a wedding ring?) tied into the next bar, followed by melismas above and below it, like the regularly "opposite" foliation of classical laurel leaves and the conventional garland. At the word "gleichen" (resemble) the continuo has the whole note and the alto voice breaks into the most florid figure of the aria, which Bach thus tells us "resembles" or represents the laurel branch (Ex. 1). On the following page (46) the text and figure

Example 1

are repeated with the bass (bars 7, 8, 9, 10) illustrating the regular foliate principle even more clearly. The chromatic setting of "fruchtbar'n Lorbeern" (objected to by Whittaker as evidence of adaptation of an earlier work),[19] is simply an illustration of the word "fruitful." Both the freely-growing spray and the plaited

---

18. Bach-Gesellschaft ed., Vol. 20, part 2. Succeeding references to this edition will be abbreviated as BG 20, 2.

19. W. Gillies Whittaker, *The Cantatas of Johann Sebastian Bach* (London, 1959), II, 681.

garland are to be seen in the coat of arms Dürer designed for Johann Stabius, in the woodcut of Stabius as St. Coloman, and in splendid examples of the garland in the woodcuts of the Triumphal Arch which Dürer designed for another Hapsburg, the Emperor Maximilian.[20]

The laurel is pleasantly decorative but it becomes much more meaningful when we realize that the laurel tree "triumphat intacta." [21] It is traditionally not injured by lightning or cold and is one of the many symbols of the Virgin Mary, the model for all women. The fruitfulness of the laurel is still proverbial—we still "flourish as the green bay tree." [22]

In Cantata 15, for Easter (BG 2, p. 153), the theme is the triumphant passage of the Tomb, "hier steht der Besieger bei Lorbeer und Fahn" (here stands now the victor with laurel and flag) and the connotation is the familiar one of victory although the sense of inviolability and fertility are included. The "flag" is represented by the fanfare (clarini) and the laurel again by an alternating, sequential melisma in the bass voice against a complementary alternating figure in the continuo (and again a tied whole note!) (Ex. 2).

Example 2

In Cantata 44 (BG 10, p. 143 Recit.), the image of the palm branch is brought vividly before our eyes with the simplest possible means, the simple subdivision—the essence of the palmate leaf form—of a single eighth note over a broken third (Ex. 3).

20. W. Kurth, *The Complete Woodcuts of Albrecht Dürer* (New York, 1946), plates 322, 294, 275.

21. Jung, *ACU*, p. 333.

22. See also *arbor philosophica* in Jung *PA*.

Example 3

de—nen Pal—men—zwei—gen

This tiny touch draws attention to the literary image and "colors" the whole line, the prosy homily,

"Allein es Gleichen Christen denen Palmen Zweigen
Die durch die Last nur desto höher steigen"
(But Christians are like those palm branches
Which, though burdened, mount but the higher).

The subject of the Cantata is St. John XVI: 2, "They shall put you out of the Synagogues, yea, when the time cometh that whosoever killeth you will think that he doeth God a service." Christ's dire prediction—here turned to exhortation—is lightened by the fleeting glimpse of the symbol of glory to come. In the seventeenth century, the palm was presented emblem-fashion as one of the attributes of the Virgin, a tree of life and here also refers to the agent of Christ's connection to divine power and victory.[23] Dürer's palm trees illustrate the principle of subdivision in several woodcuts, perhaps most beautifully in the not unrelated "Flight of the Holy Family" and in the definitely related "Christ's Entry into Jerusalem." [24]

In Cantata 86 (BG 20, 1, p. 124, Aria, alto), a magnificent rose bush flourishes and grows into a thicket of leaves, buds, flowers and thorns drawn in the decorative groups of four thirty-seconds among sixteenths and eighths

---

23. Jung, *PA*, p. 70; also the appropriate anabasis for *höher steigen*, the augmented fourth on *wider*, the diminished fifth for *Anti-Christ* and the diminished seventh for *Feuer*.

24. W. Kurth, *Woodcuts of Dürer*, plates, 187, 228.

of the violin obbligato, while the continuo portrays a sturdy scalewise vine and root (Ex. 4). The text is "Ich will doch wohl

Example 4

Rosen brechen wenn mich Gleich die Dornen stechen" (roses will I still pluck, even though by thorns I'm stuck). The voice forms folded (plica-like) figures

for "Rosen," and jagged disjunct figures for "brechen"

and "Dornen stechen"

The gospel text of the Cantata, in the opening bass aria, is St. John XVI: 23: "Verily I say unto you, Whatsoever ye shall ask the Father in my name, He will give it to you." The rose-thorn image of the alto aria is a symbolic reply, the roses are those of the "Rosie Cross." [25] The thought is that of the Rosicrucian "per cruceum ad rosam"—the divine principle, eternal life, the solar image of the rose, being the "whatsoever" vouchsafed to earth via the Cross, "in my name," and its suffering, "Dornen."

The images of root and vine of the preceding bring at once to mind the superb vine protrayed in the St. Matthew Passion, at the end of the scene of the Last Supper. Jesus' lines (Matt. XXVI: 27, 28) "trinket alle daraus . . . da ich's neu trinken werde mit euch in meinen Vater's Reich" (drink ye all of it . . .

---

25. Jung, *PA*, p. 74.

I will not drink henceforth of this fruit of the vine, etc.) are set over a bass that winds and twists, breaks forth into leaves, tendrils, and grapes—all extremely graphic—and finally goes to earth in the 'cello low *C* (Bach's earth symbol, see the "earthquake" scene)—a luxuriant "true vine." One can only think of the great vine that completely surrounds the church of St. Stephano in Monte in Bologna, carved in relief in the stone of the building. Dürer uses a similar vine in the decorative frame of his woodcut of the Crucifixion which was printed as an illustration in the 1524 Nuremburg edition of Luther's Old Testament.[26] The symbolism, bread and wine, of the whole scene relates Christ directly to the ancient Egyptian Osiris "conqueror of death . . . holder of the secret of resurrection and rebirth through which the lower power is transformed into the higher." [27]

In Cantata 114 (BG 24, p. 101, chorale), there is a memorable representation of the "Weizkornlein," the "grain of wheat" from the text of St. John XII: 24, "Verily I say unto you, Except a corn of wheat fell into the ground and die, it abideth alone: but if it die it bringeth forth much fruit," which is paraphrased here. The curious repetitious bass figure, fragmented, with each section contained between rests ("it abideth alone")

is the image of the individual grains of wheat, each tight knit, complete with its vital spark, the germ of life, *tr.,* coiled within it. These are grouped in three's with a small cadence after every third one. Each reminds us that cadence means "fall" by beginning one directly under that word (Ex. 5).

Example 5

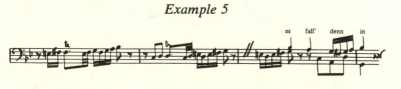

---

26. W. Kurth, *Woodcuts of Dürer,* plate 302.
27. Neumann, *OHC,* p. 239, "Osiris . . . is not a corn god only, he is also a wine god."

John's lines are, of course, a transcendent moralization on a theme which reaches far back into the vegetation myths and fertility rites of the most ancient religions,[28] to the figures of Osiris, Attis, and Dionysus. The individual Christian is likened to the separate grain whose death and resurrection is life— bread. This is behind Christ's words at the Last Supper just described and their tremendous force which is revitalized at every Communion and in myriad forms in folklore. From this, it is possible to interpret [29] the Crucifixion and Resurrection as a projection of the solar-vegetation myth whose symbolic details have been gradually added to the historical facts. Jung says, "man is fully redeemed at the moment when the Son of God returns again to the Father after undergoing sacrificial death." [30] Bach's preoccupation with fulfillment in death is well known—here it combines with a most forceful symbol in an unforgettable image of life.

The flora of the landscape of the Cantatas are perforce represented by purely visual means. In the representation of its fauna, the animals are represented by dynamic suggestion of their characteristic sound and movement (Hypotyposis) and by subjective reaction to their natures, as benign or dangerous.

In the opening chorus of Cantata 1 (BG 1) (*Wie schön leuchtet der Morgenstern*), designated for the Feast of the Annunciation, the gleaming star hangs low and sparkles warmly, its points and rays graphically and aurally represented by the six-note figures in the violins, while the camel which the star will eventually lead to Bethlehem with the Magi trudges patiently through

Example 6

28. Neumann, *OHC*, p. 223 ff. and p. 239; Jung, *ACU*, p. 117.
29. Jung, *PA*, p. 294.
30. *Ibid*. See also Jung, *ACU*, p. 11.

the desert sand below in the unusual repeated octave leaps of the continuo (Ex. 6). Dürer places such a six-pointed star in the sky in four different woodcuts of the Nativity.[31]

Another morning star sparkles, high, clear, and brightly in the opening chorus of Cantata 96, BG 22, p. 169, (*Herr Christ, der einige Gottes-Sohn* . . . Er ist der Morgenstern). The key is the same and the figuration similar, but the tempo is *vivace,* the visually and aurally descriptive passages are assigned to a high diŝcant recorder and the *violino piccolo* (Ex. 7).

Example 7

In Cantata 10 (BG 1, p. 301)—for the Feast of the Visitation of Mary—the text of the tenor aria, "Seine Same musste sich so sehr wie Sand an Meer und Stern am Firmament ausweihen" (His seed must spread as wide as the sand of the sea and the stars of the Firmament) is accompanied by two pages covered with closely set (48 per bar!), evenly spaced sixteenth-notes. The visual image is striking enough in Bach's autograph[32] and is even more impressive in the regularity of the Bach-Gesellschaft score (Ex. 8).

Example 8

31. W. Kurth, *Woodcuts of Dürer,* plates 183, 185, 226, 262.
32. E. Winternitz, *Musical Autographs* (Princeton, 1955), Vol. II, plate 36.

The opening chorus of Cantata 104 (BG 23, p. 97), *Du Hirte Israel, höre* (Shepherd of Israel, hearken) is an apocalyptic vision of the Christian allegory of the Shepherd and His flock. The radiance of the Cherubim and of Him "who is above" illumines the earthly scene of the movements of a flock of sheep, now herded closely, p. 100, now straggling, as in the long lines of pp. 101 and 104, and then finally safely in the fold, p. 106. In the same cantata (BG 23, pp. 113, 114, Aria), there is a finely observed detail. At the text, "Jesu schafe" a melisma (p. 113, bar 7, p. 114, bar 6) in the solo bass voice portrays the faster movement of the would-be stray and the consequent opening in the flock, which is deftly closed with a rhythmically complementary direct scale by the violin to the tonic at the cadence in the next bar (Ex. 9).

Example 9

In the St. Matthew Passion, the setting of Jesus' words, "I shall smite the shepherd and the sheep shall be scattered" is very simple and direct, the contrary, disjunct, rapid, staccato motion between the bass and the upper parts forming the image.

The sound and movement of a flock of pigeons is described in Cantata 71 (BG 18, p. 24, Coro). The text is Ps. 74: 19, "O, deliver not the soul of Thy turtledove unto the multitude of the wicked." The cooing is conveyed by two flutes, with oboes and violins, in a low register with many trills, and by the remarkable treatment of a violoncello (piccolo?) and bassoon, which, with an overlapping, complementary figure manage to contribute to the murmuring and also picture the strutting, purling, tumbling of the birds feeding at familiar feet in a quiet courtyard (Ex. 10). The vocal complement, *coro pleno,* might seem excessive until one recalls the following line of the Psalm, not set here: "forget not the congregation of Thy poor."

Another portrayal of the dove is to be found in Cantata 49 (BG 10, pp. 313, 330). Here, the sound and notoriously erratic,

Example 10

evasive flight of the wild bird when pursued is portrayed in the florid *organo obbligato* part. Bach makes certain that we understand the image by placing the picturesque elements directly in line with the word "dove" (Taube) in the solo bass voice, which there shares the figuration "I seek thee with longing my dove, fairest bride—where art thou gone that my eye sees thee no more?" In the final duet for soprano, the "dove" and bass, the *organo obbligato* again imitates the sound of the dove in a contented, acquiescent manner in contrast to that of the fugitive in the first aria (Ex. 11).

Example 11

The dove as the representation of the Holy Ghost of the Trinity appears in Cantata 7 (BG 1, p. 201), "der Geist erschien in Bild der Tauben." No fugitive flight this, but a serene hovering. At the word "erschien" (appeared) the two obbligato violins descend to their lowest tone (*G*) and then rise again. The soaring and hovering dominates the movement, while the Trinity is everywhere expressed by the *Dreifaltigkeit* of the meter, 9/8. The dove as a symbol of divine vision expressed in innocence, faithfulness, and simplicity, the feminine principle, *sophiasapientia,* is of great antiquity.[33] Realization and bestowal of these is symbolized in baptism, making the prominence given this image in this Cantata, which has the baptism of Christ as its theme, entirely appropriate.

Two images of a very different order complete the list of domestic animals described in the Cantatas. Bach gives Midas a bray (Ex. 12) and thus a superb set of asses' ears in Cantata 201

Example 12

denn nach mei – nen bei–den Oh – ren

(BG 11, 2, p. 52), *Der Streit zwischen Phoebus und Pan* ("denn nach meinen beiden Ohren"), ante-dating Mendelssohn's "Bottom" and S. Saëns' "Animals," while Phoebus' horses gallop rhythmically across the pages of Cantata 202 (BG 11, 2, p. 79), *Weichet nur betrübte Schatten.*

References to predatory animals bring forth several striking visual images supported by affective aural features, e.g., harmonic tension, suggesting emotional reaction. A lion shows his teeth in Cantata 178 (BG 35, p. 262) in jagged, broken seventh chords in the continuo. Bach assures us of his graphic intention by making the solo bass voice take over the same figure (Ex. 13)

Example 13

sie flet – – schen ih–re Mör–der zäh – ne

---

33. Neumann, *OHC,* p. 76; Jung, *ACU,* p. 45.

precisely on the word "fletschen" (bare, as teeth), and *nowhere else*.

Another lion roars in Cantata 63 (BG 16, p. 79) on the lowest organ tone and in snarling thirty-second note scales an octave higher. In the St. Matthew Passion, the terrible claws of the tiger, "Tieger-klauen," are graphically and aurally represented in Part II, No. 36, by the ascending thirty-second note scales and their slur, followed by the drop of the diminished seventh, and, by the upward resolution of very dissonant suspensions, bars 10–12. A wolf in sheep's clothing appears in Cantata 24 (BG 5, 1, p. 144, Recit.), represented by purely oratorical, rhetorical means—in which this recitativo is especially rich—simple antithesis, opposition of pitch level.

The eagle's wings and flight described in Cantata 137 (BG 28, p. 187) are those of Exodus 19: 4, described by the Lord to Moses at Sinai. Their strong, secure beating is portrayed in the figural violin obbligato which Whittaker rightly observes is certainly more idiomatic for the violin than for the organ as in the version included among the Schübler chorales.[34] Especially persuasive is the long arching, wheeling flight immediately following the line, "der dich auf Adlers Fittigen sicher geführst" (who bears thee safe on eagle's pinions) (Ex. 14).

Example 14

The eagle, as a symbol of power and divinity, God, is a usage of great antiquity in its various associations with the Sun, Zeus-Jupiter. Its significance in the unconscious as a symbol of the ego-self, personal consciousness, emerges from alchemical symbolism.[35]

---

34. BG 5, 1, p. 453.
35. Neumann, *OHC*, p. 352. See also Nietzsche, *Also sprach Zarathustra*.

In this light the words of God to Moses on Mt. Sinai gain interest as a commentary on the history of the emergence of personal ego and consciousness (of which the wanderings and escape from Egypt, apart from historical verity, are the allegories): "You have seen what I did to the Egyptians and how I bore you on eagles' wings and brought *you to myself*" (Exodus 19:4). And, the fact remains, Bach *did* make a solo organ piece of it—for himself to play.

The same means, harmonic tension referring to subjective dread and fear, is used to depict the "scorpion" (see Luke 10:19) in Cantata 52 (BG 12, 2, p. 38, Recit.). The scorpion's hook is the diminished seventh between the voice and the bass on the third syllable of the word. Here Bach shows discretion, necessary in recitative where images succeed one another quickly; the exotic "Skorpion" is allowed to dominate the image while the commoner "Schlange" (serpent), which follows hard upon it in the same bar, and which often receives the same treatment, is, for oratorical purpose, ignored.

The symbolic significance of serpent imagery and its universal manifestations in the unconscious are the subject of extended interpretation by Jung and his school. It symbolizes the unredeemed animality; blind, unreasoning instinct, unerringly deadly and fascinating because of the perfection of the mechanism-organism of the reptile, whose brain is incorporated into our own as the lower centers of the diencephalon and whose intolerable master, the precariously victorious cortex [36] cannot survive without it. The formulation of this tension as a symbolic struggle or (dragon) fight in Genesis and countless other places is the representation of the effort of achievement of self-consciousness —the freeing of the individual psyche.[37]

The image of the dragon fight and the emergence of the hero-ego is common to many cultures [38] and, very significantly for

---

36. Paradoxically, the evolved, adapted, and greatly developed olfactory area of the original reptile brain itself. See Nietzsche, *Also sprach Zarathustra,* Prologue 3 and 10.

37. Neumann, *OHC,* pp. 131–32.

38. *Ibid.;* Eliade, *Cosmos and History* (New York, 1959), p. 37 ff.; Jung, *PA,* p. 97.

our discussion, is the subject of the earliest evocative instrumental music of which we have record, the aulos playing at the Pythian games in 586 B.C. of "one Sakadas," . . . "illustrating the combat between Apollo and the dragon . . . which remained famous for centuries." [39] It is still with us as the basic dynamic of our sonata form.

The same theme is also, of course, the central narrative line of the Christian symbolic epic, and on which Bach and his librettists unwearyingly comment. What is begun in Genesis in the Garden is at length worked out and finally redeemed in the Gospels and Revelation in the triumph over the serpent, death, on the Mount of Olives, at Calvary, and at the Tomb.

In various mythical aspects, the serpent image takes many forms. One of the most persistent and uniquitous serpent-dragon symbols is the Uroboros, that of the serpent swallowing [40] its own tail. The Uroboros, very common in alchemical and emblem books, is generally regarded as a symbol for the concept or consciousness of time, the first step toward individuation.[41] The obsession with particularity within continuity is an emotionally intolerable, obsessive riddle of ego emergence depicted by this paradox—this image of continuity despite change.[42] Our art works are myths, which, as Eliade says of reading "yield (us) the illusion of a *mastery of Time* which, we may well suspect, gratifies a secret desire to withdraw from the implacable becoming that leads toward death." [43] That they actually contain some form of the dragon myth is the nature of the paradox. Music, like the time myth-symbol to which it ultimately, through ritual, refers, is, as a time-art the perfect means of such "withdrawal," if such it be [44] from the profane, accidental world via contempla-

39. Donald Grout, *A History of Western Music* (New York, 1960), p. 5.

40. Neumann, *OHC*, plates 2–9.

41. M. Praz, *Studies*, p. 96; Jacobi, *CAS*, p. 140; Neumann, *OHC*, pp. 5–13; Jung, *PA*, p. 45.

42. The same problem is given mathematical form by Zeno in his famous paradoxes and is visible in the abstract mathematical symbols of zero, 0, in its sense of perfection, and infinity, ∞.

43. M. Eliade, *Myths, Dreams and Mysteries* (New York, 1960). p. 36.

44. For here we are confronted with another form of the Uroboros paradox, which truly "has as many skins as a serpent." The heightened sense of time brought about by music is the surcease as well.

tion into the sacred, ordered cosmos, the paradise where time does not exist because it has no end. How correctly we say, colloquially, "killing time." No one ever understood this better than J. S. Bach.

Cantata 4, *Christ lag in Todesbanden* (BG 1, 117), is an apocalyptic recounting of Christ's victorious passage of the Tomb, and victory over the dragon, death. The text, Martin Luther's Easter hymn, employs in verse IV the image "die Schrift hat verkündiget wie ein Tod den anderen frass" (the Writ hath told how one Death devoured the other). To illustrate this, Bach has created a powerful and complex musical image.

The contrapuntal voice parts (S. T. & B., *cantus firmus* in Alto) are in imitation and finally in canon, which, against all good precepts of counterpoint, is allowed to come to an inconclusive end, to "taper off" to a single tone, while the bass maintains a futile "waving" eighth note motion over a semitone. The two Deaths [45] are conceived very naturally as serpents, with the canon, which "disappears" into a unison with the helpless, futile waving of the dead and dying snake's tail in the bass (Ex. 15).[46]

Example 15

frass, wie   ein Tod den an – dern   frass,

Jung gives a seventeenth-century illustration of the Uroboros-image of the kind that Bach and Luther may well (one might almost say must) have seen.[47] This is no accidental or unconscious image—deeply as its meaning may be embedded there—it is the work of a craftsman, poet, artist in full possession of his sacerdotal powers.

---

45. Neumann, *OHC*, p. 49, "the uroboros as a ring snake, for instance . . . the Leviathan . . . later divides or is divided into two." See also Jacobi, *CAS*, pp. 144 ff.

46. Our folklore still says "till sundown."

47. Jung, *PA*, p. 38.

However forceful and striking it may be, this image is surpassed, in scope at least, by the "subtil" serpents described in Cantata 165, *O heil'ges Geist- und Wasserbad* (BG 33). As has been observed, serpent symbolism is extremely rich and varied and in this cantata no fewer than three different, yet complementary images appear. Designed for the feast of the Trinity and on the general topic of baptism, the symbolic rebirth and unification with the Holy Spirit to which we have already referred, the libretto is by Salmo Frank, in some ways the best of Bach's librettists. He shows a refined use of imagery and provides Bach with the opportunity to demonstrate his own utter comprehension of symbolic language. In the opening soprano aria, "O, heil'ges Geist- und Wasserbad" (O, Holy Spirit and Waterbath), Bach invokes the mystical properties of water.[48] "Water," says Jung, "is the commonest symbol for the unconscious, the primordial state as described in Genesis. It is the 'original substance'— 'prima materia,' 'aqua mercuriates,' 'philosophical water' of Thales of Miletus and the alchemists." [49] It is the return to this state as preparation for rebirth which is the significance of the purification—by water—and re-identification by baptism, the subject of our present instance.

Of the relationship of the serpent-dragon symbol and that of water, it has been observed that "almost everywhere the dragon is related to . . . universal water," and, like the dragon, the snake . . . "belongs to the chthonic cold moist element of water." Like water, "the dragon symbolizes the state of primordial unconsciousness for it haunts caverns and tenebrous places." [50]

---

48. And describes it with precisely the same tonal means as would a latter-day "Impressionist," with secondary harmonies and mild dissonances. In two and three-quarters $\frac{4}{4}$ bars (13 beats) there are eight accented dissonant combinations and although the pieec is a fugue but one suspension. In the total length (fifty-two sixteenths) no fewer than twenty-four dissonant combinations are presented to the ear. The leading tone is lowered twice and such complexes as $VI\frac{9}{7}\frac{7}{5}$ (bar 2, *3*, bar 5, *3*), II^7 (bar 3, *3*), VII^7 (bar 3, *1*) and freely approached seventh and ninth echappées lend their characteristic properties.

49. Jung, *ACU*, p. 18; Jung, *PA*, p. 224; Jacobi, *CAS*, p. 144.

50. Jacobi, *CAS*, p. 148; Amos 9: 3, "in the bottom of the sea, thence will I command the serpent"; Rev. 12: 13, "And the serpent cast out of his mouth water as a flood . . ."; Jung, *PA*, p. 428.

The first serpent to appear in Cantata 4 (BG 33, p. 100, Recit.) is the primordial "original" serpent of the line "Du weisst, mein Gott, wie schmerzlich ich empfinde den alten Schlange-Stich" (Thou knowest, Lord, how painfully I feel the old serpent sting). This is the "old" Serpent of the Garden [51] visually and aurally represented by a twisting broken diminished seventh chord. It begins, tail first, with a few conjunct tones, then the twisting becomes more violent; with a lunge across the octave, the forked tongue and fangs are thrust forward on the word "Stich" (sting), the third of a minor chord.[52] (Ex. 16a).

Example 16a

der al — ten Schlan — ge Stich

The second serpent image follows almost directly on the first. In the next sentence of the Recitative ". . . helf, dass ich gläubig dich erwähle, blutrothes Schlangenbild, das an dem Kreuz erhöhet . . ." (. . . help me that I, in faith may elect thee, blood-red serpent-sign, raised upon the Cross . . .). Here we have a complex symbol which Jung [53] refers to as the "redemptive serpent," as the "serpent of Paradise who persuaded our first parents to sin and who finally leads to the redemption of mankind through the Son of God." It is the Ophitic serpent identified with the Saviour and Jesus.[54] The alchemical pictorial or emblematic representation of this concept is also a development of the Serpent of Moses,[55] as are the lines of St. John 3:14, "And as Moses

---

51. Jung, *ST*, p. 298.

52. An especially interesting detail on account of the "Schadenfreude" associated with minor triad.

53. Jung, *ACU*, p. 35.

54. See Jung, *PA*, p. 137.

55. Numbers 21: 6, "And the Lord sent fiery serpents among the people . . . and they bit the people . . ." and 21: 8, "And the Lord said unto Moses, make thee a fiery serpent and set it upon a pole and . . . everyone that is bitten when he looketh upon it shall live" and 21: 9, "And Moses made a serpent of brass and put it upon a pole. . . ."

lifted up the serpent in the wilderness even so must the Son of Man be lifted up: That whosoever believeth in Him should not perish, but have eternal life." Bach's treatment here shows his understanding; it is not the deadly serpent which hangs before us, but the inert, harmless image ("Schlangenbild"). The voice traces a broken V^7 chord, over $V\#^6_2$ harmonies—the most completely "inverted," "raised up" form of the chord; in the harmonic context the phrase is of a relatively low degree of tension. (Ex. 16b).

Example 16b

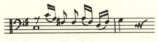

blut – ro – thes Schlan – gen – bild

The third serpent quite literally "inhabits" the final aria (BG 33, p. 101) and is referred to in the text in an affectionate diminutive: "Heilschlänglein" (savior-snakelet).[56] The text is "Jesu meines Todes Tod, lass in meinen Leben und in meiner letzten Noth mir für Augen schweben, das du mein Heilschlänglein sei'st" (Jesus, Slayer of my death, may I in my . . . final need see thee suspended before me).

Jung says "the hanging up of the god has an unmistakable symbolic value since suspension is the symbol of unfulfilled longing or intense expectation." Having already portrayed the Moses serpent, Bach goes on to portray the "little healing saviour-snake" of the text. This is, of course, the alexipharmic serpent, "the principle that brings all things to maturity and perfection." It represents the "transforming substance" of the alchemists, ferment and leaven, the spirit by which cold water and primordial being is raised to fire, divine incandescence, the *materia coelestis et divine*, the *materia lapidis Philosophorum*. In psychological terms, it is the achievement of wholeness, the master, but not

---

56. See Jung, *ST*, p. 436.

suppression of the reptilian diencephalon by the higher centers of the brain—the integration of the psyche and the acceptance of the riddle, and the defeat, of the Uroboros.[57] Instead of the knotted, dread, venomous serpent, Bach has, with great insight, portrayed here the slim, supple, mercurial, jewelled snake of the caduceus of Hermes and Asklepios. Bach's image shows that he understood this exactly. The figure of the violin obbligato with scalewise broken fourths in sixteenths, six in the first bar (like nothing else in Bach) alternating with rows of broken thirds, conveys the image and movement of the glittering scaly, sinuous creature graphically and aurally.[58] (Ex. 17).

Example 17

This realm of natural and mythical things is governed by its Creator—the Hand of God—and nowhere does Bach show such prodigal delight as in the invention of images and symbols for it. As a musician-performer, he was naturally extremely hand-conscious—he is credited with the innovation of using the whole hand at the keyboard—and for him, manual activity, thought, creation and intelligence were certainly synonomous.

The differentiation, "right" and "left" is positive and so habitual that it must be regarded in the most spontaneous and most nearly unconscious of his imagic uses. For the musician, this differentiation is even graphic. In Cantata 140, *Wachet auf* (BG 28, p. 278), the bridegroom addresses the bride, "auf

---

57. Jung, *ST,* p. 382, "The hero is himself the snake, himself the sacrificer and the sacrificed, which is why Christ rightly (!) compares himself with the healing Moses serpent"; see also p. 367; Jung, *ST,* p. 383; Jung, *PA,* pp. 128, 429; "Because of the bath and rebirth he takes a new name," Nicholas Melchior +1531, is an alchemical paraphrase of a Hymn to Mary, quoted in Jung, *PA,* p. 385; Jung, *PA,* p. 120n.

58. Alfred Dürr, *Studien über die Frühen Kantaten J. S. Bach's* (Leipzig: Breitkopf & Härtel, 1951). Dürr points out a sequence of three such fourths in Cantata 31, part 8, bar 14, which he assigns a composition date of some eight weeks before that of Cantata 165.

meiner Linken sollst du ruhn, und meine Rechte soll dich küssen" (on my left [hand] shalt thou rest and my right [hand] shall kiss thee); the notes of the first phrase lie low, and those of the second generally higher, which spells "left" and "right" to any keyboardist.

A similar configuration is found in Cantata 96 (BG 22, p. 181). The text "bald zur Rechten, bald zur Linken lenkt sich mein verirrter Schritt," (now to the right, now to the left go my erring steps) is set in uneven values and large intervals with "Rechten" as the highest tone (b♭) and "Linken" a diminished seventh below. After two repetitions of this pattern, Bach tells us of his intention by contradicting, inverting it vis-à-vis the text, to bear out the sense of the word, "erring." (Ex. 18).

Example 18

bald   zu   Rech – ten; bald   zu   Lin   –   ken   lenkt sich mein ver – irr   –   ter   Schrift

Examples of a sharp rise on or to the word "recht" are numerous; it will suffice to cite Cantata 153 (BG 32, p. 45, and also p. 52 even though here the sense is that of "correct"—not "hand!"); Cantata 43 (BG 10, p. 109, Recit.) . . . "zur rechten Hand Gottes," an octave leap; Cantata 11 (BG 2, p. 31), same text, an augmented fourth leap, i.e. "pointing."

The graphic representation of the Divine Hand is frequent in the woodcuts and engravings of illustrated religious emblem books and decorated devotional works. One of the most beautiful is the cloud-cuffed Hand of the Creator to be seen in the engravings by Michael Wolgemuth, the teacher of Albrecht Dürer, and Wilhelm Pleydenwurff, which illustrate the first pages of Dr. Hartman Schedel's *Liber Chronicorum* (Nürnberg, 1493). They relate the Biblical account of the Creation and the Hand traces the great circles of the Firmament. Such traditional representation was very common, and it is unthinkable that Bach was not familiar with the image.

In Cantata 105 (BG 23, p. 136), he offers us a very similar image to illustrate the text ". . . so wird die Handschrift ausgethan" (thus shall the handwriting be shown forth), and "wenn deine Sterbestunde schlägt dem Vater selbst die Rechnung übergeben" (when thy death hour strikes [Jesus] will himself give the Father the reckoning).

The popular concepts of a predetermined hour of death inscribed in a great Judgment or "Doomsday" Book and of an ultimate "reckoning," or evaluation of the Christian life were prevalent in Bach's day and appear in other places in his works. Here the repeated figure of the upper strings, *Recitativo stromentato,* present a graphic image of a right hand

which "traces" or writes out the text against the steady repeated eighth note bass (pizzicato octave leaps), which is often a clock or time symbol with Bach. At the words "death" and "reckoning" the activity becomes more complex as the recording angel works up the tally sheet. (Ex. 19).

Example 19

Jung has outlined the relationship between the development of the rhythmic activity of the hand and the development of consciousness and personality, "the phase of rhythmic activity generally coincides with development of mind and speech." [59] He considers this activity an auxiliary of the *libido,* or in a word, a sign of psychic force and life itself. A similar sense, that of movement, purpose, energy, dexterity, will, and ordered action is often used by Bach to convey the Hand, operative. In connection with such references and images there are recurring characteristic graphic patterns which bring to mind the structure of the hand— opposition of thumb, articulation, flexibility, and reach. In the

59. Jung, *ST,* p. 143 ff.

St. Matthew Passion, the alto aria "sehet, Jesus hat die Hand uns zu fassen aus gespannt" (Behold, Jesus has stretched forth His hand for us to grasp) these are plainly visible; e.g.

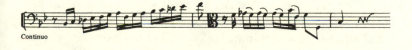

Also, in the St. Matthew Passion, at the Last Supper where Jesus blesses the bread and the cup ("dankete") the two gestures are so beautifully suggested that it is almost impossible not to think of Dürer's drawing of praying hands.

Similar figures are visible in Cantata 100 (BG 22, p. 309), on the word "Händen" itself. In Cantata 111 (BG 24, p. 15 and 26), there is another writing "God has prescribed the day" and the Hand operative, ". . . wenn seine Hand mich rührt" (when His Hand shall touch me). In Cantata 106 (BG 23, p. 163, Duet), these elements are combined in the continuo—the rhythmic force and order of the ascending scale—the articulation and span of the hand in the answering figures. (Ex. 20).

Example 20

![Musical example for Example 20, continuo part]

Continuo

A very striking and picturesque composite image is to be seen in Cantata 10 (BG 1, p. 296), at the text "will seine Hand wie Spreu zerstreu'n" (His hand will scatter like chaff). Both voice and continuo have graphic and dynamic hand images while the chaff is dispersed in a fine swirling Baroque cloud.[60]

It is again in connection with baptism that Bach offers us the most beautiful representations of the Hand of God. The Cantata

---

60. Other examples are:

Cantata 139, BG 28, p. 240 (order bringing)

Cantata 131, BG 32, pp. 12, 13 (garland weaving)

Cantata 178, BG 35, p. 253 (leading)

The instance in Cantata 187 (BG 37, p. 166), at "wenn Du Deine Hand aufthust" (when Thou open'st Thy hand) leaves no question as to Bach's intention of expressing the action of the text.

7 (BG 1, p. 179), *Christ unser Herr zum Jordan kam,* interprets the Baptism of Christ at the hands of John the Baptist. The opening chorus describes the purifying water bath ("da wollt'er stiften uns ein Bad, zu waschen uns von Sünden"). The Cross and God the Father in glory soar above all, the stream slows and eddies among the reeds (*violino concertante, oboe d'amore* 1, 2) while in the continuo we find again the same graphic hand image as at the "Handschrift" of Cantata 105 illustrating the act of washing, the hands passing down over the limbs, two and two, and the falling water. (Ex. 21).

Example 21

The succeeding aria, p. 195, "merkt und hört ihr Menschenkinder was Gott selbst die Taufe heisst" (hear ye children of men what God calls the Baptism) converts the preceding ritual purification to the transcendent concept of Christian baptism. The Hand dips up the water in its hollow and pours it on the believer's head. The image of the cupped hand with closely serried fingers (four thirty-seconds and an eighth, descending scalewise) is everywhere to be seen. It is the closest possible musical representation of the hand and action to be seen in Hans Wächtlin's beautiful woodcut of the scene from his *Leben Jesu Christ,* Strasburg, 1508. (Ex. 22).

Example 22

Bach saw the Hand of God everywhere, and surely none ever saw it plainer!

THE ARCHITECTURE OF

ST. MARK'S CATHEDRAL

AND THE VENETIAN POLYCHORAL STYLE:

A CLARIFICATION

Wilton Mason

THE UNIVERSITY OF NORTH CAROLINA AT CHAPEL HILL

Giacomo Benvenuti, Giovanni d'Alessi, William Kimmel, and other scholars have long since disposed of the notion that Willaert invented the idea of opposed choirs in a polychoral style of writing. Nonetheless there remains, in most of the literature dealing with the Venetian school, fixed conviction that the special architectural characteristics of St. Mark's cathedral did contribute in greater or lesser degree to the formation of this style. There is, of course, some truth in this as a general proposition, but the more one ponders some of the statements and tries to correlate them with the facts, the more involved does the whole question appear. A few examples will suffice to indicate some of the confusion.

Three quotations by Leichtentritt, Dickinson, and Ferguson may be cited first as more or less typical of the usual references to be found in general music histories.

"Willaert also created the new style of *chori spezzati*, in which two distinct choral bodies answer each other in dialogue and are finally combined in powerful climax. For this, the peculiar architecture of St. Mark's, with its two choirs and two organs lofts at a distance from each other, gave him his first impetus." [1]

"The founder of the sixteenth-century Venetian school was Adrian Willaert (about 1490–1562), a Netherlander. The struc-

---

1. Hugo Leichtentritt, *Music, History, and Ideas* (Cambridge, 1941), p. 83.

ture of St. Mark's church, with its two galleries and organs facing each other, suggested to him the plan of dividing his choir into two bodies, by which new combinations and effects were obtained." [2]

"The vesper services at St. Mark's at once became famous. In this extraordinary structure . . . the proud Venetians, in some earlier day had set up, in two opposing galleries, two organs whose answering echoes gave a splendor—quite befitting the jeweled magnificence of the edifice itself—to those responsive chants in which, since the foundations of Christianity, the Psalms of David had been recited." [3]

Before investigating further references it might be well to recall the actual plan of St. Mark's. The church is laid out as a Greek cross with four equal arms covered by a dome in the center and by a dome over each of the arms. The eastern end of the nave terminates in an apse which is flanked by smaller apses terminating the side aisles of the nave. A narrow gallery circles the church at the upper level. The choir is separated from the nave by two means: a raising of the floor level, which is some four feet higher than the floor of the nave to allow for a crypt beneath the high altar where the relics of St. Mark are laid, and a beautiful rood screen of eight columns, surmounted by fourteen statues. Similar screens, each of four columns, placed a little to the east, close the choir in a line with the front of the high altar. (See sketch).

In the light of this description it will be seen that some of the following observations are indeed perplexing.

Venice's musical center was the beautiful church of St. Mark's, proud witness of a thousand-year-old Byzantine culture. Its organ, on which the great masters of the time had played, had gained widespread fame. All these musicians had already adopted the new polyphonic style that had come out of the North. To facilitate the performance of these many-voiced works, requiring a multiple di-

---

2. Edward Dickinson, *The Growth and Development of Music* (London, 1921), p. 47.

3. Donald N. Ferguson, *A History of Musical Thought* (New York, 1939), p. 108.

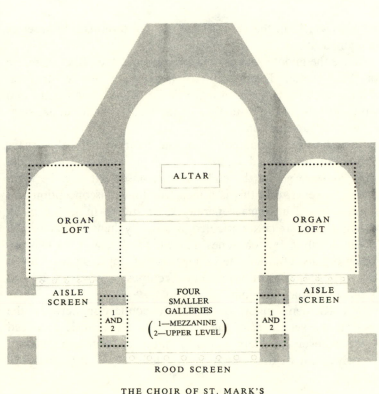

ALTAR

ORGAN
LOFT

ORGAN
LOFT

AISLE
SCREEN

1
AND
2

FOUR
SMALLER
GALLERIES
$\left(\begin{array}{l}\text{1—MEZZANINE}\\\text{2—UPPER LEVEL}\end{array}\right)$

1
AND
2

AISLE
SCREEN

ROOD SCREEN

THE CHOIR OF ST. MARK'S
(DETAILS SIMPLIFIED)

vision of choirs and instrumental groups, a second organ was
built in the year 1490, so that each of the two main naves now had
its own organ and its own choir with orchestral accompaniment,
affording the opportunity for magnificent combined effects.[4]

Here the cart has been placed before the horse, or rather, the
"new polyphonic style" before the second organ which is supposed to have called it forth. It is impossible to determine what
is meant by the phrase "the two main naves" since St. Mark's has
only one. Possibly this is intended as a reference to the aisles of

---

4. Kurt Pahlen, *Music of the World* (New York, 1949), p. 56.

the nave which, in the choir of the church, terminate in apses as mentioned above.

"Since the middle ages St. Mark's had been the center of music for the Venetian Republic. . . . Because of the construction of the church in the form of a Greek Cross, with two organs and two choir lofts in opposite ends of the transept, antiphonal singing was not uncommon." [5]

Here confusion is compounded. The choir lofts and the organs are, of course, located in that part of the cathedral called the choir, and are not at the ends of the transept. It may be mentioned, however, that this is a most common misconception and is the one which seems generally to spring to mind for many musicians who are better oriented historically than architecturally.

"Since only a few churches, like St. Mark's, with its two opposing organs, afforded the opportunity of opposing two choirs, the mass production of double-choir compositions was prohibited by practical considerations." [6]

Here Riemann insists on the close connection between the physical characteristics of the cathedral and the music produced there, and even considers such a spatial disposition as a necessity for polychoral writing which, as we shall see, is historically inaccurate.

> Willaert . . . stimulated by the architectural relationships of the interior of St. Mark's, with its two main galleries, each of which was furnished with an organ, began to experiment with the spatial separation of his singers in order to bring clarity to the intricate web of the older polyphony; but after the experiment with two choirs had succeeded brilliantly he began to use the small adjoining galleries of the church for the disposition of special choirs, finally achieving nine groups of four voices each, naturally to the much greater edification of the hearers than his predecessor Ocken-

---

5. Ernestine M. Klinzing, *Music History in Brief* (New York, 1951), p. 42.
6. Hugo Riemann, *Handbuch der Musikgeschichte, Bd. II* (Leipzig, 1920), p. 420: ". . . da nur wenige Kirchen wie die Markuskirche mit ihren zwei gegenüberliegenden Orgeln Gelegenheit boten, zwei Chöre einander gegenüber aufzustellen, so war aus praktischen Gründen eine Massenproduktion doppelchöriger Kompositionen unterbunden."

heim had been able to do with his previously mentioned 36-voice mass.[7]

In this excerpt we find the first mention of the use of the other galleries of the church. These are the smaller galleries lying one above the other just to the east of the rood screen. The supposition that these *Nebengallerien* might be those narrow galleries of the north and south transepts must, as we shall see, be ruled out from a purely practical point of view. "Willaert (about 1485–1562) was, among others, the creator, or at least the outstanding innovator, of the so-called apse-choir technique, a form of reciprocal performance of two vocal-instrumental groups derived from the disposition of the church interior into two divided spaces (apses)." [8]

The curious German term "Apsidenchore" seems to be a word coined to describe some virtually nonexistent practice. Churches with true opposing apses are so rare as to be real architectural curiosities since this would mean the placing of apses at the opposite ends of either the nave or the transept. It is true that from the end of the sixth century onward other apses were added to churches in addition to the main choir apse, but these were generally placed either at the end of the aisles of the nave or else within the eastern walls of the north and south transepts, where they were called "transept chapels." Musical forces stationed

---

7. Wilhelm Langhans, *Die Geschichte der Musik des 17., 18., und 19. Jahrhunderts* (Leipzig, 1884), p. 71. "Willaert . . . angeregt durch die architektonischen Verhältnisse des inneren Raumes der Markuskirche mit seinen zwei Hauptgallerien, deren jede mit einer Orgel versehen war, den Versuch unternahm, seine Sängerschaar örtlich zu theilen, um so Klarheit in das verwickelte Gewebe der älteren Polyphonie zu bringen; nachdem aber der Versuch mit zwei Chören glänzend gelungen war, begann er auch die kleinen Nebengallerien der Kirche zur Aufstellung gesonderter Chorgruppen zu benutzen, deren er schliesslich neun von je vier Stimmen zusammenwirken liess, nun selbstverständlich zu ungleich grösserer Erbauung der Zuhörer, als es sein Vorgänger Ockenheim mit seiner früher erwähnten 36-stimmigen Messe je vermocht hätte."

8. Hans Schnoor, *Geschichte der Musik* (Gutersloh, 1954), p. 63. "Willaert (um 1485–1562) was u. a. der Schöpfer oder zumindest der hervorragendste Neuschöpfer der sogennanten Apsidenchortechnik, einer aus der getrennten Aufstellung im Kirchenraum (Apsis) abgeleiteten Form des wechselseitigen Konzertierens zweier vokal-instrumentaler Gruppen."

in the apses of transept chapels would be isolated from each other, out of sight and, to some degree, out of hearing, and performance under such conditions would appear impractical. The same consideration holds true for apses at the end of the nave aisles. At St. Mark's the organ lofts lie above the aisle apses and face in to the choir (see dotted lines on sketch) and thus might more accurately be considered as lateral extensions of the choir area than as separate areas, since the singers and musicians indubitably faced in toward the center, stationed along the front railing of the lofts.[9]

In view of the foregoing discussion the complete confusion of the following quotation will be evident.

> The Cathedral of St. Mark's at Venice was the only important church in Christendom which was built in the shape of a Greek instead of a Latin cross. With such a floor plan the transept divides the nave into two equal parts, thus making the normal position of choir and congregation impossible. As early as the fourteenth century this problem was solved by dividing the choir into two parts, stationed in low balconies on either side of the transept. An organ was placed with each choir.[10]

---

9. It may be noted from the sketch that the musicians' galleries 1 and 2 lie well to the west of the aisle apses and, like the organ lofts, appear to belong to the choir areas, an effect which is intensified by the small balconies which extend toward the center of the chancel.

10. Theodore Finney, *A History of Music* (New York, 1935), p. 154. The quotations thus far cited have been chosen for their typical misrepresentations but they are far from being a complete roster. Many excellent and highly regarded references continue to suggest a relationship between the architecture of St. Mark's and the music produced there. Robert Haas, in his *Aufführungspraxis der Musik*, p. 129, says "Willaerts Ausbildung dieser Technik Mehrchörigkeit wurde durch die räumliche Anlage der Markuskirche begünstigt." Guido Adler in his *Handbuch der Musikgeschichte*, p. 350, makes the following observation: "Die bauliche Beschaffenheit der Markuskirche dürfte Willaert die Anregung geboten haben, eine von Josquin gleichsam ideell angewendete satztechnische Eigentümlichkeit ins Reale zu übertragen: die Mehrchörigkeit." In Manfred Bukofzer's *Music in the Baroque Era*, p. 20, we find, "The music for double chorus, or *cori spezzati*, was brought to fame (not invented, as it is frequently claimed) by Willaert, choirmaster at San Marco, the architecture of which lent itself singularly well to such experiments." And Gustave Reese, in his *Music in the Renaissance*, p. 372, says, "No doubt inspired especially by the two choir-lofts at St. Mark's, one facing the other, Willaert wrote for two choirs singing alternately."

The idea of using the transept of a church for the deployment of musical forces is an attractive one and seems, indeed, almost to be indicated when dealing with the musical dialogue of opposing groups. The fact remains, however, that there is no historical justification for such an assumption, certainly not in the case of St. Mark's, or for any other important Renaissance chapel. Sartell Prentice, in his splendid and provocative study of cathedrals and cathedral-building, speculates on the possibility that transepts might have been so used in the early days of church-construction but shows that by the time the placement of the high altar was fixed in the main apse, the placement of the choir was necessarily dictated thereby.

With one exception definite functions were assigned to each important member of the church—to the chancel, chapels, choir, and nave; only the transepts varied from age to age in the nature of the services demanded of them. Apparently first added to the basilica to accommodate the increasing number of the clergy, it is probable that they were early utilized to accommodate a choir, recruited from the minor orders of the priesthood.

This explanation answers one perplexing question that would otherwise remain unanswered and unexplained. Granted that the transepts were intended for the many clergy that flooded the church after the Edict of Milan, what function did these clergy perform? Were they present merely as detached members of the congregation, or did they share in the performance of the liturgies?

It must be remembered that, by the Fourth Century, the liturgy of the Church had developed complicated forms and had become rather too difficult for the ordinary clergy who, however consecrated, were not always vocally gifted or musically trained, and also that the congregations had been progressively excluded from all participation in the musical portion of the service. The organization of a priestly choir had, therefore, become increasingly imperative.

Shortly after the Edict of Milan, the Council of Laodicea issued a decree which stated, "Beside the appointed singers others shall not sing in church." The importance of the action lay more in the spirit it revealed than in its general effectiveness for, beyond the boundaries of its own jurisdiction, the action of the Council could only be accepted as a recommendation; it was not an Ecumenical

Edict. In some of the great Eastern liturgies the part permitted to the people was restricted to a few brief responses: the "Amens," the "Kyrie Eleisons," "And to thy spirit," with a few others of equal brevity. By the middle of the Fourth Century the change had become general, if not universal; the laity had been silenced, and only the voices of the priests might be heard in the various offices and liturgies of the Church which now demanded, for their rendition, the voices of a large and trained choir recruited from the ranks of the minor clergy. Schools for the training of ordained choristers were established by the metropolitan churches—in Rome, in Lombardy, and elsewhere—and a portion of the nave was walled off to form the Schola Cantorum, the "place of the singers," as in S. Clemente in Rome.

But the introduction of antiphonal singing immediately gave a practical value to the transepts for the priests, if they might not easily sing in unison when widely scattered in the two wings of the Crossing, in the schola cantorum, and in the chancel, could render the antiphonals of the liturgies with great effectiveness when seated in the transepts. Whether these transepts were so used is a possibility worth considering.

It is true that neither history nor tradition bears witness to this use for the transepts so that we are driven to mere conjecture as to its probability, but the argument from silence is never convincing especially when, as now, the failure of the witnesses to testify is far from inexplicable.

The use of the transepts for a priestly choir must have been of too short duration to have left any deep impression on the Church, for the early removal of the altar from its primitive place in the Crossing to the depths of the apse forced the transference of the choir from the transepts to a new location in the long axis of the church. Then the appearance of the symbolist, with his dramatic and appealing interpretation of the transepts as the silent proclamation of the gospel of the Cross of Christ, supplanted and drove from memory the more practical, if less emotional, explanation of the transepts as having been utilized by the Church for the accommodation of a double choir.[11]

The choir, as an architectural term, refers to any part of the church intended for choir use or, more commonly, the eastern

---

11. Sartell Prentice, *The Heritage of the Cathedral* (New York, 1936), p. 43.

end of the church, in which case it is practically synonymous with the term chancel. Already by the time of the Tudor church composers of England the choral forces had been split into opposing groups stationed on either side of the choir area. The side on the north was known as the *cantoris* side because of the presence there of the cantor or precentor; the south side, by the dean's stall, was known as the *decani* side. Nor did these distinctions hold for English usage only; Ockeghem is mentioned as one of the 25 singers who served on the *cantoris* side at Our Lady in Antwerp.[12] Evidently, then, it was a well-established procedure in the fifteenth and sixteenth centuries (as indeed it is today) to divide cathedral choirs into facing groups separated by the width of the chancel. In most cases the seats for the choir are elevated into ranks above the floor level of the chancel.

When this customary deployment of musical forces is compared with that of St. Mark's it becomes evident that the only real difference of disposition in the latter case is one of height. The organ lofts of St. Mark's lie at an upper level on the sides of the choir. The musicians' galleries lie one above another just east of the rood screen. Choir groups or instrumentalists stationed in them would occupy, relatively, mezzanine and upper floor levels. Whether this vertical displacement would really have an acoustical effect, as so many authors seem to imply, is highly debatable. As far as the horizontal scale is concerned the musical groups would actually be somewhat closer to each other in St. Mark's than in many other cathedrals of Europe since the chancel there is not a notably wide one.

A mid-nineteenth century description of the interior of the choir area is of interest here in clarifying the picture:

> Nowadays, on entering the choir by the center steps you may see on the right the doge's seat, and the *schenale,* or back of this, fashioned of inlaid walnut, finely worked, having Justice in the center with a sword in her right hand and balances in her left. . . . Around the choir, similarly inlaid, were the seats for the senators and for the clergy participating in the solemn ducal functions. . . . The seats of the choir were covered on solemn occasions with

---

12. Gustave Reese, *Music in the Renaissance* (New York, 1954), p. 118.

tapestries worked with figures of gold and silk, executed sometime before 1551 in Florence. Above these seats there are four balconies, or boxes, or porches, two on each side of the chapel, one above the other. In the lower ones there are Sansovino's gleaming bronzes with scenes from the life of St. Mark; the two upper ones are nothing but open-work parapets jutting out. All four of these balconies were, in times past, given over to the musical chapel, but those with the bronze parapets were also used for ambassadors or foreign residents. Today they are exclusively for the use of distinguished persons.[13]

In the light of this clear description we may examine one further quotation which betrays again the now familiar misconception.

Although the Venetians are frequently accorded the distinction of having invented the opposed choir, polychoral style of writing by taking advantage of the fact that Saint Mark's possessed two organs in choir lofts opposite each other in the northern and southern extremities of the transept of the cathedral, this (invention) concept has long since been superseded by the researches of Giovanni d'Alessi, William Kimmel, and others.

Basic to the polychoral style is the principle of tonal contrast achieved by the opposition of differently placed vocal or instrumental groups whose performers are either of similar or different ranges and colors. Disparity in the physical placement of the groups

---

13. Francesco Caffi, *Storia della musica sacra nell' già capella ducale di San Marco in Venezia,* Vol. II (Venice, 1855, repr. Milan: Bollettino Bibliografico Musicale, 1931), pp. 116–17:

"Ai tempi nostri vedevasi nel coro, alla destra di chi entra per la gradinata di mezzo, il sedile del doge; e lo schenale o dorse di esso di noce intarsiato di minuto lavoro, avente nel mezzo la Giustizia con la spada nella destra, e le bilancie nella sinistra . . . Allo intorno del coro i sedili lavorati parimenti a tarsie, erano per li senatori, e per la chieresia nelle solenni funzioni della ducale. . . . I sedili del coro ne' tempi solenni coprivansi de arazzi contesti d'oro e di seta a figure, ed erano state eseguiti, poc'anzi il 1551, in Fiorenza. Sopra questi sedili veggonsi tuttora quattro pergoli, o palchetti, o poggiuoli, due per lato della Capella un sopra l'altro. Negl' inferiori sonvi i nitidissimi getti di bronzi del Sansovino can fatti de san Marco; i due superiori non hanno che li parapetti traforati sporgenti in fuori. Tutti e quattro cotesti poggiuoli erano ne' tempi andati a disposizione della musicale Cappella; ma quelli che hanno i parapetti di bronzo servivano eziando agli ambasciadori o residenti esteri presso la Veneta repubblica; ed oggidi sono esclusivamente ad uso di personaggi distinti. . . ."

is of primary importance, particularly at Saint Mark's where the resonant intermingling of the opposed sounds in the lofty spaces of the cathedral in part defines the special quality of this music. Elsewhere it may at times have been performed by two or more groups in the same gallery. However, such a practice would not appear to represent the essence of polychoral music as conceived by baroque composers, but an adaptation necessitated by the physical limitation of a given church.[14]

Here we find the musical forces again consigned to the transept. There is an implication that "disparity in the physical placement of the groups" was an exclusive St. Mark's prerogative when in actual fact it was standard practice everywhere for the two halves of the choir. As we have already seen, it is doubtful whether the opposed sounds would "intermingle more resonantly in the lofty spaces" of St. Mark's than they would in the even more lofty spaces of the cathedrals of York, Halberstadt, or Beauvais when similarly initiated there from opposing sides of the chancel. Finally, one wonders exactly what were the "physical limitations" referred to, since each church of necessity had a choir.

An examination of the vocal literature of the Renaissance shows clearly that the composers of sacred works for double chorus felt themselves to be under no handicap in their lack of a Venetian ambient. Giovanni d'Alessi has published excerpts from the polychoral works of various North Italian precursors of Willaert, showing choir alternation to be a well-established regional specialty. There is a *Regina coeli* by Rousée for double chorus, an *Alma Redemptoris Mater* by Palestrina, to say nothing of his Masses for double chorus, numerous pieces by D. Phinot, chansons for double chorus by Lassus, a Mass by Nanino, a *Salve Regina* by Goudimel, and many other examples by Spanish, German, and even Polish composers. The authors of these works may (or may not) have regarded polychoral writing as a Venetian specialty but they evidently did not feel that the spatial characteristics of St. Mark's were a *sine qua non* for the successful performance of such pieces.

14. John A. Flower, *Giovanni Gabrieli's Sacrae Symphoniae (1597)* Vol. I (Unpubl. Ph.D. Diss., University of Michigan, 1955), pp. 11–12.

Let us now turn our attention to the organs which are supposed to have been of such importance in the inception of the polychoral style. Caffi tells us that the organ on the right (that is, the sacristy side) was the work of one brother Urbano. Behind it were the bellows and alongside them were chests and cabinets containing the music of various masters. Then there is an extremely interesting statement: "I do not need to tell you that the musicians and singers used to be, and are still today stationed by this organ." [15]

Viadana, in the preface to his *Salmi a 4 chori per cantare e concertare nelle gran solennita di tutto anno,* Venice 1612, speaks of the performance practice of divided choral groups and insists that in the *tutti* sections all pauses, syncopations, breathing spaces, etc., must be accurately observed, otherwise the music will fall apart and be harsh and unpleasant. He stipulates that the chapel master should be stationed with the first choir in order to indicate the tempo from the basso continuo of the organist and to lead solos, duos, and movements of few voices. At the entry of the ripienists he is to turn his face to all the choirs and give a sign by raising both hands. The first choir stands by the main organ and comprises five good singers, accompanied by no other instruments except for this organ and occasionally a chitarrone. The organist may improvise or ornament his part during a *tutti* but not during the singing of the choir, which he must accompany in a plain fashion, without figuration. The second choir, called the chapel, is four-voiced and is the basis of the whole. It should consist of at least 16 singers, and if it numbers around 20–30 voices and instruments, this constitutes an excellent group. The third choir contains only high voices and the fourth choir is composed of four deep voices. The psalms may be performed, however, by merely two choirs, the first and the second.[16]

Since Viadana did not come to Venice until 1612, the year of publication of this work, it is doubtful if he was referring to a specifically Venetian practice here, though it was surely regional since his previous posts were at Mantua and Fano. Nonetheless

---

15. "Non e uopo ch'io ti dica che i musici e i cantori usavano ed usano pur oggi di stare in quest' organo."

16. Robert Haas, *Die Musik des Barocks* (Wildpark-Potsdam, 1928), p. 79.

it is of interest that no mention is made of a second organ for use with the second choir, though it is, to be sure, not excluded either. Of even greater interest is the simple injunction that the chapel master must turn his face *to all the choirs* to bring them in at the proper time. This common-sense advice indicates clearly that all the musical forces, even for a disparate four-choir aggregation, had to be disposed somewhere within the confines of the chancel in order to have a clear sight-line to their director. This simple and obvious fact seems to rule out the fanciful placement of choirs and instrumental groups in transepts, transept galleries, or "blind" apses. They evidently had to be where they could see and be seen.

It may be mentioned in passing that the slightly naïve insistence on the importance of the two organs at St. Mark's as instigators of the double-chorus style of writing completely overlooks the fact that many of the Gabrieli works are for triple choirs and even quadruple choirs. Goudimel and Victoria, among others, also wrote works for triple choirs, showing that not even a second organ was necessary for such a concept. It is of interest to note that such present-day recordings of these pieces as we have use only a single organ and it may be surmised that the idea of using a second organ was never even considered at the recording sessions.

It is difficult, if not impossible, to stipulate exactly as to performance practice with regard to the organ accompaniments of these pieces. The scores of Willaert's *Salmi spezzati* of 1550, generally considered as the starting-point of Venetian *cori spezzati* technique, contain no organ parts but merely the parts for the two choirs. Even these were originally issued in part books. What, then, was the role of the organ or organs? In Kinkeldey's opinion the organists of the time developed an astonishing ability to play from the part books or, more likely, from the choir-book form which gave several parts on a large double folio page. Bermudo and others attest to this practice and make no effort to conceal its difficulties for the performer.[17] Since we know that it was customary for the organist thus to improvise an accompani-

---

17. Otto Kinkeldey, *Orgel und Klavier in der Musik des 16. Jahrhunderts* (Leipzig, 1910), p. 98.

ment to a choral work, we may readily concede that two organists might similarly accompany a double chorus. Praetorius, Artusi, and others tell us of the customary practice of doubling voices with instruments, the selection of which was usually left up to the arranger or chapel master, the choice being usually made on the basis of the clefs employed. But from a purely practical standpoint the idea of two organists, each improvising freely during the *tutti* sections when their respective choruses coincide, seems a somewhat hazardous procedure.

Reese has called attention to works by Victoria for two or three four-part antiphonal choruses with organ, and one for antiphonal four- and five-part choruses with organ.[18] In these the organ always has merely a reduction of the music sung by Chorus I and does not play when that chorus is silent. It may be that, as in the Gabrieli practice, Choruses II and III were accompanied by other instruments, but only the part for the single organ survives in the prints.

An organ part for Banchieri's *Concerti ecclesiastici a 8 voci,* published in Venice in 1595, gives a score for the organist who accompanies the first choir but has nothing for the sections where the second choir is singing.

Examples such as these cited show that a constant underlay of organ tone was not considered indispensable by all composers of the time. These early prints may betoken a conscious use of organ sound as part of a particular choral composite, to be contrasted with other choral components either unsupported or else supported by contrasting instrumental timbres.

It is evident that the exact role of the organ in the support of the choral music of the time is not clear, but it is equally evident that the mere presence of a second organ at St. Mark's cathedral was not so important a determinant as it has usually been considered.

In conclusion, several opinions may be cited in support of the ideas advanced in this study. The relationship between the archi-

---

18. *Music in the Renaissance,* p. 604. See also Kinkeldey, *Orgel und Klavier,* p. 201.

tecture of St. Mark's and the music composed there has been called into question as early as 1929 in an article by Erich Hertzmann in which he says, "The reiterated, widely circulated view that the origin of polychorality is necessarily connected with the spatial lay-out of St. Mark's in Venice has been questioned for some time." [19]

Hermann Zenck, in his study of Willaert's *Salmi spezzati,* states firmly that the disposition of the choir lofts and galleries of St. Mark's is not to be regarded as a basis or an instigation of polychoral practice, but merely as an especially favorable setting for it.

The management of two independent and complete 4-voice choirs obviously requires their spatially separated disposition. But in St. Mark's the opposing galleries of the side apses, each with its own organ, can in no way be considered as a point of departure, or even as a cause for the "founding" of double-choir music-making. Rather they constitute only an especially favorable opportunity, implicit in the architecture, for the traditional antiphonal performance of psalms, and for the previously mentioned choral alternation practiced in upper Italy; they were a musically profitable potential which was to find its baroque instrumental-vocal performance realization first in works like Giovanni Gabrieli's Concerti ecclesiastici.[20]

---

19. "Zur Frage der Mehrchörigkeit in der ersten Hälfte des 16. Jahrhunderts," *ZfMW,* XII (1929–30), 142 "Die vielfach verbreitete Ansicht, dass die Entstehung der Mehrchörigkeit schlechthin mit der räumlichen Anlage der Markuskirche zu Venedig in Verbindung zu bringen sei, ist schon seit langem in Frage gestellt worden."

20. Hermann Zenck, "Adrian Willaerts 'Salmi spezzati' (1550)," *MF,* II (1949), 106. "Die Disposition zweier selbständiger und in sich geschlossener vierstimmiger Chöre fordert endlich auch deren räumlich getrennte Aufstellung. Aber die einander gegenüberliegenden, mit Orgeln versehenen Emporen der Seiten-Apsiden in S. Marco können keineswegs als Voraussetzung oder gar Anlass für die 'Erfindung' des doppelchörigen Musizierens betrachtet werden. Vielmehr stellten sie für den althergebrachten antiphonischen Psalmenvortrag und für das in Oberitalien geübte *chörische* Alternieren, das wir eingangs erwähnten, nur eine besonders günstige und in der Architektur gegebene Gelegenheit und musikalisch nutzbare Möglichkeit dar, die dann erst in Werken wie den Concerti ecclesiastici Giovanni Gabrielis ihre barocke, instrumental-vokal konzertierende Verwirklichung finden sollten."

The simplest and most unequivocal statement comes from
Denis Arnold, editor of the collected works of Giovanni Gabrieli,
who in his General Introduction to Volume I says, "The usually
held view that the poly-choral style originated and was greatly
popularized by the architecture of St. Mark's is now thoroughly
discredited. Divided choirs were used in many places lacking
lofty choir galleries, and the antiphonal nature of psalm singing
is part of a tradition never entirely forgotten from the earliest
times." [21]

As a final citation it will be of interest to turn to the perspica-
cious Dr. Burney, who found himself in the enviable position of
having to record his own estimates and reactions instead of per-
petuating the opinions and errors of other historians. This statement, from his *Present State of Music in France and Italy,* shows
that at the beginning of the eighteenth century the practice of
divided musical forces was still going strong at St. Mark's, but
with somewhat less felicitous acoustical results than most historians would have us believe!

> Wednesday 15. I went this morning to St. Mark's church, at
> which, being a festival, the doge was present. I there heard high
> mass performed under the direction of Signor Galuppi, composer
> of the music. Upon this occasion there were six orchestras, two
> great ones in the galleries of the two principal organs and four less,
> two on a side, in which there were likewise small organs. I was
> placed very advantageously in one of the great organ lofts, with
> Signor L'Attila, assistant of Signor Galuppi. The music, which was
> in general full and grave, has a great effect, though this church is
> not very happily formed for music, as it has five domes or cupolas,
> by which the sound is too much broken and reverberated before it
> reaches the ear.[22]

21. Denis Arnold (ed.), *Giovanni Gabrieli, Opera omnia,* I (Rome: American Institute of Musicology, 1956), p. 1.

22. Charles Burney, *The Present State of Music in France and Italy* (London, 1721), pp. 173 f.

ISORHYTHMIC DESIGN

IN THE MOTETS OF JOHANNES BRASSART

Keith E. Mixter
THE OHIO STATE UNIVERSITY

Johannes Brassart was a composer of the first half of the fifteenth century whose significance has been overshadowed by that of the chief figures of the epoch—Dufay, Dunstable, and Binchois. The master deserves critical appraisal, however, both because of the importance of the positions which he held and because of the very considerable merit of his compositions.

Brassart may have been born about 1405 in the Flemish part of present-day Belgium, in the village of Lowaige, not far from Tongeren (which itself lies about nineteen kilometers north and slightly east of Liège).[1] From 1422 to 1431 Brassart held the position of succentor in the collegiate Church of Saint-Jean l'Evangeliste in Liège. He said his first Mass in 1426. In 1431, the composer was a member of the Papal Chapel in Rome.

In 1433, Brassart stood in the service of the Council of Basel, but he had left this august body by the end of 1434 for employment with the Emperor Sigismund. He remained in Imperial service at least until 1443, with the exception of intermittent employment in the Church of Our Lady in Tongeren. The last record of his life is from the latter place, dated February 7, 1445.

The corpus of Brassart's compositions is, as far as we know it

---

1. Brassart's Liège period has been treated by Suzanne Clercx in her article "Jean Brassart et le début de sa carrière," *RbM*, VI (1952), 283–85; further documentation and biographical details are to be found in the present author's "Johannes Brassart: A Biographical and Bibliographical Study; I: The Biography," *MD*, XVIII (1964), 37–62.

now, entirely of a religious or quasi-religious nature. It includes eight Introits, nine Mass Ordinary movements, twelve motets, and one *geistliches Lied*. The compositions are to be found in eight manuscripts of the fifteenth century, of which the Aosta codex is the most important for our purposes. The texts of the motets are varied in nature, and they have given us, for the most part, a new fund of Latin Christian poetry. Four of these motets are either partially or completely isorhythmic. We shall examine them in the order of progressive complexity.

The motet *Ave Maria—O Maria*,[2] for two rather flowing superius voices, contratenor and tenor, is provided with a double text consisting largely of trope insertions to the prayer "Ave Maria." The sources for this composition are the manuscripts Bologna, Civico Museo Bibliografico Musicale (CMBM), formerly the Liceo Musicale "G. B. Martini," Cod. Q 15 (hereafter abbreviated BL), ff. 234'–235, and Trento, Castello del Buon Consiglio, Ms. 87, fol. 51. This is the only one of Brassart's isorhythmic motets in which the tenor (the sole isorhythmic voice) is written out, i.e., not provided for by way of a canonic inscription.[3]

We may not say that *color* (or melodic repetition) is present, although the first isorhythmic period of the tenor is repeated literally, together with the first twelve measures of the contratenor. During this repetition superius II reiterates the melody which superius I sang in the first twelve measures, but to a different text. The isorhythmic construction may be represented as follows.

$$
\begin{array}{lll}
[\mathbb{C}] & /:A^1:/ & (\text{mm. }1\text{–}12 \text{ and } 13\text{–}24) \\
 & A^2 & (\text{mm. }25\text{–}36) \\
 & A^3 & (\text{mm. }37\text{–}48) \\
O & A^4 & (\text{mm. }49\text{–}60) \\
 & A^5 & (\text{mm. }61\text{–}72)
\end{array}
$$

2. Printed in Guido Adler and Oswald Koller (eds.), *Sechs Trienter Codices, geistliche und weltliche Kompositionen des XV. Jahrhunderts, erste Auswahl* (Vols. XIV–XV of *Denkmäler der Tonkunst in Österreich*) (Wien, 1900), pp. 95–97.

3. The isorhythmic construction of the tenor was commented upon by Hellmuth Christian Wolff in his book *Die Musik der alten Niederländer* (*15. und 16. Jahrhundert*) (Leipzig, 1956), pp. 95–96.

As may be seen, there are six statements of a twelve-measure rhythmic pattern, the *talea,* in the tenor. The first four are in *tempus imperfectum, prolatio major* mensuration, while the last two are in *tempus perfectum, prolatio minor* mensuration. The different mensurations do not affect the likeness of the *taleae* except in one place, where two different solutions of the values semibreve-semibreve-breve are produced, as shown in Example 1.

Example 1

Ave Maria - O Maria

The use of *taleae* in varying mensurations with a continuous tenor, rather than with a series of *colores,* may be viewed as a departure from practice customary at this time.

A. W. Ambros has stated that the motet *Magne decus potencie—Genus regale esperie* was written in honor of a Pope, but without verification and without identification of the pontiff concerned.[4] If this is true, it would suggest that the composition of the work may be placed in the year 1431, when we know Brassart served at the Curia. The motet bears a resemblance in the structure of the opening duo and the terminology of the canonic inscription to Dufay's motet *Apostolo Glorioso—Cum tua doctrina—Andreas Christi famulus,* for which De Van suggests the date 1424–28.[5] If Ambros' assumption is correct, perhaps Brassart came to know the Dufay work when the two were colleagues in the Papal Chapel.

The unique source of the Brassart motet is the manuscript BL, ff. 253'–254. The composition utilizes two superius voices, contratenor and tenor, but isorhythmic construction is found only in the tenor.[6] The entrance of the tenor is preceded by an *introitus* in the upper two voices, in which superius I sings alone for six

4. August Wilhelm Ambros, *Geschichte der Musik* (3rd ed.; Leipzig, 1887–1911), III, 511.

5. Guillelmus Dufay, *Opera omnia* (Rome, 1947–), Vol. I, Part II, p. iii; the motet is printed on pp. 11–16 of the same volume.

6. This motet, together with the other Brassart pieces discussed in the following pages, is printed in the author's edition of Johannes Brassart, *Sechs Motetten* (Graz, 1960).

measures and is then joined by superius II, which sings in exact imitation of superius I, the latter having counterpoint against this. This opening is much more typical of the fifteenth-century isorhythmic motet than is that of *Ave Maria—O Maria*.

The tenor itself is given in *integer valor*. It is divided into three *taleae*. According to the accompanying instructions ("iste dicitur bis, primo de modo et tempore perfectis, secundo per tercium sed prime pause non dicuntur"), the repetition of the *color,* with its three *taleae,* should be performed by disregarding the initial rests (over which the *introitus* was sung) and by dividing the note values by three. The construction of the motet may be represented in each of the following two ways.

a.   Duo (6 + 6 measures)
I,A^1 (mm. 13–33), A^2 (mm. 34–54), A^3 (mm. 55–75)
Transition independent of isorhythmic scheme
  (mm. 76–78)
II, a^1 (mm. 79–85), a^2 (mm. 86–92), a^3 (mm. 93–99)
Finalis (m. 100)

b.   (c/3t) $\times$ 2 [1:1 + 3:1 without introductory rests]

In the analyses for this and the following Brassart motets the first of each pair shows the construction of the entire composition. The Roman numerals are used to indicate the *colores,* while the isorhythmic periods are represented either by letters with exponents (if they are repeated exactly), or by Arabic numerals (if they are subject to proportions). The second of each pair of analyses employs a modification of symbols proposed by Willi Apel for other isorhythmic instances.[7] In Professor Apel's schemes, "t" and "c" represent *talea* and *color,* respectively, and while these show accurately such proportions as may be involved, they do not describe the free sections.

Example 2 shows how the first *taleae* of each of the two *colores* compare in transcription.

7. Willi Apel, "Remarks about the Isorhythmic Motet," *Les Colloques de Wégimont* (Paris, 1954–), II, 143.

Example 2

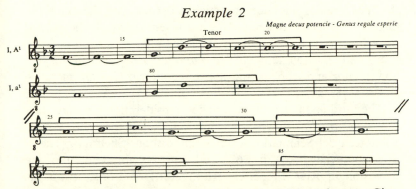

Magne decus potencie - Genus regale esperie

The "per tercium" idea can also be found in Johannes Ciconia's motet *Petrum Marcello venetum—O Petrum antistes.*[8] It is completely isorhythmic. *Color* obtains in the contratenor and tenor, both of which subscribe to the same isorhythmic and isomelic design. The entire melodic line, the *color,* is divided into two halves, A and B, each of which is repeated to a 3:1 diminution of the *talea.* This construction may be represented as follows (again, the symbol following the comma in each line stands for the *talea* or its diminution).

A^1,A^1 (mm. 1–41)
A^2,a^1 (mm. 42–56)
B^1,A^2 (mm. 57–97)
B^2,a^2 (mm. 98–114)
Finalis (m. 115)

Immediately below the tenor of the Brassart motet the manuscript provides, in a slightly different hand, a "Tenor ad longum." [9] In this, the *modus* is considered imperfect, the longs therefore being dotted where appropriate and the breves doubled in places where alteration would have applied in the original tenor. The *integer valor* statement is followed by a resolution of

---

8. This motet is described by Samuel E. Brown, Jr. in "A Possible Cantus Firmus Among Ciconia's Isorhythmic Motets," *JAMS,* XII (1959), 12–13; the composition is to be found in Suzanne Clercx, *Johannes Ciconia: Un musicien liégeois et son temps (Vers 1335–1411)* (Bruxelles, 1960), II, 193–96.

9. A facsimile of the folios containing this motet is provided in Brassart, *Sechs Motetten,* p. [xiii].

the "per tercium" instruction, which is correct with the exception of m. 85, where two semibreves are given, of which the second must be altered in violation of the *integer valor* version of long-breve. Similar "ad longum" *resolutiones* are provided for the contratenor and tenor of the above-mentioned Ciconia motet in BL, ff. 248'–249.[10]

The third and fourth motets under consideration here are state motets. *O rex Fridrice*, whose unique source is the codex Aosta, Biblioteca del Seminario, Manuscript without Shelfmark (here-after abbreviated Ao), ff. 262'–264, was probably written for the accession of King Frederick III in April of 1440, or for his coronation in June of the same year. The text is laudatory in nature, but reminds Frederick of the virtues of his immediate predecessor Albert II, who is held up as a model.

The *introitus*, sung by superius I and II, is unlike that of the foregoing motet, for both voices begin simultaneously, singing the same text, with a considerable amount of rhythmic agree-ment, but without the occurrence of imitation. Again, isorhythm is present only in the tenor. The *color* is not divided into *taleae*, but rather the *taleae* and the *colores* coincide exactly. The *taleae* themselves are repeated in lessening augmentation. There is a postlude free of isorhythmic structure. The canonic inscription accompanying the *integer valor* statement of the tenor is as follows.

Ca	Si me cupis promere sic dic quater sine fine.
non	In primo cupio me subsestupla / que secundo
teno	Subquadrupla iunge sed si vis nunc ter habere
ris	Sic studeas canere me subdupla sit sine veve
	Pausas obmitto quarto vt jaceor promor ego.

The *color/talea* unit is to be stated four times: the first in six-fold augmentation, the second in fourfold augmentation, the

10. Willi Apel, in *The Notation of Polyphonic Music, 900–1600* (5th ed.; Cambridge, Mass. [1961]), p. 184, has commented upon sixteenth-century *resolutiones* of canonic tenors for readers "of merely average training and ability"; however, such *resolutiones* as those found in these motets of BL would seem to anticipate this use considerably.

third in twofold augmentation, and the fourth in *integer valor,* but without observing the rests. The isorhythmic detail may be represented by either of the following two schemes.

    a.   *Introitus* (mm. 1–27)
        I,1 (mm. 28–72)
        II,2 (mm. 73–117)
        III,3 (mm. 118–147)
        IV,4 (mm. 148–155)
        Postlude (mm. 156–169)

  b.   (c/t) × 4 [1:6 + 1:4 + 1:2 + 1:1 without rests]

Example 3 illustrates the beginning measures of each isorhythmic section and how these relate one to another.

Example 3

O rex Fridrice

Although the same text obtains in superius I and II, and although the two show points of imitation, there is a high degree of independence, especially in the use of varying mensurations. The basic mensurations are *tempus perfectum, prolatio minor* and *tempus imperfectum, prolatio minor,* but these are complicated by the insertion of sections of *proportio tripla* (really *proportio sesquialtera* at the level of the minim). In addition, these sections contain occurrences of both *color temporis* and *color prolationis.* The third *color/talea* period in the tenor is accompanied in the upper voices by a change to *tempus perfectum diminutum* mensuration. A reduction of note values by half over that of the preceding *integrum* sections is necessary here if the letter of the tenor canonic inscription is to be carried out.

Another *unicum* of the Aosta codex is the motet *Romanorum rex,* found on ff. 276′–268.[11] This four-voice motet employs superius, two contratenors, and tenor. It is without ascription, but De Van has assigned it to Brassart since his name figures so prominently in the text and because the composition immediately follows *O rex Fridice* in the codex.[12] The primacy of Brassart's name among those of other chapel singers may be due to his rank of "rector capelle," which he held as early as 1437.[13] This lamentation motet for Albert II may have been sung at the funeral of the King at Stuhlweissenburg following his death on October 27, 1439.[14]

The motet employs a *cantus prius factus* in the tenor, the incipit of the Introit of the *Missa pro Defunctis*.[15] The quotation of the chant is carried only through the words "Requiem aeternam." In this, the technique is similar to that which Dufay used in the motet *Nuper rosarum flores,* based on the Introit *Terribilis est locus iste (ad Missam in Dedicatione Ecclesiae)*.[16] Brassart uses the plainsong quotation as a *color,* which is sung three times. The *color* is divided into four sections by groups of rests to the value of three breves each. Each of these sections acts as a *talea* consisting only of three breves. Isorhythm is present in all parts, but *color* only in the tenor. There is no introductory duo, and the isorhythmic scheme begins immediately. There is a free section, a six-measure postlude, at the end of the isorhythmic structure. The inscription accompanying the tenor is as follows.

---

11. A facsimile of the folios containing this motet is provided in Brassart, *Sechs Motetten,* p. [xiv].

12. Guillaume De Van, "A Recently Discovered Source of Early Fifteenth Century Polyphonic Music," *MD,* II (1948), 14.

13. Johannes Haller *et al., Concilium basiliense: Studien und Quellen zur Geschichte des Consils von Basel* (Basel, 1896–1926), VI, 21.

14. Hellmut Federhofer, "Die Niederländer an den Habsburgerhöfen in Österreich," *Anzeiger der phil.-hist. Klasse der Österreichischen Akademie der Wissenschaften,* 1956, No. 7, p. 104.

15. *Liber usualis* (Tournai, 1944), p. 1807.

16. Dufay, *Opera omnia,* Vol. I, Part II, pp. 70–76.

Tenor iste qui dicitur: primo modo, prima tallea
in subdupla superbipartiente proportione,
secunda tallea in subdupla proportione, tertia in subsesquitertia,
quarta vero in sesquialtera. Secundo modo, prima
tallea dicitur in tripla proportione, secunda in emiolia,
tertia sicut iacet, quarta in subdiatessaron. Tertio modo
dicitur in dyapenthe. Et est notandum quod secunda et tertia vice
capitur in dyapenthe.

This terminology is very interesting. The isorhythmic period is
called the "tallea," but the *color* itself (the isomelic period) is
referred to, at least indirectly, as the "modus." The use of the
words "subdiatessaron" and "dyapenthe" for the proportions $3:4$
and $3:2$ respectively, where *subsesquitertia* and *sesquialtera*
would be more common, is substantiated by Tinctoris.[17]

As mentioned above, the *color* of the tenor (which is stated
three times, the second and third times with transposition to the
lower fifth) is divided into four *taleae*. Of the resulting twelve
isorhythmic periods within the *colores*, all but one are subject to
proportion, a highly complex and unusual manifestation. The
entire last statement of the *color* is in the proportion $3:2$. The
isorhythmic design of the tenor might be formulated as follows.

$$(c/4t \times 3) \; [3:8 + 3:6 + 3:4 + 3:2; \; 3:1 + 3:2 + 3:3 + 3:4; \; 3:2]$$

Example 4 shows the first *talea* of each statement of the *color* and
how each relates to the *integer valor*. As in previous examples,
the reduction of the original note values is by half.

Turning to the upper parts of this pan-isorhythmic structure,[18]
we see that although there is no *color* involved, there are three
large sections (progressively shorter in length, with changing
mensurations), each divided into two *taleae*. Three different isorhythmic periods are therefore involved, each repeated once. The

---

17. Johannes Tinctoris, *Terminorum musicae diffinitorium,* ed. Armand
Machabey (Paris, 1951), pp. 21 and 17.

18. "Pan-isorhythmic" is a term employed by Willi Apel to refer to compositions in which isorhythm obtains in all parts; cf. *Colloques de Wégimont,*
II, 139.

Example 4

large sections of the isorhythmic scheme of the upper voices and of the tenor are of the same length, but within these sections the periods overlap, as may be seen in the following analysis.

Section 1 (mm. 1–60)	Upper voices: A^1 (mm. 1–30), A^2 (mm. 31–60) Tenor: I,1 (mm. 1–24), 2 (mm. 25–42), 3 (mm. 43–54), 4 (mm. 55–60)
Section 2 (mm. 61–120)	Upper voices: B^1 (mm. 61–90), B^2 (mm. 91–120) Tenor: II,1 (mm. 61–66), 2 (mm. 67–78), 3 (mm. 79–96), 4 (mm. 97–120)
Section 3 (mm. 121–144)	Upper voices: C^1 (mm. 121–132), C^2 (mm. 133–144) Tenor: III,1 (mm. 121–126), 2 (mm. 127–132), 3 (mm. 133–138), 4 (mm. 139–144)
Postlude (mm. 145–150)	All voices free

Through excessive trimming of the leaf containing contratenors I and II, some of the music of the latter voice has been lost. Restoration is considerably facilitated by the observance of the isorhythmic configuration of this voice.

These four motets of Johannes Brassart form a significant part of the repertory of fifteenth-century isorhythmic compositions available to us for study, because of the variety of their design and the circumstances of their composition. Two of the motets come from the Aosta codex, whose importance for the history of music in the fifteenth century was realized only in 1948, not long after its discovery.

The element common to these motets is a tenor of isorhythmic construction. In three of the four pieces we find *colores* treated in a proportional manner, and in these a canonic inscription accompanies the notated tenor. In only one motet does the isorhythmic organization extend to the upper voices. This limitation of isorhythm to the tenor in three of the motets both rounds out the history of the isorhythmic motet, since it reaches back to the prototype to be found in De Vitry and his contemporaries, and anticipates the gradual abandonment of isorhythmic technique.[19] At the same time, however, the "pan-isorhythmic" motet *Romanorum rex* shows a structure so involved that it might well be classed among the monuments of the most intense period of isorhythmic composition.

These compositions are among the final documents of isorhythm, and they mark the wane of that type of treatment. Rhythmic complexities will increase, but they will do so, except for isolated instances, apart from isorhythmic design, largely a manifestation of the fourteenth and early fifteenth centuries.

---

19. For the latter observation I am indebted to Professor Richard H. Hoppin.

THE HYMNS OF GIACHES DE WERT

Melvin Bernstein
UNIVERSITY OF MARYLAND

The sacred vocal compositions of Giaches de Wert are a part of the approximately two hundred manuscripts which constitute a large segment of the musical archives of S. Barbara, the ducal chapel of the Gonzaga family at Mantua, and which are now preserved in the library of the Conservatorio Giuseppi Verdi of Milan. The present study confines itself to a description of the contents of two of these manuscripts. A later study will present a style critique of the Wert hymns and attempt an evaluation of their importance both as a major segment of the Mantuan liturgy and in relation to the period generally. Wert's sacred compositions include motets, Masses, hymns, psalm-settings, Magnificats, a Passion, and a *Te Deum*. Of all these works, only the motets were printed and published as complete sets of compositions. Of the remainder, only one Mass and one Magnificat are known to have appeared in published editions.[1]

The hymns, by far the largest known collection by a sixteenth-century composer, are contained in two of the S. Barbara manuscripts. The first group appears in manuscript 167 under the title: *Inni in festis S. Barbare virginis et martyriis, a 4 et 5 voci-*

---

1. The Mass appears in: *Missae Dominicales quintis vocibus auctorum, a F. Julio Pellinio Carmel. Mant. collectae. Mediolani: Michaelis Tini. 1592.* The *Magnificat* appeared in: *Psalmi ad vesperas . . . quatour vocibus cum Cantica B. Virginis Excellentiss . . . Jaches Vuerth.* R. D. Jacobi Gastoldi Caravagiensis (Venetiis, 1588). A complete edition of the Wert compositions, undertaken jointly with Carol MacClintock, is being published in the *Corpus Mensurabilis Musicae* series of the American Institute of Musicology, Rome.

bus. Mantuae (at bottom of f. 2ʳ) *Per Francisco Sforza. 1590.*
The name, Jaches Wert, appears at random on numerous folios.
The second book of hymns appears earlier in the collection in
manuscript 155 under the listing: *Inni a 4 et 5 voci. Saeculo XVI.*
There is no other title folio. At the bottom of f. 2ʳ, again appears
the scribe's inscription: *per Franciscum Sforzum, 1613.* Here,
too, Wert's name is inserted at random throughout the manuscript.[2]

As far as can be determined, none of these hymns, in the
present settings, was ever published, although many are well-
known hymn texts. They were apparently intended for use only
in the chapel of S. Barbara. A number of the hymns may have
been composed much earlier than the dates of the Sforza manuscripts. Wert's hymn cycle in honor of St. Barbara, which appears
first in the 1590 group, and his motet, *Beata Barbara,* may be a
case in point.[3] Wert was first summoned to Mantua in the autumn
of 1564 for the express purpose of composing the music for the
December fourth celebration of the Feast of St. Barbara. There
is, however, no date on the manuscript version nor any indication as to authorship of the text.

At least two of the hymns exist in separate form and may date
from Wert's first appointment at Mantua. The first of these,
Exultet celebres, is identical with the first hymn of the 1590
Sforza collection.[4] The second separate hymn, *Verbum supernum
prodiens,* appears in our catalogue as the second hymn in the
1613 Sforza collection. Since others were written for the same

---

2. The fact that the Wert collection of hymns is a work of such large proportions was obscured by an error in the catalogue of the Verdi Conservatory
Library. The catalogue indicates that manuscript #155 contains mainly the
work of Giacomo Gastoldi; that Wert's compositions begin with f. 64 and continue through f. 104. Aside from the fact that Wert's name appears at random
through the manuscript, the catalogue division is erroneous since both of the
folio numbers listed fall clearly in the middle of compositions.

3. Jaches Wert. *Modulationum cum sex vocibus liber primus* (Venetiis: apud
Haeredem Hieronymi Scoti, 1581). *Beata Barbara* is number ten of this group.

4. A. M. Bautier-Regnier, "Jacques de Wert," *RbM,* IV (1950), 40–70. On
p. 64, the author refers to this hymn as *Virginis inclitae.* Upon examination of
the hymn in the separate version, it is immediately obvious that the incipit and
chant are missing. Both are given in the Sforza manuscript immediately preceding an identical setting of the *Virginis inclitae* section.

liturgical festivals, they were likely written at the same time. It seems reasonable to assume, however, that the two great collections which Sforza copied and compiled represent the compositional activity of a long period of time.

Indeed, upon examination, it is seen that the two books of hymns, one hundred and twenty-nine compositions, cover an entire liturgical year, at least as it must have been observed at

Table I

LITURGICAL ORGANIZATION OF THE HYMNS

Ms. 167, 1590

	FEAST	HYMN NOS.
I.	*S. Barbare*	1– 9
II.	*B.M.V.*	10–13
III.	*Cathe. S. Petri*	14
IV.	*Convers. S. Pauli*	15
V.	*Annunciat. BMV*	16–19
VI.	*Invent. S. Crucis*	20–22
VII.	*S. Joannis ante Portae Latinae*	23
VIII.	*Aparit. S. Michael Archan.*	24
IX.	*Nativit. S. Joannis Baptiste*	25–27
X.	*S.S. Apost. Petri et Pauli*	28–30
XI.	*Comm. S. Pauli Apost.*	31–32
XII.	*S. Margaret. virg. et mart.*	33–34
XIII.	*Marie Magdalena*	35–36
XIV.	*Invent. S. Stephanie*	37
XV.	*B.M.V.*	38
XVI.	*Transfig. Domini*	39–40
XVII.	*Decollation. S. Joannis Bapt.*	41
XVIII.	*Adriani Mart.*	42–44
XIX.	*Exaltation. S. Crucis*	45
XX.	*Dedication. S. Michael Archang.*	46–47
XXI.	*Dominum Sanctori.*	48
XXII.	*Omnium S.S.*	49–51
XXIII.	*Dedication. Basilicae S. Barbare*	52–56
XXIV.	*Translation. S.S. Reliquiarum*	57–59
XXV.	*Sabb. per annum*	60
XXVI.	*Dup. Apost.*	61–64
XXVII.	*Semidupl. Maior. Apost.*	65
XXVIII.	*Dupl. Apost. Temp. Pasch.*	66–67
XXIX.	*Semidupl. Maior. Apost. Temp. Pasch.*	68
XXX.	*Unius Martyris.*	69–71
XXXI.	*Plurium Martyriis.*	72–75

Ms. 155, 1613

	FEAST	HYMN NOS.
I.	*Vigil. Nativit.*	1 – 3
II.	*Nativit. Domini*	4 – 5
III.	*Die Nativit. Domini*	6*–12
IV.	*Die S. Stephanie Protomartyris*	8 –11
V.	*Die S. Johannis Apost. et Evange.*	12–15
VI.	*Dominicis infra Oct. Nativit. Domini*	16
VII.	*S. Silvestri pape et conf.*	17–20
VIII.	*Epiphanie Domini*	21–24
IX.	*Dominica infra Oct. Epiphanie*	25
X.	*Dominicis ab oct. Epiph. usq. ad Septuagesima*	26
XI.	*A Septuages. usque ad Quadrages.*	27
XII.	*A Dominica Quadrages. usque ad Domin. Passionis*	28
XIII.	*In Passione*	29
XIV.	*Resurrec. Domini*	30–37
XV.	*A Dominica Post. Pasch. usq. ad Ascens.*	38
XVI.	*Ascens. Domini*	39–41
XVII.	*Dominica infra oct. Ascens.*	42
XVIII.	*Pentecost.*	43–47
XIX.	*Sanctiss. Trinit.*	48–50
XX.	*Sacratiss. Corpus Domini*	51–53
XXI.	*Dominica infra oct. Corp. Domini*	54

*The numbering represents hymns probably present in this section. This is a conjecture owing to the missing folios mentioned in the text above. Thus, the overlapping numbers of section IV represent a continuous numbering of compositions actually present.

Mantua. Book I, 1590, comprises seventy-five hymns; Book II, fifty-four hymns. Because the two books present one continuous liturgy, it will be more convenient to discuss them together. Table I indicates the continuity of the Mantuan Liturgy of the Daily Hours as reflected in Wert's two books of hymns. Although the hymns *In Festo S. Barbare* were probably written first, the 1613 manuscript begins with hymns of the season of the *Nativity* and probably should be considered first.

From the list in Table I, it can be determined that each collection condenses into several basic classes. The 1613 group is devoted primarily to the liturgies of the Nativity and Eastertide; the first, including Advent; the second, the period of Epiphany to the *Resurrection,* and the traditionally associated festival of

Pentecost. The 1590 group, being much longer, covers many more liturgical classifications, principally: the festivals of St. Barbara, the Blessed Virgin, Apostles, Saints, Martyrs, the Church, and Holy Relics.

Sforza's organization of the two books appears to be somewhat arbitrary. In the 1613 collection, for example, the festivals of St. Stephen and St. John are implied to be in their traditionally celebrated position during the Octave of the Nativity. The four hymns devoted to Stephen are entitled, *In Die S. Stepheni Protomartyris Ad* (:) *tertiam, sextam, vesperam, complectorium hymnus.* The corresponding section of the 1590 collection, XIV, is entitled, *In Festis Invent. S. Stephani ad vesperam hymnus.* Since this hymn is apparently for the service of the preceding evening, it should appear before the other St. Stephen hymns. Similarly, the four St. John hymns of section V, 1613, are entitled, *In Die S. Joannis Ad* (:) *tertiam, sextam, vesperam, complectorium hymnus.* However, the following St. John group, IX, is, *In Festis Nativitatis S. Joannis Baptiste ad* (:) *vesperam, complectorium, tertiam hymnus.* These hymns, numbered twenty-five, twenty-six, and twenty-seven in our catalogue, should precede all the other St. John hymns.

Many discrepancies of this type may be found in the Sforza manuscripts. Only one other need be mentioned. The two main groups of *BMV* hymns appear in sections II and V of the 1590 collections; a single hymn, *In Festis Beate Marie Virginis ad vesperam hymnus,* appears as number thirty-eight and differs from the first BMV hymn of section II (#10), also *ad vesperam.* Number ten is a part of the famous hymn, *Ave Maris Stella* while number thirty-eight, lacking the incipit, contains settings of verses two, four, and six of the same hymn text. In any event, the existence of these two hymns for ostensibly the same purpose, in addition to being so widely separated in the book, is unexplainable.

In general, hymns of unknown source, or those which may be original, usually appear *ad vesperam,* although a few appear *ad mattutinum* and *ad complectorium.* Since Vespers was the only daily service of the Roman liturgy in which music other than Gregorian chant might be used, we may reasonably assume

Table II

Section One

that this service would ordinarily contain the most significant musical changes, particularly at centers such as Mantua.

In order to further visualize the interrelation of the two sets of hymns, a list of chant incipits may be found in Table II. Although there is generally little musical overlap between the two books, certain aspects of similarity may be noted and the Table sheds much light on the structure of this type of liturgy. The first section of the Table presents all the chant incipits of both books

Table II

Section One (*continued*)

of hymns. Each chant, designated by Roman numeral, bears the text of its first appearance. In Section 2 of the Table, all of the hymns are listed in order following the Roman numeral of the melody to which each is related or from which each is derived. Those hymns which are not directly related or which cannot be definitely identified are further indented. In addition, an effort has been made to indicate the interrelation of the melodies and/or texts with subsequent hymns in each book as well as between the two books.

Table II

Section Two

TABLE OF HYMN CHANTS

Book I, 1590

I.	#1.	*Exultet celebres (Virginis inclytae)*
II.	#2.	*Te lucis ante terminum* (p. 8)
	#3.	Incipit and chant missing.
	#4.	*Sancte triumphum virginis* (p. 15)
	#5.	*Iam lucis orto sydere* (p. 21)
	#6.	*Nunc sancte nobis spiritus* (p. 24)
	#7.	*Rector potens verax Deus* (p. 26)
	#8.	*Rerum Deus tenax vigor* (p. 28)
	#9.	Incipit and chant missing. Probably same as #1. V. 1 & 2 same as #2 & 3 above.
III.	#10.	*Ave maris stella* (p. 36)
IV.	#11.	*Te lucis ante terminum* (p. 44)
	#12.	*Nunc sancte nobis spiritus* (p. 49)
	#13.	*Rector potens verax Deus* (p. 54)
	#14.	Incipit and chant missing. From *Aurea luce*. Setting different from #28 & 31 below.
	#15.	Incipit and chant missing.
	#16.	Incipit, chant & V. 1 missing. May be *Te lucis*.
V.	#17.	*Nunc sancte nobis spiritus* (p. 62)
	#18.	*Rector potens verax Deus* (p. 63)
	#19.	Incipit, chant, V. 1 missing.
VI.	#20.	*Equeva ingenito* (p. 64) Cf. #45 below; V. 2 & 4 of same hymn; same setting.
VII.	#21.	*Te lucis ante terminum* (p. 71)
	#22.	*Nunc sancte nobis spiritus* (p. 75)
	#23.	Incipit and chant missing. Setting related to #68 below, & to Bk. II, #31–37.
	#24.	Incipit and chant missing. Related to Bk. II, #51 & 54, last verse.
VIII.	#25.	*Ut queant laxis* (p. 88) Cf. #41 below. Additional text of same hymn; different setting.
IX.	#26.	*Te lucis ante terminum* (p. 95)
	#27.	*Nunc sancte nobis spiritus* (p. 98)
X.	#28.	*Aurea luce* (p. 99) Cf. #14 & 31; additional texts of same hymn.
XI.	#29.	*Te lucis ante terminum*
	#30.	*Nunc sancte nobis spiritus*

XII.	#31.	*Doctor egregie*
		Text derived from #28; different setting.
XIII.	#32.	*Nunc sancte nobis spiritus*
XIV.	#33.	*Virginis sancte*
XV.	#34.	*Nunc sancte nobis spiritus*
XVI.	#35.	*Voce Jesu quem*
XVII.	#36.	*Nunc sancte nobis spiritus*
	#37.	Incipit and chant missing.
	#38.	Incipit and chant missing.
		From *Ave maris stella*; same setting as #10 above.
XVIII.	#39.	*Laude mater pietatis*
XIX.	#40.	*Nunc sancte nobis spiritus*
	#41.	Incipit and chant missing. *O nimis felix meritque celsi,* from *Ut queant laxis,* #25; different melody.
XX.	#42.	*Ut fidem sanctam*
XXI.	#43.	*Te lucis ante terminum*
	#44.	*Nunc sancte nobis spiritus*
	#45.	Incipit and chant missing; may be same as #20; identical setting.
XXII.	#46.	*Tibi Christi splendor Patris*
XXIII.	#47.	*Nunc sancte nobis spiritus*
XXIV.	#48.	*Christe redemptor omnium—famulos*
XXV.	#49.	*Te lucis ante terminum*
	#50.	*Nunc sancte nobis spiritus*
	#51.	*Rector potens verax Deus*
XXVI.	#52.	*Urbs beata Hierusalem*
	#53.	Incipit and chant missing. Probably *Te lucis,* beginning XXVII. V. 2, *Deo Patri* is the same.
XXVII.	#54.	*Nunc sancte nobis spiritus*
	#55.	*Rector potens verax Deus*
	#56.	Incipit and chant missing.
	#57.	Incipit and chant missing. Probably *Te lucis,* beginning XXVIII. Setting of V. 2, *Te nunc redemptor,* same as #58.
XXVIII.	#58.	*Nunc sancte nobis spiritus*
	#59.	*Rector potens verax Deus*
	#60.	Incipit and chant missing. From *O lux beata trinitas*
XXIX.	#61.	*Aeterna Christi munera*
XXX.	#62.	*Nunc sancte nobis spiritus*
	#63.	*Rector potens verax Deus*
	#64.	*Rerum Deus tenax vigor*

	#65.	Incipit and chant missing. From *Aeterna Christi* munera; same setting as #61, different strophes.
XXXI.	#66.	*Tristes erant apostoli* From *Aurora lucis rutilat*; same melody as Bk. II, #31–37.
	#67.	*Nunc sancte nobis spiritus*
	#68.	Incipit and chant missing. *Sermone blando* section of *Aurora lucis rutilat*. Melody & setting related to #23 above & Bk. II, #31–37.
XXXII.	#69.	*Deus tuorum militum*
XXXIII.	#70.	*Nunc sancte nobis spiritus*
	#71.	Incipit and chant missing. *Hic nempe saxis* section of *Deus tuorum militum*; same setting as #69 above.
XXXIV.	#72.	*Sanctorum meritis*
XXXV.	#73.	*Nunc sancte nobis spiritus*
	#74.	*Rector potens verax Deus*
	#75.	Incipit and chant missing. Part of *Sanctorum meritis*. Setting identical to #72.

Book II, 1613

I.	#1.	*Nos qui vivimus* (invitatory)
II.	#2.	*Verbum supernum prodiens*
	#3.	*Te lucis ante terminum*
	#4.	*Christus natus est* (invitatory)
III.	#5.	*A solis ortu cardine*
IV.	#6.	*Christe redemptor omnium* Text continuation in #16 below; identical setting.
V.	#7.	*Te lucis ante terminum*
VI.	#8.	*Nunc sancte nobis spiritus* Cf. Ave maris stella, but transposed.
	#9.	*Rector potens verax Deus*
VII.	#10.	*In hoc precandidi*
	#11.	*Te lucis ante terminum* Setting identical to #8 above.
VIII.	#12.	*Nunc sancte nobis spiritus*
	#13.	*Rector potens verax Deus*
IX.	#14.	*Evangeliste maximus*
	#15.	*Te lucis ante terminum.* Setting identical to to #12 above.
	#16.	Incipit and chant missing. *Jesu redemptor omnium.* Setting identical to #6 above.
X.	#17.	*Clara silvestri*

XI.   #18.   *Te lucis ante terminum*
         #19.   *Nunc sancte nobis spiritus*
         #20.   *Rector potens verax Deus*
XII.   #21.   *Hostis herodis impie*
                Text from *A solis ortu cardine*
                #5 above; setting different
XIII.   #22.   *Te lucis ante terminum*
         #23.   *Nunc sancte nobis spiritum*
         #24.   *Rector potens verax Deus*
         #25.   Incipit and chant missing. *Crudeles herodes*;
                               text part of #5 above. Setting identical to
                               #21 above.
         #26.   Incipit and chant missing. *Lucis creator optime.*
         #27.   Incipit and chant missing.
         #28.   Incipit and chant missing. *Audi benigne condi-
                               tor.*
         #29.   Incipit and chant missing. From *Pange lingua
                               gloriosi—certaminis.*
XIV.   #30.   *Ponatur lacrimis*
XV.   #31.   *Te lucis ante terminum*
         #32.   Incipit and chant missing. An Easter invita-
                               tory; not a hymn.
         #33.   *Aurora lucis rutilat*
                Cf. Bk. I, #66 & 68.
         #34.   *Iam lucis orto sydere*
         #35.   *Nunc sancte nobis spiritus*
                               Cf. Bk. I, #23, 66–68.
         #36.   *Rector potens verax Deus*
         #37.   *Rerum Deus tenax vigor*
         #38.   Incipit and chant missing. Melody related to
                               #31–37 group.
XVI.   #39.   *Te su nostra redemptio*
                Settings 2 & 3 same as #42, 1 & 2 below.
XVII.   #40.   *Te lucis ante terminum*
         #41.   *Nunc sancte nobis spiritus*
         #42.   Incipit and chant missing. From *Jesu nostra
                               redemptio* (Roman *Breviary: Salutis huma-
                               nae sator*). First setting identical to #39,
                               V. 2; 2nd identical to #39, *Gloria tibi
                               Domine.*
XVIII.   #43.   *Veni creator spiritus*
XIX.   #44.   *Te lucis ante terminum*
XX.   #45.   *Iam Christus astra ascenderat*
         #46.   *Rector potens verax Deus.* Setting identical to
                               #44.
         #47.   *Rerum Deus tenax vigor.* Setting identical to
                               #44.

XXI.	#48.	*Adesto sancta trinitas*
XXII.	#49.	*Te lucis ante terminum*
	#50.	*Nunc sancte nobis spiritus*
XXIII.	#51.	*Pange lingua gloriosi—corporis*
		Cf. #54; continues same text; identical setting.
XXIV.	#52.	*Te lucis ante terminum*
	#53.	*Nunc sancte nobis spiritus*
	#54.	Incipit and chant missing. Continuation of *Pange lingua gloriosi*—corporis. Setting identical to #51.

A number of well-known hymn titles are, of course, much in evidence. Forming the core of the set are the following:

1.) *Te lucis ante terminum*   (*Compline*)
2.) *Nunc sancte nobis spiritus* (*Terce*)
3.) *Rector potens verax Deus*   (*Sext*)
4.) *Rerum Deus tenax vigor*   (*None*)

While one or more of this group may be omitted from the hymns of any given feast day in Wert's collection, either *Te lucis* or *Nunc sancte nobis* is always present. Thus, an interesting quantitative comparison can be made with the Roman liturgy of the period. *Te lucis* appears in the Roman liturgy with twelve different melodic settings. All the Wert polyphonic compositions are cantus firmus pieces whose melodic sources must have been included in the Mantuan liturgy created mainly under Guglielmo Gonzaga.[5] Wert's settings reflect sixteen different melodic sources. As is the case with all of Wert's hymns, these bear only marginal similarities, if any, to the Roman melodies. Similarly, *Nunc sancte nobis* appears in the Roman liturgy in thirteen different settings according to the Proper of the Time. In Wert's collection—reflecting Mantuan liturgical usage—*Nunc sancte nobis* appears in twenty-four different settings. This is made possible, of course, by either changing the settings for the various

---

5. That such a chant book must have existed is suggested by the cover title of the recently discovered *Kyriale* at Mantua: *Mantova, Archivio Musicale di S. Barbare. Libro di Coro Nr. 1*. For a description of this chant book and the contents of the Mantuan manuscripts, see Knud Jeppesen, "Pierluigi da Palestrina, Herzog Guglielmo Gonzaga und die neugefundenen Mantovaner-Messen Palestrinas," *AM*, XXV (1953), 132–79.

Offices for a single day or Proper; or, by assigning new settings to feasts which the Roman church considered of less importance.

A further distinction may be mentioned in the usage of the two hymns, *Te lucis* and *Nunc sancte nobis,* as compared to the procedure in the Roman liturgy. Wherever these two hymns appear within the same day of a given feast in the Mantuan version, the musical settings are invariably identical. This was not always the case in the Roman practice, nor is it today. For example, while these two hymns have identical settings for Compline and Terce during the Proper of the Nativity, the settings for the same services for the Proper of the first Sunday of Advent differ from one another. In the Wert collection, the other two hymns of the group listed above, *Rector potens verax Deus* and *Rerum Deum tenax vigor,* when present, are always in settings identical to *Te lucis* and *Nunc sancte nobis* on any given feast day, at least one of which they always follow.

Since section I of the 1590 manuscript is in honor of the patroness of the Mantuan chapel and contains several original hymns, it seems appropriate to cite this section in some detail to exemplify further both the structure of the Mantuan liturgy and Wert's settings. Section I comprises a group of hymns in honor of St. Barbara, providing for all of the daily hours. In the manuscript, the hymns of Compline and Matins are out of place. The text of the first hymn, *Exultet celebres,* mentioned above, is of unknown origin and may be original, as is its musical setting. St. Barbara is given only the briefest notice in the Roman calendar and none of these hymns appear in her service. Since the remainder of the text has not been found, the choice of verses used here cannot be determined precisely. However, the three strophes set polyphonically appear to be the second, fourth, and sixth. There seems never to be a deviation from the *alternatim* structure.

The second hymn of section I is the first of many *Te lucis* groups. The Table of Chant Incipits indicates that the five remaining St. Barbara hymns are based on the *Te lucis* melody. In fact, among them are many strophes in identical settings. For example, the opening choral setting of hymn four, *Sancte triumphum,* is identical to the first setting of *Te lucis,* beginning at *rerum creator poscimus.*

Noteworthy in this section is the use of a single strophe as a refrain throughout most of the hymns of the section. This strophe, entitled, *Per Te Beata Barbara,* first appears in the place of a standard doxology at the conclusion of *Te lucis,* of which it is obviously not an original part. This strophe recurs at the end of the fourth, fifth, sixth, seventh, and eighth hymns. Wert's setting follows in Example 1. While the strophes of the hymns are all *a4,* nearly all of the doxologies are *a5;* in the present case, the quintus' canon at the fifth to the tenor is written out.

This text is a revision of the fifth stanza of Marc-Antoine Muret's hymn, *Sancte triumphum virginis,* the hymn for Lauds of the St. Barbara group which in the original begins: *Aeterne cunctorem Pater.* Several others of Muret's texts were set in both the 1590 and 1613 collections. *Aequeva ingenito,* also in the 1590 collection, numbers twenty and forty-five; *Ponatur lacrimis,* in the 1613 collection, number thirty.[6]

Of the three remaining hymns of the St. Barbara section, two are of unknown origin, numbers three and nine. Only one of the three, (number four) *Sancte triumphum virginis,* has an incipit. In addition to previous remarks concerning *Sancte triumphum,* the final verse, *Simplex etherii,* must be mentioned. This portion of the Muret hymn appears as a final stanza or doxology in all thirty-one hymns of the Muret collection cited in footnote 6. Wert does not use the text here, but employs the *Per Te Beata Barbara* as a doxology. However, *Simplex etherii* appears in Wert's setting of *Aequeva ingenito* and occasionally is borrowed as a verse or doxology for hymns other than those by Muret, as in hymn seventy-five of the 1590 collection.[7] In general, the choices of doxologies in the Wert collection do not agree with those found in the Roman versions of the standard hymns. However, the doxology texts most frequently used by Wert are the following three, musical settings of which vary as much as do the hymn texts proper:

---

6. The Muret hymn texts cited above are from the first of two collections commissioned by Guglielmo Gonzaga: *Hymnorum sacrarum liber . . . post primam editionem* (Romae: ex officium Georgii Ferrarii, 1581).

7. The practice of borrowing a strophe of a hymn for use as a doxology is fairly common in the Wert hymns. Besides *Simplex etherii,* another strophe popularly used in this way is the final strophe of the hymn, *Iste confessor: Sit salus illi.*

Example 1

Per te beata Barbara (Hymns, Book I, 2, v.2)

1.) *Gloria tibi Domine*
2.) *Te nunc redemptor quesumus*
3.) *Gloria Patri melodis*

The ninth and last hymn, *In Festis S. Barbare,* may be a setting of other verses of number one, *Exultet celebres.* Often in this liturgy a hymn text of many verses is divided so that the several sections are used for different occasions; this practice is found in the Roman liturgy, also. In the case of our ninth hymn, besides the relation of text subjects, the first choral setting, beginning, *In Patris valida,* is identical to the second choral setting (strophe four) of *Exultet celebres,* which begins, *Vincitur premitur.* The second choral setting of hymn nine, *Dextra cesa Patris (a5),* the text of which has a specific reference to Barbara as well, is identical to strophe six of *Exultet,* beginning *Trino unique Deo.*

In addition to the many interesting examples of intricately interrelated texts and musical structures, certain implied differences from the conduct of the Roman service, relative to musical performance, may be pointed out. One of the most interesting of these may be cited in the 1613 Sforza manuscript. Section II of this collection, *In Festo Nativitatis Domini,* was apparently the most complete group of hymns in the entire collection. Unfortunately, our study is complicated by the fact that ff. 11–16 are missing from the manuscript and space does not permit a discussion of the probable organization of this section.

However, the first of the two preserved compositions of this section is the only instance of utilizing a text which is not, properly speaking, a hymn. It is well known that often many types of texts were used in the manner of hymns, particularly the tracts, sequences, and the greater antiphons. In the present case, the text, *Christus natus est nobis,* is an Invitatory which introduces the first nocturn of Matins for the Feast of the Nativity. Depending upon the elaborateness of a particular service, this brief passage was performed in a variety of ways. In the Roman service (*Liber,* p. 368), the Invitatory follows in order: *Pater noster, Ave Maria, Credo,* and *versicles,* ending with *Deus, in adjutorium.* The celebrant then intones the complete text: *Christus*

natus est nobis: Venite adoremus, after which the choir responds
with the same text.

The Mantuan service likely began similarly. However, in view
of the choral setting given below in Example 2, the Invitatory
was probably performed in a somewhat different manner. It appears that following the intonation of the complete text the choir
responded with the complete text; the celebrant then repeated
the *Venite adoremus,* after which the choir repeated *Venite adoremus,* which is duplicated in the manuscript in all parts. This
very forceful setting is entirely chordal in contrast to Example 1.
The repeat of the *Venite adoremus,* identical from measure five
to the end, has been omitted in the present version.

Example 2
Invitatory, Service of the Nativity

Section XIV of Book II, *In Festo Resurrectionis Domini,* is, next to the Nativity section, the largest group in the collection. The third hymn of this group bears the heading Invitatory, *Christum resurgentem ex mortuis* and, as in the case of the Nativity Invitatory, a repeat section is provided, this time consisting of an Alleluia. The Roman liturgy, however, does not have an Invitatory in the resurrection service. The closest parallel, even in contemporary practice, appears at Mass for the fourth day after Easter in the form of an Alleluia verse (*Liber,* p. 827). The two texts differ in many ways and the chants are totally dissimilar.

PARODY TECHNIQUE

IN THE MASSES OF COSTANZO PORTA

Lilian Pibernik Pruett
NORTH CAROLINA COLLEGE

In the second half of the sixteenth century, Masses patterned after pre-existent polyphonic pieces assume a position of primary importance in almost every Mass composer's output. Such parody or transcription Masses display remarkable variety in their treatment of the borrowed material, thus making it quite difficult to formulate a universally valid definition of parody technique. That such problems exist is clearly evidenced in the rather divergent modern interpretations of the term *missa parodia* which range from ". . . a Mass built upon the tenor of a familiar motet" [1] to ". . . [a Mass] which uses the theme of a familiar motet as a *cantus firmus,* or draws on its music in a more elaborate way . . . ," [2] from ". . . underlaying of a new text to a composition, e.g., the Mass-text to a motet," [3] to ". . . that peculiar Mass type that is patterned after a model not only in its themes but also in the working-out of these themes. . . ." [4] The problems of the historical concept of parody have been dealt with extensively in several recent articles [5] and will not be reviewed here; rather,

1. Translated from Hugo Riemann, *Musik-Lexikon* (11th ed., 1929), II, 1346.

2. *Grove's Dictionary of Music and Musicians* (5th ed., 1954), VI, 559.

3. Translated from Hans Joachim Moser, *Musik-Lexikon* (4th ed., 1955), II, 930.

4. Translated from Peter Wagner, *Geschichte der Messe* (Leipzig: Breitkopf & Härtel, 1913), p. 447.

5. Cf. Ludwig Finscher, "Parodie und Kontrafaktur," *Musik in Geschichte und Gegenwart,* X, 815–26; Hellmuth Christian Wolff, "Die ästhetische Auffassung der Parodiemesse des 16. Jahrhunderts," *Miscelánea en homenaje a Mons.*

the present study hopes to show in a somewhat detailed manner one major composer's approach to parody procedures. Quite special problems, apart from the difficulties in formulating a definition, will be posed by the material of this study, as will be seen shortly.

Upon recommendations of Cardinal Giulio Feltre della Rovere, a member of the ducal house of Urbino and Archbishop of Ravenna, Costanzo Porta was appointed to the position of *maestro di cappella* at the Cathedral of Ravenna in January, 1567, and again to a similar position at the renowned basilica in Loreto in September, 1574. On the latter occasion the Cardinal commissioned Porta to compose some Masses in honor of the celebration in 1575 of the Year of the Sacred Jubilee, the eleventh such celebration in the history of Christendom. Despite his indebtedness to the Cardinal, Porta was somewhat slow in fulfilling this commission. In the summer of 1578, three years after the Year of the Sacred Jubilee, and barely a few weeks before Cardinal della Rovere's death, Angelo Gardano of Venice finally brought out the *Missarum liber primus* containing twelve Masses. Two others, one a *Missa mortuorum* (*a4*), the other an eight-voice *Missa Da pacem,* are preserved in a partially damaged manuscript in the Archives of the Santa Casa in Loreto.[6] The thirteen-voice *Missa Ducalis* honoring Duke Cosimo de' Medici survives in Florence,[7] bringing the total number of known Masses by Porta to fifteen. These Mass settings represent, as do Porta's other sacred works, an interesting admixture of apparently contradictory stylistic qualities. Some of these qualities are reminiscent of earlier practices in Mass composition while others are more indicative of the modern trends at the end of the sixteenth

---

Higinio Anglés (Barcelona: Consejo superior de investigaciones científicas, 1958–61), II, 1011–17; Lewis Lockwood, "A View of the Early Sixteenth-Century Parody Mass," *Twenty-fifth Anniversary Festschrift,* Queens College, Department of Music (New York: Queens College Press, 1964), pp. 53–77, and "On 'Parody' as Term and Concept in 16th-Century Music," *Aspects of Medieval and Renaissance Music* (New York: W. W. Norton, 1966), pp. 560–75.

6. Archivio della Santa Casa, Codex 34, 133–75.

7. Biblioteca Mediceo-Laurenziana, Codex Palat. VI.

century. Among the retrospective tendencies may be enumerated Porta's frequent reliance on strict cantus firmus style, a style generally considered quite old-fashioned that late in the century; his conservative modal usage (e.g., the unmistakably Lydian settings); and his predilection for the contrapuntal ingenuity normally associated with the Franco-Netherlanders of the first part of the sixteenth century which, however, receives less clear expression in Porta's Masses than it does in his motets. Nevertheless, we find such devices as mirror canon, diminution canon, and a puzzle canon—albeit a simple one—in these Mass settings.[8] On the other hand, some details of melodic construction and of structural treatment seem to be progressive traits.

A tabulation of Porta's fifteen Masses by types presents us with a major problem which, I fear, shall remain unsolved for some time. At first glance the Masses seem to conform to three types: the freely composed Mass unified by mode, the cantus firmus Mass, and the parody Mass. The free type is apparently represented by six Masses (composed according to the first six modes), the cantus firmus type by six, and the parody type by three. Since Porta himself makes so much of the fact that the six Masses in four voices were written as an illustration of the proper usage of the respective modes [9] the question was never raised in any of the discussions of Porta's music [10] that there may be some additional formal organization present in these Masses. The suggestion of some closer structural relationships occurring among the several movements of the individual Masses first presented itself to me while undertaking a close study of the works in preparation of a dissertation on the Masses and hymns of Porta. Quite recently this suggestion of something unusual led to the

8. *Missa de beata Virgine,* Agnus Dei II; *Missa Da pacem,* Agnus Dei II; *Missa Audi filia,* Agnus Dei II, respectively. The ingenious construction of the *Missa Ducalis* merits an individual study.

9. Cf. the dedication of the *Missarum liber primus,* translated in L. Pruett, The Masses and Hymns of Costanzo Porta (Unpublished Ph. D. dissertation, Department of Music, The University of North Carolina, 1960), pp. 7–11.

10. Cf. Antonio Garbelotto, *Il P. Costanzo Porta da Cremona, O. F. M. conv., Grande polifonista del '500* (Roma: Editrice Miscellanea Francescana, 1955); Oscar Mischiati, "Costanzo Porta," *Die Musik in Geschichte und Gegenwart,* X, 1464–71.

realization that at least some (and very probably all six) of the so-called free Masses are, in fact, parody Masses.

In describing a hitherto largely unknown anthology of sixteenth-century music N. Bridgman and F. Lesure [11] list among the contents a *Missa secundi toni Vestiv' i colli* and a *Missa tertii toni Com' havran fin le dolorose tempre* by Costanzo Porta. Nowhere else do these titles appear in connection with Porta's works. Although I have been unable to examine this anthology as yet, there is no doubt that the two Masses in question are the *Missae secundi* and *tertii toni* from the *Missarum liber primus*. The title given to the former in the anthology made tracing easy; a comparison of the Mass with the similarly named famous madrigal by Palestrina reveals that Porta did, indeed, derive his Mass from the Palestrina madrigal. The third-mode Mass was more difficult to identify; a slow, page-by-page, check through the Vogel bibliography of sixteenth-century secular works [12] produced a madrigal *Come havran fin* by Cipriano de Rore, which turns out to be the source for Porta's *Missa tertii toni*.[13]

The question presenting itself immediately is, why did Porta not indicate in the print that these are parody Masses, as he did in three other Masses contained in the same book? My conjectural answer is quite simple. Could he have concealed intentionally the worldly origins of these Masses, having in mind the general sentiment of the church authorities of his time that secular compositions were not suitable models for Mass compositions? The book of Masses is dedicated to an important church figure, and we know from the dedicatory statement that Cardinal della Rovere urged Porta to keep the settings simple so as not to obscure the liturgical text by polyphonic intricacies—another generally shared sentiment of the sixteenth-century church. In any case, the three admitted parody Masses of Porta are based on motets; I strongly suspect that we should seek sources for some

11. "Une Anthologie 'historique' de la fin du XVIᵉ siècle: le manuscrit Bourdeney," *Miscelánea en homenaje a Mons. Higinio Anglés,* I, 161–74.

12. Emil Vogel, *Bibliothek der gedruckten weltlichen Vokalmusik Italiens aus den Jahren 1500–1700* (Berlin: A. Haack, 1892), II, 152.

13. This work was originally published in 1547 and then underwent some fifteen reprints by various publishers; it is now available in the *Smith College Music Archives Series,* No. 6, ed. Gertrude Parker Smith.

of the remaining modally identified Masses among the secular
works of the Renaissance. The following table will afford a concise descriptive summary of the Masses before we enter upon
more detailed discussion of parody procedures.

Table I

Source	Title	No. of voices	Type	Remarks, references to pre-existent materials
Missarum liber primus, Venice, 1578	*Primi toni*	4	Suspected parody	Unidentified
	Secundi toni	4	Parody	*Vestiva i colli* by Palestrina
	Tertii toni	4	Parody	*Com' havran fin . . .* by Cipriano de Rore
	Quarti toni	4	Suspected parody	Unidentified
	Quinti toni	4	Suspected parody	Unidentified
	Sexti toni	4	Suspected parody	Unidentified
	De beata Virgine	4	Cantus firmus	Mass XI, Mass XVII
	Descendit angelus	5	Parody	Motet by Hilaire Penet
	Mortuorum	5	Cantus firmus	Requiem Mass
	Quemadmodum	6	Parody	Unidentified
	Audi filia	6	Parody	Motet by Nicolas Gombert
	La sol fa re mi	6	Cantus firmus	Original
Loreto, Codex 34, *ca.* 1574–79	*Mortuorum*	4	Cantus firmus	Requiem Mass
	Da pacem	8	Cantus firmus	Antiphon
Florence, Bibl. Med. Laur. Palat. VI, date?	*Ducalis*	13	Cantus firmus	Original

The relationship between Palestrina's *Vestiva i colli* [14] and the
Missa secundi toni is very close throughout the Mass. The five-
voice madrigal is in two *partes,* the first cast in *AAB* form and
yielding five distinctly recognizable motives, the second *pars*
furnishing seven more motives. Porta's four-voice setting of *Kyrie*

---

14. Cf. Casimiri, ed., *Le Opere complete di Giovanni da Palestrina* (Roma:
Edizione Fratelli Scalera, 1940–XIX), IX, 117.

I uses the first motive in melodically unchanged form in bass and alto, somewhat embellished in cantus and tenor; the quintus is omitted and the polyphonic entries of the four borrowed voices are compressed. The result is a setting unmistakably related to, and yet, distinctly different from the madrigal. The *Christe* employs motive no. 3 as it appears in the bass and tenor of the model, combining it with free material in the upper two voices. The bass of *Kyrie* II is a virtually literal quotation of motives 4 and 5 of the madrigal bass while the upper voices intermingle snatches from different parts of the madrigal.[15] The same procedure may be seen in the *Gloria* and the remaining movements of the Mass: the bass is always the most clearly derived voice, stringing borrowed motive after borrowed motive with little new material added. The upper voices are at times almost identical with those of the madrigal, but not necessarily with their corresponding parts, that is, borrowing may occur from different voices of the madrigal; at other times they may be quite free. Using one voice less than the model provides, much variety is available to Porta as he may draw from two different voices to come up with one melodic line. A noteworthy feature is that the borrowed segments do not always appear in the order in which they stand in the madrigal but may be freely rearranged, apparently to suit the composer's fancy. The frequent use of borrowed materials in all four voices simultaneously makes the dependence of Mass upon madrigal quite obvious.

The reliance of Porta's *Missa tertii toni* upon Cipriano de Rore's four-voice *Com' havran fin le dolorose tempre* is no less extensive yet quite different from that described above. The difference is caused primarily by the nature of the madrigal. The motives are less well-defined rhythmically and melodically than those of Palestrina and therefore much more unobtrusive. Though borrowing is almost ever-present, much of it passes unnoticed; the clearest recognition of it comes in the opening and concluding measures of the Mass sections. Again, simultaneous borrowing is not unusual.

---

15. E.g., Porta's cantus quotes from Palestrina's cantus and altus, Porta's altus from Palestrina's altus and tenor, and Porta's tenor resembles portions of Palestrina's tenor.

The structural similarity among these two identified parodies and the remaining four modally unified Masses is so pronounced that I have little doubt that they, also, are parodies. Not having any titles for them the identity of their sources will remain unknown unless, and until, by a stroke of luck, someone may discover additional information; if their models are found it almost certainly will be through serendipity.

The three admitted parody Masses all give the names of their models in their titles, but to date only two of the models have been identified. The *Missa Audi filia* in six voices is based on a five-voice motet by Nicolas Gombert which appeared in *Musica Excellentissimi Nicolai Gomberti vulgo Motecta Quinque Vocum . . . liber primus* published by Scotto in Venice, in 1539. It appears to have been a well-liked motet, for it is included in several later collections and is even found in tablature arranged for instrumental performance.[16] The motet is quite typical of Gombert's motet style with a structure consisting of two *partes* of about equal length. Unlike many other contemporary two-part motets this one does not follow the familiar *aBcB* motet form but is through-composed. The outstanding feature of the motet is pervading imitation; each line of text (and sometimes even a part of a line) is set to a new motive which provides the material for a point of imitation. There is little relief in this severely polyphonic texture, neither chordal sections[17] nor any simultaneous cadences in all voices until the final cadence of each *pars* is reached. The opening points of imitation of the two *partes* show great similarity in the disposition of voices. In both instances the composer makes use of paired imitation, juxtaposing the altus-cantus pair with the quintus-bassus pair; the tenor is the last voice

16. E.g., it was reprinted by Scotto of Venice in various editions in 1541, 1550, and 1552; by Jacques Moderne of Lyon in 1542; and it appears in a lute tablature manuscript in the Bayrische Staatsbibliothek in Munich. For a complete listing of the occurrences, cf. Joseph Schmidt-Görg, *Nicolas Gombert: Kapellmeister Karls V.* (Bonn: Ludwig Röhrscheid Verlag, 1938), p. 362. The relationship of Porta's Mass to the motet by Gombert was discovered by Joseph Schmidt-Görg.

17. A quasi-chordal effect is created at times, however, when all imitatively treated voices proceed in relatively uniform rhythmic values, as at the text *et concupiscet Rex* in the *prima pars*.

to enter. Imitation between the voices within a pair occurs at the time interval of two measures, i.e., two breves, and at the pitch interval of the lower fifth; imitation between the pairs is in both cases at the time interval of six measures. The paired imitation at the openings of both sections is exceptional; the remainder of the setting maintains a uniform texture, permitting all voices to remain more or less equally active in the continuous flow of the imitative process. In a number of instances a motive is used repeatedly for imitative entries instead of being limited to a single working-out. This, of course, becomes the standard motet treatment among central and north Italian composers in the second half of the sixteenth century, but is still new with Gombert.

Porta's exploitation of the model material is clear, yet by no means obvious. Knowing his inclination to use paired imitation from a study of his motets as well as knowing the general practice of the time to borrow opening and closing passages of the model in the manner of a framework, one should expect to find a clear reliance on the Gombert motet in the individual movements of the Mass. Instead, Porta seems to be making a special effort to avoid congruences. Taking each line of the motet text as a point of departure he isolates seventeen recognizable motives from the Gombert motet, eight from the first *pars* and nine from the second. In the course of the Mass all seventeen motives are touched upon, some more extensively than others, but seldom bearing resemblance to their original treatment in the motet. As a rule the borrowed motive is used imitatively, sometimes in all six voices (to the CATTB voicing of the motet Porta adds a cantus secundus), at other times in only two or three, with new material appearing in the remaining voices. Occasionally the vertical relationship of two borrowed parts is maintained for short stretches, but the addition of other voices obscures the original relationship.

Each of the five main movements of the Mass begins with a reference to the first motive of Gombert, but other than that there seems to be no particular system to the order in which the borrowed motives are employed. There is no textual relation between the Mass and the motet that might be taken to account in the borrowing of the material. Sometimes the motives are used in the order in which they appear in the original; at other times they are mixed seemingly at random. For example, Kyrie I is based on motives 1 and 2, Christe on motives 3 and 4, Kyrie II on motives 9, 10, 11, and 17, quite in order except for the gaps between 4 and 9 (between sections), and 11 and 17 (within a section). The final Agnus Dei, on the other hand, refers to motives 1, 2, 17, 6, 13, 5, and 17, in that order. The endings of the main sections have reference to the closing motives of either the first or second *pars* of the motet (motives 8 and 17, respectively), but the subsections may end with other borrowed or original material. In all cases, whether the borrowed material be treated imitatively or not and whether it be in consecutive order or not, the bass part quotes most literally as well as most extensively from the model. The other voices tend to be limited in their references to the borrowed material to the first four or five notes of the motives. Since the most characteristic intervallic relationships occur at the head of the motives, the abbreviated references, though not overly obvious, are nevertheless clearly recognizable.

Space does not permit an extended description of the manipulation of borrowed material as it occurs in this Mass, but our remarks should suffice to indicate that here we are presented with a parody technique whose main characteristics consist of the extraction of individual motives from the model and the rearrangement of them in new ways, vertically as well as horizontally, without great alteration of the motives themselves. Simultaneous drawing upon all voices of the model is absent.

The other admitted parody Mass for which the model is known, *Missa Descendit angelus,* proves even more interesting than the *Missa Audi filia,* both on its own merit and because it may be compared to Palestrina's setting based upon the same motet. In fact, it was a comparative study of the two Mass settings, prompted by the identity of the titles, that enabled me to identify the model for Porta, since Palestrina's model was known. The model is a two-part, *aBcB* responsory form motet for four voices by the relatively obscure French composer Hilaire Penet who was employed as a singer in the Papal Chapel from 1514 to 1521. Palestrina's and Porta's works are apparently the only two parody Masses of the period which draw upon the Penet motet. That Palestrina should compose a Mass based on a composition by one of his predecessors at the Papal Chapel seems reasonable enough.[18] In view of the fact that the other identified sources for Porta's parodies were apparently famous and oft-reprinted works, his reasons for choosing this relatively obscure motet as a model for his Mass are open to conjecture; perhaps it was nothing more significant than that the motet was accessible in two collections brought out by Porta's own publishers, the house of Gardano in Venice.[19]

A comparative examination of the Masses *Audi filia* and *Descendit angelus* reveals certain similarities in borrowing procedure while also illustrating notable dissimilarities in the manipulation of the borrowed material. Porta adds a new voice to those of the original, as he does in the *Missa Audi filia*. To the CATB parts of the Penet motet is joined a *quinta pars,* in tessitura a second tenor. Again, individual motives are culled from the model, fewer in number in this case (ten), since the responsory form of the motet allows substantial repetition of material. The texture of the Penet motet is characterized by consistent imitation, often not strict, but nevertheless unmistakable. Both *partes* open with imitative entries marked by the modification which corresponds to the later concept of "tonal answer," somewhat unusual for the time of Penet. More characteristic of his generation are the several, at times extended, instances of paired imitation. In another apparent attempt to avoid a too direct dependence upon his model Porta refrains altogether from using paired imitation in the Mass setting. As is the case in the *Missa Audi filia,* the bass is the voice that relies most heavily on the corresponding voice of the motet, often consisting of nearly literal quotations of the original motives. Again, these motives may follow the order in which they appear in the original or they may be scrambled. In the following example is given the entire bass

18. Although the motet is not represented in the surviving manuscripts of the Chapel, it is contained in one of the printed collections held by the library; cf. J. M. Llorens, *Capellae Sixtinae Codices* (Città del Vaticano: Biblioteca Apostolica Vaticana, 1960), p. 282.

19. The two collections are *Primus liber . . . Fior de mottetti . . .* (RISM 1539[12]) and *Flos Florum . . . Motteti del fior* (RISM 1545[4]).

part of the *prima pars* of Penet's motet and the bass part of Porta's *Et in terra*. The relationship between the two parts may be seen by following the numbered phrases. Note that in some instances Porta telescopes the borrowed material by eliminating the middle of the phrase, employing only the beginning and the end.

Example 1

A curious treatment is given to some of the more lengthy motives: Porta divides them into several fragments which he then may use in isolation without further reference to the remainder of the motive. As illustration we quote the material

taken from the beginnings of the two *partes* of the Penet motet
(motives 1 and 7) and indicate the fragments as used by Porta
by the letters *a, b,* and *c.* While these motives, or fragments

Example 2

thereof, may be used imitatively, such is not always the case. In
several instances two motives are used simultaneously in the two
outside voices with new material appearing in the inner voices.
Quite curiously, the new material given to the inner voices in
these instances in itself becomes a unifying factor in the Mass. It
is used repeatedly, as illustrated in the four excerpts below.

Example 3a

Porta, *Missa Descendit angelus,* "Kyrie I."

Example 3b

Porta, *Missa Descendit angelus,* "Et in terra."

Example 3c

Porta, *Missa Descendit angelus,* "Et incarnatus."

Example 3d

Porta, *Missa Descendit angelus,* "Et in spiritum."

This procedure is strongly reminiscent of that found in several of the modally identified Masses, where the same material is used in similarly unifying fashion at the beginnings and endings of several sections. But, whereas it appears in at least two of the modal Masses that the recurring material is taken *in toto* from their respective models (that is, the usual "framing-in" parody procedure is applied), the recurring measures in the *Missa Descendit angelus* are not so derived from the motet but represent original material.

A comparison of the Palestrina and Porta Mass settings proves fruitful concerning these composers' respective parody procedures. Generally speaking, the relationship between model and Mass is a much closer one in Palestrina's setting than in Porta's. Palestrina's utilization of the borrowed material is very systematic. He, too, isolates motives from the model, in the same way as does Porta. These motives are, however, treated with much greater consistency throughout the Mass setting: they provide material for points of imitation, thus appearing in equal distribution in all voices (Palestrina retains the original four voices of the motet). Moreover, they are used mostly in the order in which they occur in the original, with little new melodic material added. Palestrina retains the borrowed motives in virtually unchanged outline rhythmically and melodically, in contrast to the motivic modifications encountered in Porta's setting. Although Palestrina follows the model very closely in individual lines his ingenuity in seeking new ways of polyphonically combining these borrowed lines is admirably revealed in this Mass. Within the framework of a strictly imitative texture he discovers possibilities of simultaneous alignment of individual parts that go far beyond the pre-Gombertian imitative procedures employed by Penet. The result is a tight, closely knit structure, thoroughly homogeneous. The less intense reliance upon the model revealed in Porta's setting need not, however, be taken as an indication of lesser ingenuity. Contrapuntal complexities attesting to Porta's technical skill are amply represented among his other sacred compositions. I prefer to interpret this difference in treatment as a basic difference in the conception of the nature of the parody.

Despite some dissimilarities in details the parody procedures observed in the Masses *Audi filia* and *Descendit angelus* are essentially the same. Porta extracts salient motives from his models and subjects these motives to imitation, chordal treatment, fragmentation, telescoping, rhythmic and melodic modification, and combination with new material. In both cases the outer voices of the model are most heavily drawn upon, particularly the bass. In fact, the bass lines of certain sections of the Masses are a veritable patchwork of quotations from the model basses. That this is an essential procedure in Porta's parodies is borne out by yet a third parody Mass, the six-voice *Missa Quemadmodum*. The title probably refers to Psalm XLI, *Quemadmodum desiderat cervus ad fontes aquarum,* which was occasionally used for motet settings during the sixteenth century. The text is better known in another version, *Sicut cervus desiderat ad fontes aquarum,* in which it was set by Palestrina. I have had occasion to examine several of these *Quemadmodum* motets including one by a pupil of Porta, Ludovico Balbi, but so far the model for the Mass remains unknown. Yet, in addition to the title, there is quite substantial stylistic evidence in the Mass setting that identifies the work as another transcription Mass. The bass lines of all five movements of the Mass are put together in phrases that keep recurring through the entire setting. Only about five short phrases are used only once; the others recur from two to fifteen times. In these recurrences the consecutive order is sometimes retained repeatedly; at other times it is altered. Similar, though not as numerous, recurring elements may be noted in the other voices as well. The textural treatment is comparable to that found in the other two admitted parody Masses. The recurring motives may be treated in various degrees of imitation, that is, strict, free, or combined with new material, or they may occur in familiar style sections. In short, the technical features of the Mass correspond precisely to the type of parody observed in the two confirmed instances. From the manner in which the motives are used in the Mass it seems feasible to assume that the model, when it is found, will prove to be in two *partes,* cast in the *aBcB* responsory form. This much I deduce from the fact that most sections and subsections of the Mass setting conclude with references to the same closing motive, whereas different ones may appear at the beginnings of sections. Three of the four known models of Porta's parodies are works by composers older than Porta; quite possibly the *Quemadmodum* model should be sought among older works, too. This preference—if such it be—for compositions from earlier times would not be unique with Porta. Palestrina, too, drew his models from among older composers, except when parodying one of his own compositions, and ignored the work of his contemporaries.

As revealed in the three named and two unnamed parody Masses Porta's parody techniques may be summarized as consisting of these characteristic points:

(a) Extraction of motives from the model. The choice of motives is determined by the individual lines of text in the model and relies primarily on the bass part; in the two unadmitted parodies reliance on the other voices is almost equally heavy, but in the named parodies the cantus and the remaining voices are distinctly secondary sources of borrowed material.

(b) The borrowed motives appear most literally and most frequently in the bass voice of the parody, either in the order in which they are extracted from the model or in random rearrangement. This random order is stressed here as an important point of difference between Porta and Palestrina, who rarely departs from the original order of borrowed motives, and then only for systematic reasons, not arbitrarily.[20]

(c) The borrowed motives may be subjected to the following modifications: melodic alteration consisting of elimination of inessential notes while the characteristic framework is clearly retained; melodic alteration consisting of addition of new notes to the characteristic framework; rhythmic alteration to fit the demands of the different texts; telescoping consisting of elimination of the middle of a lengthy phrase, fastening the conclusion directly onto the head; fragmentation of lengthy motives into several units which may then be used consecutively, separately, and/or simultaneously.

(d) The textural treatment of the borrowed motives may range from strict imitation in all voices to imitation in some voices combined with new material in the other voices; from chordal treatment with the borrowed material in the bass to original imitative treatment in the upper voices combined with the borrowed bass. At no time is there a perfunctory adoption of the texture of the model; on the contrary, there seems to be a constant effort to avoid too obvious relationships.

(e) Simultaneous exploitation of all the voices of the model is encountered only in the unnamed parodies. In the named parody Masses it is conspicuously absent. This difference in treatment may perhaps have chronological significance. I am inclined to believe that the parody Masses on Palestrina's and de Rore's madrigals, which show heavy reliance on their models, are among Porta's earlier works. The apparently intentional avoidance of too easy adaptation, characteristic of the three named parody Masses, would seem to reflect the mature composer's pleasure in exerting full control over his materials.

The question arises: why did Porta concentrate his borrowing on the lowest part of his models and why is the bass time and again the only voice referring to the models? I have no answer, but I shall venture to propose a theory. This practice perhaps

---

20. This question is thoroughly treated in Johannes Klassen, "Zur Modellbehandlung in Palestrinas Parodiemessen," *Kirchenmusikalisches Jahrbuch,* XXXIX (1955), 41–55.

reflects the emergence of what becomes one of the chief Baroque innovations, the awareness of the bass as the foundation, the fundamental supporting voice. Looking at some of the recurring bass motives of the *Missa Quemadmodum* such a theory does not appear inconceivable, for that bass line is particularly harmonic in nature, as these excerpts show:

Example 4

IS THERE A RATIONALE FOR

THE ARTICULATION OF J. S. BACH'S

STRING AND WIND MUSIC?

*William S. Newman**
THE UNIVERSITY OF NORTH CAROLINA AT CHAPEL HILL

There has been more than one occasion to remark that in all the vast literature that has accumulated on nearly every aspect of music so few fundamental studies have been dedicated primarily to music's most basic phenomena—to rhythm, or texture, or the phrase, or the motive, or such an essential of performance practices as articulation. But, of course, further consideration suggests the explanation. Fundamental studies of this sort must be the ultimate goal, not the starting point, of musical scholarship. To arrive at the broad, generalized view that they require presupposes a rich background of more localized and specific studies.

Articulation as a significant problem of performance practices is our case in point in this little study. Although the primary sources, especially the autographs and contemporary treatises, often lie ready to yield substantial information, the actual number of systematic studies into specific articulation problems is small; and as for any generalized, comprehensive view of the articulation problem, only one consequential study has been discovered here up to the time of this writing (spring of 1965). This last is Hermann Keller's *Phrasierung und Artikulation*, published in 1955 [1] as a complete revision of his doctoral dissertation issued

* *I welcome the privilege of contributing to this commemorative volume, honoring as it does an outstanding musician and musicologist (as well as a longtime colleague and valued friend) who, in both his writing and teaching, steadfastly expounded, maintained, and exemplified the highest ideals of musical scholarship.*

1. Kassel: Bärenreiter-Verlag. Also published in English translation by Leigh Gerdine (New York: Norton, 1965).

thirty years earlier. Those more specialized studies that do exist occur primarily as extended digressions or episodes in the course of broader studies. Thus, to confine ourselves more nearly to the topic at hand, which is articulation in J. S. Bach's music, the chief study of this sort written before Keller's book is the total of nearly seventy pages that pertain directly or indirectly in Albert Schweitzer's *J. S. Bach*.[2] A more objective, systematic, and fuller discussion, written in cognizance of Keller's dissertation rather than his 1955 revision, is that in *The Interpretation of Bach's Keyboard Works,* by the late Erwin Bodky.[3] An actual monograph is the careful, enlightening article by Henry S. Drinker, "Bach's Use of Slurs in Recitativo Secco," which is based on the cantatas, Passions, and oratorios.[4]

The concentration here on the end of the Baroque Era rather than any subsequent period is determined partly by the fact that the late-Baroque Era was the last period before the editorial designation of articulation became more the rule than the exception. In the high-Classic Era of Haydn and Mozart, articulation, with all its niceties and refined practice, developed into one significant aspect in itself of Classical style. Even so, the editorial designations for this articulation remained inadequate, inconsistent, and contradictory enough that they have seldom survived without "improvements" in the hands of later editors. One even finds such a remedial experiment as Professor Jacob Fischer's edition of pieces from Bach to Mendelssohn, published in Vienna in 1926, which introduces and substitutes new designations, especially the familiar punctuation signs of literary writing.

The concentration here on articulation in Bach's music rather than that of any one of his contemporaries is determined only

---

2. Originally published in Paris in 1905. The reference here is to the 1947 reprint (London: Adam & Charles Black), I, 365–80 (most pertinent to the present study); II, 25–30, 74–122, of Ernest Newman's English translation of 1911.

3. (Cambridge: Harvard University Press, 1960), including all of Chapter VII (pp. 202–22) and copious examples in the concluding sections (pp. 382–400) of Appendix B. This book is, of course, much more than an expansion and reworking of *Der Vortrag alter Klaviermusik* by Bodky (Berlin: Max Hesse, 1932).

4. Published privately by the author (Merion, Pennsylvania, 1946).

partly by the fact that the lion's share of such limited research as has already appeared has emphasized Bach, thus clearing the way for more in the same channels. Also favoring this concentration are the exceptionally rich indications for articulation in at least certain categories of Bach's music, the relatively fewer categories of music that pertain in the output of most of his contemporaries, and the much greater accessibility of Bach's autographs in facsimile (which necessarily constitute a prime source for this sort of investigation).

The concentration here on Bach's string and wind music rather than his choral or his solo keyboard music is determined by a simple process of elimination. Drinker has already made a significant attack on the choral problem (which adds extraneous considerations of symbolism and word painting, in any case), and all too little in the way of articulation indications occurs in the solo keyboard music.[5] The indications in the string and wind music are frequently considerable, varied, and intriguing. Furthermore, the autographs of a substantial portion of this music are extant, and from these a fair number have been published in excellent facsimiles. Four facsimiles have sufficed as bases for the present study.[6]

They are:

> *Sei Solo* [sic] *à Violino senza Basso accompagnato,* dated 1720, published in facsimile by Bärenreiter (Kassel, 1950).
>
> *6 Suites a Violoncello solo senza Basso* (undated), published in facsimile by Ludwig Doblinger (Vienna, 1944?).
>
> *Sonata a cembalo obligato e Travers solo* (undated), published in facsimile by Deutscher Verlag für Musik (Leipzig, n.d.).
>
> *Six* [Brandenburg] *Concerts Avec plusieurs Instruments,* dated 1721, published in facsimile by Argonaut Books (Larchmont, N.Y., n.d.).

---

5. Bodky (pp. 202–4) finds indications in only about 5 per cent of the keyboard music. He gives a summary of these, including full details on both volumes of *The Well-Tempered Clavier.*

6. All findings here have been based on these facsimiles. But three of the works—that is, all but the cello suites—have also appeared to date in the careful Bach *Neue Ausgabe,* along with the supplementary *Kritische Bericht* for each, and these have been consulted here, too, as a double-check on the findings.

The object here has been to find some rationale for the articulation of Bach's instrumental music. The method has been, first, to summarize and, where necessary and possible, reconcile the somewhat divergent conclusions of Schweitzer, Keller, Drinker, and Bodky, as well as a few hints by contemporaries of Bach; and second, to put these conclusions to the test by checking them against the editorial markings that do occur in the four autographs by Bach listed above. The conclusions of Schweitzer and the others are divergent partly because the approaches differ. Much of what Schweitzer says relevant to phrasing or the details of articulation concerns matters of prosody and word painting in the choral music. But he does get down to specific examples of articulation in keyboard and other instrumental passages by Bach. The relatively few citations of Bach's own articulation marks then become the basis for increasingly subjective conclusions. These conclusions show the strong influence of Rudolf Westphal and Hugo Riemann, especially the uncompromising view that every musical idea must begin with an anacrusis.

Drinker's study is at once more systematic and more limited than Schweitzer's. It is pertinent here mainly to the extent that it provides one excellent model for the present sort of investigation. Otherwise, it is less pertinent because it considers only the short slur among articulation devices, and only in vocal *recitativo secco*, at that. Keller begins by making the distinction between phrasing and articulation that is understood here. In our own words, phrasing is the organization of musical thought into sentences and clauses, whereas articulation is the more local grouping or detachment of the individual notes within the phrase—that is, what might be likened to the delivery, elocution, and facial expressions of speech. After devoting the first half of his book to a general survey of phrasing and articulation, both historical and analytic, Keller deals more specifically, in separate chapters, with the particular problems in Bach, Mozart, Beethoven, and the nineteenth century. Actually, he gives three chapters to Bach, including one on phrasing, one on articulation in the chamber music, and one on articulation in the unmarked keyboard music.

Because Bodky's discussion is written in cognizance of Schweitzer's and Keller's and because it applies more directly to the present discussion it may be summarized a bit more fully. Lamenting the lack of more studies, Bodky notes that Schweitzer and Keller conflict when they get down to specifics. He also regrets the remarkably few editorial indications for articulation in Bach's keyboard works and admits that those he does find (as in Two-Part Inventions 3 and 9) are not at all those he might have discovered had he had to arrive at them by deduction and analogy. He notes that the longtime confusion created by using the slur both to indicate legato articulation and to define phrases [7] is no problem in Bach's keyboard music, where only the articulation use occurs, and is sometimes resolved in his chamber music by the use of double slurs—that is, individual articulation slurs under the longer phrase slur. But Bach's few original fingerings merely seem to add confusion, he notes. Only further experimentation with older instruments is likely to bring additional clarification, he suggests. Bodky pays special attention to the *Affektenlehre* and its bearing on styles of articulation, citing Emanuel Bach, Quantz, Marpurg, and the exceptionally rich editorial markings and prefatory advices of Couperin.

Perhaps Bodky's most important conclusion is the disappointing one that the principle of articulation by analogy, advocated by Schweitzer, Keller, and others—that is, derivation from analogous passages that do have editorial indications—is generally inconclusive, untenable, and sometimes actually misleading in Bach's music. Prompted to make an over-all survey of Bach's articulation marks by the conflicting and uncertain conclusions of Schweitzer and Keller, Bodky is forced to acknowledge that the broad unity of style in Bach's musical language still does not preclude idiomatic, often very different treatment of the inexhaustibly varied ideas in each scoring category of his music. Extensive tables in the appendixes of Bodky's book illustrate how Bach often changes the articulation as he transfers the same or similar motives from the influence of words in vocal music to bowing in string music, blowing in wind music, and so on.

As for early sources on articulation, a fair number of statements on the need for articulation can be found at least as far

---

7. Cf. W. S. Newman, "The Enigma of the Curved Line," *The Piano Teacher* I[5] (May–June 1959), 7–13.

back as the sixteenth century, but prior to the death of Bach any statements supplying a rationale—that is, a clear, practical, musical basis—for articulation seem to be almost nonexistent.[8] Thus, in 1553, Diego Ortiz could already write in his *Tratado* on string playing that "when two or three semiminims occur in one [metric] group ['regla'] only the first is to be defined [by a new bow] and the others are to be passed over without [a change of] bowing." [9] And in 1635 Frescobaldi could call for as complete a legato as the performer's technique would permit in the Gregorian *canti fermi* of his *Fiori musicali*.[10] But not until just after Bach's death is a clearer relationship suggested between the style of the music and the style of the articulation. In 1752 Quantz wrote in his celebrated *Essay* (Chapter VII) that

> . . . It is necessary to avoid slurring notes which ought to be detached and detaching notes which ought to be slurred. . . . It is the quick passages in Allegro which must above all be performed briskly, clearly, with liveliness, with articulation and distinctly. . . . Long notes ought to be given fulness in a manner characterized by the increase and diminution of the volume; and the quick notes which follow ought to be well separated in a lively idiom. . . . But when after quick notes there follow several slow and singing notes, the fire must at once be restrained, and the notes performed with the feeling which they require, in order that the hearer shall not experience any tedium.[11]

A year later Emanuel Bach wrote still more specifically in his own much celebrated *Essay* (Chapter III) that

> In general, the liveliness of allegros is conveyed by detached notes, and the feeling of adagios by sustained, slurred notes . . .

---

8. The best known statements and a few others on phrasing and articulation are all brought together in translation by Robert Donington in *The Interpretation of Early Music* (London: Faber & Faber, 1963), pp. 184, 211, 404–15, 485, and 513.

9. From Donington, p. 411, but retranslated from the original Spanish as reproduced in Max Schneider's reprint of 1913 (Berlin: Leo Liepmannssohn), p. 1.

10. The remark occurs in the last paragraph of his preface "al lettore," as reprinted in Joseph Bonnet's edition of 1922 (Paris: Editions Salabert).

11. Excerpted from passages translated by Donington, pp. 412–13.

even when not so marked . . . I realize however that every style of performance may occur at any tempo. . . . Notes which are neither detached, slurred nor fully sustained are sounded for half their value. . . . Crochets and quavers in moderate tempo are generally performed in this half-detached style.[12]

Other, more limited advices that contribute to a rationale of articulation occur occasionally in Baroque treatises, such as the instruction to slur a trill into the note to which it leads even when not so marked (for example, as stated by Bacilly in 1668 and cited by Donington, p. 184). But the generalizations at which our modern writers have arrived with regard to J. S. Bach derive mainly from the basic principles most clearly stated by Emanuel Bach. And well they might, for though one ordinarily tries to insure that Emanuel's generation is not too closely identified with his father's, it is hard to see why his remarks about articulation are not equally applicable to the music of his father. The modern generalizations, most of which are systematically and fully summed up by Bodky (p. 222), are tabulated in the following chart. Some of these generalizations cannot be related directly to Baroque writings but are derived merely by inference and longtime association with the music.

Legato is more likely in	*Staccato is more likely in*	*The mean or half-staccato touch may prevail in*
adagio tempo	allegro tempo	allegro tempo, or quarter- and 8th-notes "in moderate and slow tempos" (Emanuel Bach, III, 22), or "ordinary movement, which is always understood" (Marpurg, *Anleitung,* 1765, I, vii, p. 29—i.e., in the absence of articulation marks, but this advice is very risky to follow)
smallest intervals	larger intervals	
regular rhythms	irregular rhythms	
middle pitch ranges	outer pitch ranges	
soft passages	loud passages	
shortest and longest notes	notes of average length	

---

12. Excerpted from passages translated by Donington, p. 413.

Legato is more likely in	*Staccato is more likely in*	*The mean or half-staccato touch may prevail in*
connection of trill, turn, and appoggiatura to note of resolution	first note of any rhythmic change that occurs in a zigzag line (Schweitzer, I, pp. 272–73)	
short to long note of , etc.	the long note in	
(Schweitzer, I, p. 371), but vice-versa in Keller (p. 79) and Bodky (p. 219)! in the familiar, "sighing," two-note, often stepwise groups (frequently slurred anyway by Bach) that repeat or sequence up or down the scale	(Schweitzer, I, p. 371), but vice-versa in Keller (p. 79) and Bodky (p. 219)!	
clavichord music	harpsichord music	harpsichord music

Before testing the above generalizations against certain string and wind works by Bach, we ought to recall two related considerations. First is the fact, briefly suggested in the chart, that the choice of instrument can be a determining factor in articulation. As far back as *Il Transilvano* by Diruta (Venice, 1597; p. 12 in the 1625 reprint used here), distinctions were made in the smooth legato style appropriate to the playing of organ music in church and the nonlegato style appropriate to the playing of dances on the harpsichord. One would expect the differences between bowing and blowing to affect the slurs and staccatos on string and wind instruments accordingly, but whether Bach makes these distinctions editorially will be seen in the discussion that follows. Second is the need to list the most frequent means by which the articulation may be indicated editorially in late-Baroque music. These are the slur (except when it is used for other purposes, as it sometimes is by Couperin with reference to *notes inégales*), the rest, the dot, the wedge, the dash, the dots under a slur, the broken balkan (or beam), the fermata, the apostrophe, and such clues as a shift of manuals on the organ or harpsichord. Although all these means can be found in one passage or another of Bach's music, it is the slur that concerns us almost exclusively in the four autograph facsimiles at hand.

It cannot be claimed here that the findings on articulation arrived at by examining the four autograph facsimiles listed earlier are either very surprising or extensive. Their ratio to the introductory matter of this article is almost as one-sided as that of the clinching couplet to its three antecedent quatrains in the English sonnet. Furthermore, although the approach and method have been different, these findings are often no more conclusive than Bodky's. Where they fail to abet our search for a rationale of articulation, one can only fall back on the hope that the very fact of the inconclusiveness has significance for the understanding of Bach's musical articulation.[13]

Taking the generalizations in the order by which they were tabulated above, we find, first, considerable validity in the assumption that legato is more likely at a slow than at a fast tempo. The most obvious evidence is the presence of the largest number of bowing and blowing slurs at an adagio tempo (as in BC 1/ii), somewhat fewer at an andante tempo (as in BC 2/ii), and the least in the outer or inner fast movements (none, in fact, in BC 2/iii). When an extended legato slur occurs in a faster movement, the passage is likely to stand out, especially when its context suggests a more detached style (as in Ex. 1, from a gavotte, Vn 6/iii/86–90). Of course, even without the evidence of the increased slurs one would be safe in assuming that a prime concomitant of slow, expressive music is legato playing.

Example 1

Violin

---

13. In the statement of the findings that follows, BC stands for the six Brandenburg concertos, Vn for the six unaccompanied violin "soli" (numbered 1–6 because of the title "Sei Solo," rather than Sonata I, Partita I, and so on), Vc for the six violoncello suites, and Fl for the Sonata in B Minor for flute and realized harpsichord. The movements and measure numbers are given in a short form, too, so that, for example, BC 1/ii/13–14 means Brandenburg Concerto I, movement two, measures 13–14.

The second assumption, that legato is more likely in smaller rather than larger intervals, has somewhat less validity. This time one would assume that because stepwise motion and other small intervals prevail in so much melody writing of the Baroque and Classic eras they also identify primarily with legato playing. Often Bach's slurs do support this assumption (as in BC 1/ii or Vn 1/iv). But Bach's melodies depart from the contemporary norm in their many jagged, tortuous, or tenderly yearning leaps. Hence it is not surprising that there are numerous instances where his slurs embrace wide leaps, including, for example, an 11th (Vn 2/iv/Double/55), a minor 9th followed by a minor 6th in the same direction (Vc 3/i/50), and a succession of two major 6ths and a diminished 7th in one direction (Ex. 2, from Vn 4/iii/6). A practical justification for detaching the notes of most leaps is technical convenience. On the keyboard the span of

Example 2

an 11th means a literal leap for most hands. (Yet just such a leap is slurred in the right hand of the harpsichord part in Fl i/13!) But melodic leaps that can be encompassed in one position through string crossing on a stringed instrument, or with the same fingering through "overblowing" on a wind instrument, do not require a physical leap at all and can be slurred both practically and easily.

In the generalization to the effect that regular rhythms are more likely to be legato than irregular ones, the implication is that patterns of steady, unchanging note values are smoother than patterns made up of assorted note values. But to judge again by the slurs he inserts, Bach seems to make no such distinction in the four autographs examined here. Or, to state it differently, when the patterns are steady he seems to make a special point of interrupting them with slurring that is almost fussy in its detail (that is, when slurs are present at all). Numerous illustrations over both regular and irregular rhythms occur in the richly slurred pages of the cello suites. As one instance, compare the first and second movements of the well known Suite III in C (Ex. 3, from Vc 3/i/24 and 3/ii/1).

Example 3

The same conclusion, or lack of conclusion, must be offered with regard to the idea that tones near the center of the pitch range are more likely to be legato than those at the extremes. Insofar as Bach gives indications he shows no distinction. Melodic lines that reach the extreme ranges usually have no special reason to be detached if they are moving in stepwise fashion, and may well be slurred even if peaking on wide leaps, as noted above. It is probably the fact that the extremes of the range are frequently approached and left by leaps and that they invite climactic rhetorical emphasis that has given rise to this generalization. Nor can the idea be substantiated by Bach's own markings that soft tones are more likely to be legato than loud ones. A glance, for example, at the second movement, "Andante," of Brandenburg Concerto II indicates that the numerous slurs are distributed about equally both between the extremes and the center of the range and between passages marked *forte* and those marked *piano*.

Taking Bach's own markings as evidence again, we would have to revise the generalization that the notes with the longest and shortest values are more likely to be legato whereas the notes with prevailing (or average) values are more likely to be detached. Instead, we would have to conclude that the shortest and average notes are legato and the long ones detached. Thus, there are slurs over the 8th-, 16th-, and 32d-notes in BC 1/ii ("Adagio") but not over the quarter- or half-notes. BC 4/ii is similar. And the relatively few slurs in the outer, fast movements of this same concerto (BC 4/i and iii) occur almost exclusively over the shortest note values—that is, 16th- and 32d-notes. However, one has to remember that the longer and longest note values imply legato by their very length, and do not offer the motivic or figural occasion for slurs that the shorter note values do. It would be hard to think of detaching the longest note values in most of Bach's music (for instance, in the first subject of the fugue in C-sharp minor in Book I of *The Well-Tempered Clavier*), especially in his slower music.

Appoggiaturas are usually slurred to their note of resolution by Bach (as in Fl i/22). And there are practical arguments once more, but no concrete support in his own markings, for slurring the resolution of the trill and turn, and for detaching the first note of a musical idea that changes rhythm and direction. If a trill or turn continues throughout the value of the note, or if the trill concludes with a suffix anyway, the legato resolution becomes a technical necessity. Although there is not an equivalent necessity for detaching the start of a musical idea that changes rhythm and direction, one can argue on musical grounds that the upbeat start of so many of Bach's musical ideas is certainly pointed up in this manner. To be sure, as the music gets slower, and presumably if not by designation more legato, the detached upbeat may become less and less appropriate. With further regard to the trills, it is interesting that even in the most expressive and richly slurred movements Bach slurs them only infrequently and then almost exclusively in but two somewhat irrelevant circumstances—that is, when the trill happens to occur during a longer slurred passage and when the trilled note descends one step from the previous note (Ex. 4, from Vn 1/i/2 and 4, respectively). The slurred descent by one step was in keeping with the usual prac-

Example 4

tice then of tying the preceding note under such circumstances to the first (upper) note of the trill itself.[14]

---

14. Cf. the examples cited by Donington, pp. 178–79.

With regard to the slurring of the dotted-note pattern, wherever the slurs do occur the evidence is all against Schweitzer
and in favor of Keller and Bodky. That is, the slur does not cross
but encompasses the beat, as in Ex. 5 (from Vn 5/1/i–ii). But
bearing in mind the problems of both technique and fluency, one

Example 5

is reluctant to suppose, especially in Bach's faster movements,
that there are not frequent passages of long-short patterns in
which the short note must be slurred to the long one. An unmarked example is the triplet figure of long and short in the
harpsichordist's left hand of Fl iv(12/16)/5–6 (and *passim*),
where the ties across the beats in the right hand (and in the
flute part) seem to justify a short-long slur (Ex. 6).

Example 6

By far the largest number of Bach's slurs appear over recurring two-note figures, confirming with little doubt the legato, frequently "sighing" effect of these characteristic figures. Among
many instances, they are inserted scrupulously throughout BC
4/ii ("Andante") and BC 1/5 ("Poloinesse"; Ex. 7, from the
opening). Next in order of frequency are the slurs that embrace
two notes of a triplet and three notes of a quadruplet (as in
Vc 6/i and BC 6/i, respectively). And next are the slurs that
give rhythmic definition to triplets and quadruplets of repeated
note accompaniment figures (as in BC 1/iii and BC 2/i, re-

Example 7

spectively), implying *portato* in spite of the absence of dots under the slurs. But there are enough clear examples of slurs that depart from these more routine figures, often shifting to a crossing of the beats and even the barlines, to prove Bach's concern with more subtle articulation, too, as in Ex. 8 (from Fl i/15).

Example 8

The fact that most of Bach's slurs do not cross the barline cannot be taken too literally, of course, because they indicate bowing and blowing techniques, first of all, rather than phrases. Even so, the not infrequent slurs that do cross the barline (as in BC 4/i/116–17, 193–94, etc.) or sometimes include and sometimes stop short of a tie (BC 2/ii/63–64) leave one puzzled as to what if any distinction is intended (Ex. 9, from BC 1/ii/7–9). Some

Example 9

of Bach's longest slurs are those that cross the barline. Ex. 9 above illustrates some of the longest slurs in the concertos. Numerous longer ones occur in the unaccompanied string sonatas, including one encompassing thirty-eight notes in Vc 4/i/49–51 (Ex. 10). In this last instance, one is puzzled again, for no cellist would actually attempt to play all those notes in one bow.

Example 10

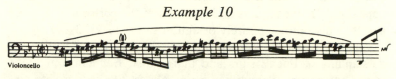

Yet this slur cannot indicate phrasing either, or it certainly would have extended over the barline to take in the one additional, low note.

The distinctions that one might expect in the idiomatic treatment of individual instruments do not show up in any conclusive manner in the slurring, within the limits of our four Bach autographs. Thus, there are no slurs over the virtuoso runs of the "cembalo concertato" part in BC 5/i, such as one might find in somewhat similar passages for the stringed and wind instruments in these concertos or the unaccompanied pieces. On the other hand, the harpsichord right hand gets more and longer slurs (over more expressive lines, to be sure) than the flute or violin in the "Affettuoso" second movement of this same work.[15] In other ways Bach's slurs do not necessarily seem to reflect idiomatic treatment of individual instruments. The converse of the slurred leap of an eleventh for harpsichord mentioned earlier might be what seem to be slurs that are too few and too short in Vc 1/i. Certainly, most cellists today would regard a literal reading of those slurs and the presumably separate notes as too

---

15. In any case, with the slurs being as unpredictable as they are, one can see the absurdity of such categorical statements as the one made by Fritz Rothschild with regard to "keyboard touch" (*Musical Performance in the Times of Mozart and Beethoven* [New York: Oxford University Press, 1961], p. 40): "What is important is that throughout the entire 18th century one did *not play legato unless it was indicated by signs*" (italics his). Rothschild had in mind the "ordinary movement" cited in our table of generalizations. But where would this advice leave us, then, in the most expressive pieces of the almost unmarked volumes of *The Well-Tempered Clavier*?

"choppy," the usual preference being eight notes to a bow. Even allowing for different techniques, instruments, and musical attitudes in Bach's day, one has to keep reminding himself that Bach's slurs seem to have been inserted more at random and less consistently than those of Haydn, Mozart, and Beethoven in their most mature works, not to mention the still more meticulous editing done by the chief Romantics. Very often Bach's slurs appear only at the start as an indication of the performance style, and then discontinue entirely or almost so (as in Vn 3/iv).

Finally, one needs to keep remembering one factor in the understanding of Bach's slurs and that is their frequent ambiguity in the autographs. Sometimes sitting almost like incomplete circles high above the notes, they often leave considerable doubt as to where they begin and end. Usually their limits can be guessed fairly safely by analogy with clearer slurs over similar passages. But as we saw, Bach is not always that routine. Modern editors, including those of the remarkably fine *Neue Ausgabe*, having to commit themselves one way or another, have generally felt safer when they at least make the slurring consistent. But in not a few instances here, including two of the foregoing examples, a different reading has seemed more likely.[16] Two other problems of legibility hamper the study of articulation in the autographs (over and above any decay of the autograph itself). One is Bach's habit of letting individual parts extend beyond the barline when they cannot be squeezed into the measure (as in BC 1/ii/8). The other is the familiar and ubiquitous problem of distinguishing between the remarkably few dots, wedges, and even dashes (as in BC 4/i/231–33), not to mention mere smudges and ink blots. Although distinctions in the latter are undoubtedly intended at least some of the time, most modern editors have preferred to give up this battle, simply reducing all such marks that seem to be intentional to dots.

---

16. For example, the editors of the *Neue Ausgabe* are probably right in the consistent slurring of BC 3/i/2 and 3, but they seem less justified in their decisions in Vn 4/v/216–224 ("Ciaccona"), where several of the slurs apply more likely to the last three notes, only, of the quadruplets. The sharply differentiated slurrings in the triplets at measures 244 and 245 of the same piece are unequivocal in the autograph. But the ambiguity of the slurs in Vc 3/iii is as great as in Bach's fair copy of his ninth Two-Part Invention.

INSTRUMENTAL SCORING IN THE

CHAMBER CANTATAS OF FRANCESCO CONTI

Efrim and Caroline Fruchtman
MEMPHIS STATE UNIVERSITY

The first quarter of the eighteenth century saw both the fruition of the Italian chamber cantata and its decline as an intimate vocal solo or duet with *basso continuo*. Francesco Conti (1682–1732) is one of the Italian composers whose secular cantatas represent both the stereotyped formal design associated with A. Scarlatti and his contemporaries and also the trend toward a more pretentious, instrumentally accompanied festival piece. As court composer in Vienna, Conti preserved in his cantatas the traditional alternation of *da capo* aria and recitative and, like many of his European contemporaries, also utilized instrumental resources available to him in at least fourteen of his secular cantatas. Our purpose here is to examine these works with reference to their instrumental scoring.

Twelve cantatas exist in manuscript at the Österreichische Nationalbibliothek, Vienna, and presumably were composed in Vienna or were intended for performance at the court. The thirteenth cantata, a wedding cantata in honor of the betrothal of Maria Gioseffa, daughter of Joseph I, to the Elector of Saxony, is preserved at the Sächsische Landesbibliothek in Dresden. The fourteenth cantata is in manuscript at the Deutsche Staatsbibliothek, Berlin. The authors have made no study of Conti's holographs and cannot suggest the possibility of autographs for any of these cantatas.[1]

---

1. See the Appendix to this article for complete titles and scoring of the fourteen cantatas. Cantatas will be cited according to their number in the Appendix.

The Italian chamber cantata as associated with the earlier works of A. Scarlatti, Handel, Ristori, Marcello, Caldara, etc. consisted almost always of two or three arias, usually preceded by recitatives: *r-a-r-a, a-r-a, a-r-a-r-a.*[2] Ternary structure, the prevailing pattern of the aria, was set to a four-line stanza. The first two lines, immediately repeated, furnished the text for the *A* section of the music. The second two lines, set to a somewhat different melody from the *A* section and composed in a different key, provided the text for the *B* section of the music. The return of *A* was understood and was almost always indicated by the *da capo* sign.

The *secco* recitative had, as in opera, become the standard procedure and was characterized by a bass mostly in half-note values progressing in fast harmonic rhythm. Likewise similar to the opera, the explanatory narrative of the recitative gave the factual background to the sentiments of the succeeding aria. The *basso continuo* was realized by the cembalo player alone or together with a bass string instrument: violoncello and/or violone.

By the end of the first half of the eighteenth century the cantata had lost some of its intimate chamber music quality and was moving toward the grand cantata type, which is stylistically related to opera and oratorio. This more ambitious cantata was often scored for strings plus oboe or flute, and occasionally brasses and tympani were included as accompanying instruments. Throughout the first quarter of the century, however, the grand cantata with instruments was not yet commonplace.

Most European composers during the first half of the eighteenth century were equally at home writing operas, cantatas, or oratorios; Conti also created in all these genres.[3] Born in Florence January 20, 1682, he went to Vienna in 1701 and was em-

2. References to the form of the Italian secular cantata and chamber duet may be found in Edward Dent, *Alessandro Scarlatti* (London, 1905); *Ibid.,* "The Italian Chamber Cantata," *The Musical Antiquary,* II (1910–11), 189–95; Eugen Schmitz, *Geschichte der weltlichen Solokantate* (Leipzig: Breitkopf und Härtel, 1955); Hans Engel *et al.,* "Kantate," *MGG,* VII, 553–80.

3. Robert Eitner, *Quellen-Lexikon* (Graz, Austria, 1959), III, and Bernhard Paumgartner, "Francesco Conti," *MGG,* II, 1640, account for about 10 oratorios, about 28 operas (including *Serenata, Festa teatrale, Intermezzo,* etc.), about 60 solo cantatas with *Bc,* and 14 cantatas with instruments.

ployed as theorbo player at the emperor's *Hofkapelle*. Later, from January 1, 1713 until his death July 20, 1732, Conti served as court composer. At this time Vienna was an artistic and cultural center where three successive emperors were not only devoted patrons of music and the arts but were performers and composers themselves: Leopold I (d. 1705), his sons Joseph I (d. 1711), and Charles VI (d. 1740).[4] The Hapsburgs attracted to their court the composers A. Pancotti (*Hofkapellmeister*), M. A. Ziani (*Vizekapellmeister*), G. B. Bononcini, P. F. Tosi, J. J. Fux (*Hofkapellmeister*), F. T. Richter, C. Draghi, and J. G. Reinhard. The court theater under Joseph I performed twelve to fourteen new operas a year and employed the poets P. A. Bernardoni and S. Stampiglia, who furnished libretti for such court composers as A. Ariosti, A. Caldara, and Conti. Official poets under Charles VI were Apostolo Zeno and Pietro Pariati. Besides J. J. Fux and the Italian composers just mentioned, Charles also employed Nicola Porpora and Antonio Lotti.[5]

At the Viennese court was one of the largest orchestras of the eighteenth century. According to Köchel (*Die Kaiserliche Hofmusikkapelle zu Wien von 1543 bis 1867*, Vienna, 1869) the instruments at the *Hofkapelle* in 1721—a date approximately the same as two of the cantatas in the appendix—numbered 23 violins, 4 violoncelli, 3 contrabassi, 5 oboes, 4 bassoons, 1 horn, 16 trumpets, 2 drums, a gamba, lute, 2 cornetti, and 4 trombones.[6] Of these instruments horn, viola da gamba, cornetto, and trombone are not specifically indicated in any of the fourteen cantatas. Conti did score for chalumeau, although this instrument is not included in the orchestra census above. The first five cantatas in the appendix specify the use of chalumeau, and much other music composed for the Viennese court also required its use.[7]

---

4. Hugo Hantsch, *Die Geschichte Österreichs* (Graz-Wien, n.d.), II, 140–41; Franz Mayer, *Geschichte Österreichs* (Wien: Braumüller, 1909), II; Othmayer Wessely, "Joseph I," *MGG*, VII, 181–85.

5. Hantsch, *Die Geschichte Österreichs*; Wessely, "Joseph I."

6. Adam Carse, *The Orchestra in the XVIIIth Century* (Cambridge: W. Heffer, 1940), p. 27. The 1730 listing includes one theorbo in addition to lute. Heinz Becker, "Orchester," *MGG*, X, Plate XIII, lists two theorbos for 1729.

7. J. J. van der Meer, "Letter to the Editor: The Chalumeau Problem," *Galpin Society Journal*, XV (1962), 89–90, identifies this chalumeau as probably being an instrument with seven holes, two keys and a range from f' up

Although details of instrumentation vary in the fourteen manuscripts, the basic ensemble consists of violins (sometimes divided), a continuo line, and one pair of soprano woodwinds (flute, oboe, or chalumeau). A part for viola may be designated by the name of the instrument or simply by the presence of the part in alto clef. Cantatas XIII and XIV indicate the use of the bassoon, and cantata XIII requires in addition the use of two trumpets and tympani. Cantatas I through V contain lute parts in French tablature, and cantata XIV includes a bass part for the theorbo.

The flute and the chalumeau are the only instruments for which Conti wrote extended solo parts. Solo passages for these instruments are present in cantatas II, III, IV, V, and X. These vary in character from simple, folk-like melodies of the type found in the second cantata to highly florid obbligatos. The chalumeau obbligato in the aria, "I bei fregi, ch'adornan," (cantata III) is especially characteristic of this latter type. The spun-out part with its expressive skips is reminiscent of *adagio* obbligatos in the music of J. S. Bach (Example 1). A similarly ornate obbligato for solo flute is found in "Nella Rosa mi piace," from cantata X, where the scoring reflects the technical resources

Example 1

to b-flat" or even b" or c". The chalumeau was indicated in the instrumentation for M. A. Ziani's *Cajo Pompilio* (1704); in G. B. Bononcini's *Endimione* (1706), *Turno Aricino* (1707), and in *La conquista delle Spagne* (1717); in M. A. Bononcini's *Trionfo della Grazia* (1717); in Ariosti's *Marte placato* (1707); and Fux's *Julio Ascanio* (1708). All these operas were written for the Viennese court where the instrument was fairly regularly in use from the first decade of the century to the time of Bonno, Dittersdorf, and Gluck, the latter scoring for chalumeau in *Orfeo* and *Alceste*. The chalumeau parts in the Conti scores are written within the pitch range described above by van der Meer.

of the instrument (Example 2). An interesting contrast in textures is achieved in "Un pensiero meno sognero," from cantata
V. In section *A unisoni* violins are used, giving way to solo
chalumeau in section *B*.

Example 2

Instrumental doubling is indicated by the use of the term "*unisoni*" and by the plural form of the name of the instrument
(*violini, leuti, viole,* etc.).[8] Sometimes doubled parts are actually
written out. In cantata X the two violin and the two flute parts
are scored on four staves even though much of the first violin
and first flute parts are sounded in unison, as are also the second
violin and second flute parts. The most common doubling occurs
when the two woodwinds reinforce the two violin parts. There
are instances, as in cantata XII, where the violins and the woodwinds are given separate, unison parts. A rather unusual doubling
occurs in cantata XI in which appears the direction: "*Tutti
l'hautb. all'primo violino.*" The lute tablatures of the first five
cantatas reveal a doubling of the continuo bass, the treble instrumental part, and sometimes also the vocal line.

---

8. The chalumeau is always indicated in its plural form even when one
instrument must obviously be intended. The instrumental part in the aria cited
in Example 1 appears designated "*chaloumaux solo.*"

These lute tablatures are, in effect, the composer's realization of the continuo bass. In addition to doubling the parts just referred to, the tablatures also provide the chordal harmony and sections of descant. Conti, of course, used other instruments in the ensemble to reinforce and sustain these filler materials. In one instance the violins (*sordini*) are assigned the task of reinforcing an arpeggiated accompaniment in the lute (Example 3).

Example 3

"Lontananza dell'amato."   Cantata I.

Since the cantatas containing the lute tablatures also contain *basso continuo* parts, the possibility should be considered that two instruments were intended to realize the continuo. It should be noted in this regard that two other cantatas, IX and XI, contain the indication "à 2" beside the bass line. Two different bass lines are written in cantata X, and apparently both of these would require realization (See Example 8). The Berlin cantata, No. XIV, contains three written-out bass lines: one each to the bassoon, the theorbo, and the cembalo. The theorbo line, frequently more ornate than the other two basses, contains occasional indications for the arpeggiation of chords (Example 4).

Example 4

"Si trovero Bella che m'ami."   Cantata XIV.

Continuo realization responsibility is delegated to the violins in the only accompanied recitative in *secco* style, "Vaghi flugelletti che d'amor," from cantata IV. Here the two violins sustain chord tones that are also present in the lute score and figured in the continuo part. Passages of this kind alternate with passages of *secco* recitative for the voice and continuo alone (Example 5). Of the nonrealizing bass instruments, the bassoon is specifi-

Example 5

"Vaghi flugelletti che d'amor." Cantata IV.
Con violini, leuti, chaloumeux.

cally indicated in cantata XIV. There also appears the direction, "*Violoncelli soli*," in portions of the continuo line in this cantata. Obviously, any bass instrument of reasonable flexibility would serve to reinforce the continuo line.

Except in solo passages the woodwind parts supplement the basic orchestration. They are usually withdrawn when there is a change in dynamics from loud to soft and at entries of the voice. There is usually little evidence of instrumental style in scoring except in the extended solo sections. There are, however, passages that indicate concern with the use of instrumental combinations in relation to the musical context. These contrast remarkably with other passages in the cantatas reflecting older practice. Illustrative of the latter is the introduction to the aria, "Giunga presto il lieto," from cantata VII. Here terrace scoring is the result of juxtaposing the full orchestra with a string ensemble of violins and violas (Example 6). Suggestive of orchestration prac-

Example 6

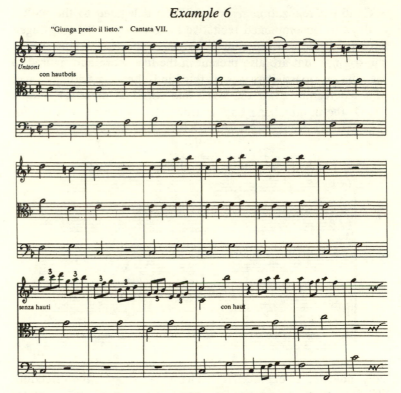

"Giunga presto il lieto."   Cantata VII.

tice in some of the music of Haydn and Mozart is the passage from "Vola à tempo," from cantata VII in which the *violini soli* execute a scale passage leading to the cadence figuration reinforced by the entire orchestra (Example 7). And finally, the opening portion of cantata X indicates a feeling for individual

Example 7

"Vola à tempo."   Cantata VII.

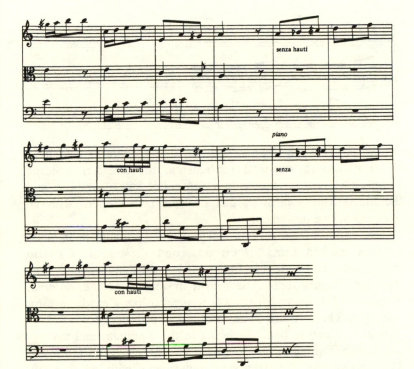

instrumental colors. In this example three different groupings are used: flutes and violins; violins and basses; and the entire ensemble (Example 8).

Conti's scoring for instruments affects the formal structure of these cantatas. Thirteen follow the traditional plan of three or four arias alternating with recitative, and one has five arias with

Example 8

recitatives. However, two of the three-aria cantatas also have self-contained instrumental movements: the Dresden wedding cantata (XIII) that opens with a *sinfonia* of four movements and the Maria Teresa birthday cantata (XII) that opens with an overture of one movement.

The *sinfonia* from cantata XII has a first movement in three sections marked *Introduzioni*; a second movement, *L'istesso tempo*, which is a double fugue; and a third movement, *Larghetto*, in binary form. The fourth movement of the *sinfonia*, *Allegro*, defies categorizing but is somewhat like a rondo in form and style. The overture to cantata XII is in binary form—*Allegro assai* of sixteen bars cadencing in the dominant and twenty-one bars beginning in the dominant and cadencing in the tonic. The appearance of instrumental movements with no thematic relation to the arias in early eighteenth-century secular cantatas is one indication of the direction toward the grand cantata and away from the intimate solo cantata.

The basic plan of these cantatas, except for the additional instrumental movements, is essentially the same as that found in most secular cantatas. A study of the aria, however, shows several departures from the traditional *da capo* form. While the majority of the arias are *da capo* in form, there are five that adhere to what might be described as a four-part, cumulative scoring plan. The final arias in cantatas I, II, IV, and V all follow this procedure:

A   scored for soprano and *Bc*
A   (*Rittornello*) scored for instruments only
B   scored for soprano, instruments, and *Bc*
A   scored for soprano, instruments, and *Bc*

The phrase structure, moreover, unlike the melismatic-type of vocal line in the traditional *da capo* aria, is symmetrical, being generally in four-bar segments. Although these arias are basically tripartite in the use of musical ideas, there is no real return to the *A* section as it first appeared. Here the use of instruments influenced the *da capo* structure, since the immediate repetition of *A* scored for instruments alone results in four sections, not three. The *B* section loses its former prominence and the aria is lent a quality of the strophic song.[9]

Cantata XII has two arias that fit neither the *da capo* plan nor the structure described above. The first, from the Maria Teresa birthday cantata, was mentioned previously as being preceded by an instrumental overture (37 measures in length). The aria, "Fermate, fermate," is very short (15 measures) and is more in the nature of an arioso or accompanied recitative. It is followed by a *secco* recitative, "Qui dove scorgerete." A shortened version of the instrumental movement returns (12 measures), and is followed by a repetition of the aria (10 bars). Such an arrangement resembles a *scène* from a French cantata, a form that shows operatic and instrumental influences to a greater extent than does the Italian counterpart.[10] The final aria, "Contente ad altra riva," has an *A* section scored for voice and *Bc*; a *B* section for instruments alone; a return of *A* extended for voice and instruments; and still another version of *A* for voice and *Bc*. The final seven bars bring back the instruments alone. In both these instances the presence of instrumental scoring in the chamber cantata brings about modifications in the form of the *da capo* aria.

In the unaccompanied chamber cantata, the *A* section usually begins with an introduction for the *Bc*, or with a motto beginning that is immediately followed by a *Bc* introduction. This introduction is usually not long (averaging about eight measures) and presents the same bass line as that of the opening vocal phrase.

---

9. A variation of this plan is found in cantata VIII (a duet), last aria, where the conventional *da capo* aria is scored for soprano and *Bc*. After the return of *A* (indicated by the sign) there is a written-out *A* section scored for instruments alone, so that the *rittornello* ends the aria: ABAA.

10. *See* Louis Nicholas Clérambault, "Fidelles echos," from *Orphée* (*Cantate francaise a voix seule avec symphonie* No. 3 in *Livre I* (1710).

In Conti's cantatas, on the other hand, the use of accompanying instruments provides an opportunity for longer introductions (rarely under eight bars in length and often up to 24). The lengthening of this introductory section of the aria changes the proportion between purely instrumental sections and vocal sections, since the introduction, or most of it, usually is written out at the end of the *A* section and is often heard the third time if repeated with the return of *A*. Furthermore, in nearly half the arias from these cantatas the musical material of the introduction is not the same as that of the later vocal entry. The introduction does often contain material that appears throughout the *A* section, but such use is usually confined to the instrumental parts. On occasion, melody playing instruments in the introduction present a modified version of the theme sung by the vocal soloist, pointing up divergencies in instrumental and vocal style (Example 9).

Example 9

"Quando veggi un'usignolo."   Cantata IX.

The presence of instruments in Conti's cantatas adds new dimensions to the basic *basso continuo*-voice framework. Greater dynamic contrast is now possible through orchestration and is evidenced in the handling of woodwinds and other doubling instruments. Harmonies normally provided by the continuo instruments are now frequently sustained and augmented in the assigning of chord parts to the instruments of the orchestral ensemble. The use of instruments for their characteristic colors adds still another dimension. In addition, the somewhat superficial modifications in the cantata structure indicate the gradual transformation of the secular cantata from a truly vocal solo intended for the salon and capable of improvisation by both soloist and *Bc* player to an ensemble work calling for a less casual performance at a concert or royal occasion.

APPENDIX

Österreicheische Nationalbibliothek, Vienna.
Codex 17593.
Cantate con Instromenti di Francesco Conti.

I.   Cantata Prima. "Lontananza dell'amato" Poesia del P.
     Savallia, [scored for] Chaloumaux, Flutte Allemand au
     Hautbois, Violini Sordini, Leuti Francesi, Soprano, and
     Continuo.

II. Cantata Seconda. "Ride a prato e fra'l'erbe" con Violini,
     Leuti, Flauto ò Chaloumaux, Soprano, and Continuo.

III. Cantata Terza, "Con più Luci" [scored for] Chaloumaux
     e due Violini con Leuto, Soprano, and Continuo.

IV. Cantata 4ª. "Vaghi flugelletti che d'amor" con Violini e
     Leuti con Chaloumaux, Soprano, and Continuo.

V.   Cantata 5ª. "La beltà chei core adora" Poesia del C.
     Stella, con Leuti e violini e chaloumaux, Soprano and
     Continuo.

VI. Cantata 6ª. "Gira per queste" Poesia del Stampiglia, con
     Violini [I and II] e Hoboa, Soprano, and Continuo.

VII. Cantata 7ª. "Fugga l'ombra tenebrosa della Aurora"
     Poesia di F. Savallia, con Violini [I and II], e Haubois,
     Soprano, and Continuo.

VIII.   Cantata à due Voci con Instromenti. "Fra questi colli" [scored for] Violini [I and II], Haubois, Soprano, Soprano, and Continuo.

Codex 17582

IX.   Cantata à 2 Soprani con Instromenti di Francesco Conti. "Clori nemica ed Irene Seguace d'Amore" [scored for] Violini e Hautbois Unissoni, Viola, Clori [Sop.], Irene [Sop.], Continuo à 2.

Codex 17589

X.   Cantata à Voce sola con Violini, e Flauti. "O nasca, ò muora il giorno" [scored for] Flauto Primo, Flauto Secondo, Violino Primo, Violino Secondo, Soprano, Continuo, and Continuo.

Codex 17590

XI.   Cantata à due Voci. Clizia, e Psiche. Per il Felicissimo, e glorioso Nome dell'Augustissima Imperadrice Regnante, [scored for] Violini et Haubois, Viola, Clizia [Sop.], Psiche [Alto], Continuo à 2.

Codex 17651

XII.   Cantata Allegorica. Festeggiandosi il Felicissimo Nome di Maria Teresa, Infanta di Spagna et Arciduchessa D'Austria, L'Anno 1720, Poesia di Pietro Pariati, Poeta di S.M.C. e Catt^{ca}, Musica di Franc:^{co} Conti Comp:^{re} di Cam:^a di S.M.C. e Catt:^{ca}. [scored for] Violini I, Violini II, Viola, Soprano, and Continuo.

Sächsische Landesbibliothek, Dresden.
Mus. 2190/1/1

XIII.   L'Istro. Cantata per Musica. Da Cantarsi per ordine Cesareo, la sera delli sponsali del Sereniss:^{mo} Principe Elettorale di Sassonia con la Serenissima Maria Gioseffa Arciduchessa d'Austria. Poesia dell' Apostolo Zeno, Poeta di S:M:C: e C:^{ca}. Musica di Francesco Conti Comp:^{re} di S:M:C: e C:^{ca} [scored for] Tromba prima,

Tromba seconda, Timpano, Violini et Haut:, Viole, Soprano, and Bassi.

This marriage took place 1719, but there is no date on this manuscript.

Deutsche Staatsbibliothek, Berlin.
No. 159
XIV.   "Lidia giá mi vedesti" Cantata in Soprano, 2 Hautbois, Violino all'Unissono, Violetta, Fagotti, Tiorba, Cembalo.

MUSICOLOGY IN THE UNITED STATES:

A SURVEY OF RECENT TRENDS[1]

Gwynn S. McPeek
UNIVERSITY OF MICHIGAN

The appropriation of cultural heritage and its interpretation by the present are not constants but historical variables; in other words, they belong themselves to our own past.

. . . The age of discovery, the bringing to light of new sources, is on the whole over, though it is not unlikely that some new and important sources will be brought to light in the future, but on the whole we must resign ourselves to the fact that future progress will lie primarily not in the further accumulation of material but in the close and necessarily slow investigation of the material presently known. The turn from breadth to depth in musicological study is a clear indication that we have arrived at a stage of stylistic study which concentrates on the music itself and relies on the analysis of the music as its primary method and evidence.[2]

It is now a decade since Bukofzer wrote those words for a public that did not see or hear them during his lifetime. In the light of his prognostic and diagnostic remarks it may be beneficial to examine the recent past to see what points of view have

---

1. Glen Haydon gave this title to an article published in *PMTNA,* 1947, pp. 321–41. In view of the purpose for which these remarks are intended, as well as their content, it seems appropriate to apply the same title here.

2. Manfred Bukofzer, "Changing Aspects of Medieval and Renaissance Music," *MQ,* XLIV (1958), 1 and 3. Published posthumously, it is believed to have been intended for the Oxford Congress of the International Musicological Society in 1955.

emerged, what matters have concerned musical scholars, and what it all means with respect to the evolving and developing field of musicology. These years have seen a dramatic growth in musical scholarship; in the number of persons dedicated to the discipline; in breadth and depth of interests. In addition, various methods of approach reflect important changes of attitude.

The primary concern here is neither the statement and justification of a new systematization of American musicology, nor a critical evaluation of any that have been stated. Neither is it a history of it, nor a bibliography of its accomplishments, nor a statement of the problems and difficulties that face it. Instead, our subject is the philosophy of American musicology as revealed in what musicologists have written and said; in other words, our concern is with the record and significance of recent American musicology.

Bukofzer draws attention to the fact that the interpretation of cultural heritage is a historical variable. The truth of his statement is nowhere in greater evidence than in the comparison of current with former attitudes toward the scope and aim of musicology. In the early years of American musicology the name, the definition, the scope, and the aim of the field were considered more frequently, perhaps, than any other topics both in published form and in public and private forum. The first decade after the founding of the American Musicological Society in 1934 saw the appearance of no fewer than sixteen articles and papers (some of considerable length), and one complete book, all dealing with the field as a whole—more than three times the number that appeared in the ensuing two decades. The authors' names are familiar: Otto Kinkeldey, Harold Spivacke, Otto Ortmann, Roy Dickinson Welch, George Sherman Dickinson, Oliver Strunk, Donald Ferguson, Gustave Reese, Charles Seeger, Curt Sachs, Glen Haydon, Paul Henry Lang, and Willi Apel. They represent the strong, sound foundations on which our present and future edifice stands. Whatever the view presented, and there was no more unanimity of opinion then than now, the discipline received comment.

In contrast, during the fifteen years from 1944 to 1959 only one article dealt with the field as a whole: Paul Lang's "On

Musicology," in 1947.[3] Statements by others touch upon the problem, but are concerned primarily either with some aspect or branch of the field, or with musicology and its relation to another field or within a larger setting.[4] In short, concern with the aim and scope of American musicology practically disappeared from public discussion and was relegated to the classroom or to informal dialogues. It is significant that no new schematization of the field was offered, and that when a new scheme finally did appear, it took a sharply different form.

Reawakened interest in defining American Musicology is evidenced by the appearance in 1959 of Lloyd Hibberd's article, "Musicology Reconsidered." [5] From a philosophical point of view he presents the first of the new schematizations. Two articles followed in 1961, both bearing on the impending international congress in New York: "The Growth and Influence of Musicology in the United States," by Scott Goldthwaite; [6] and "Codetta: Some Details of Musicology in the United States," [7] by Jan LaRue. Although Goldthwaite and LaRue were not concerned with the field as a whole, the timeliness of their articles aroused still further thought and comment.

In 1963, two books appeared that deal extensively with the problem. The earlier by a matter of weeks was *Historical Musicology* by Lincoln Spiess,[8] which contains supporting essays bearing on our problem by Ernst Krohn, Lloyd Hibberd, Luther Dittmer, Tsang-Houei Shu, Tatsuo Minagawa, and Zdenek Nováček. Intended as a reference manual for research, the book

3. *MQ*, XXXIII (1947), 557–64.

4. For example: "Musical Scholarship at the Crossroads," *MQ*, XXXI (1945), 371–80 by Lang; "Historical Musicology," in *The Music Journal* (Nov.–Dec.,1946), pp. 19–27, by Bukofzer; "Musical Scholarship and the University," *MD* (formerly *The Journal of Renaissance and Baroque Music*), I (1948), 10–18 by Kindeldey; "Systematic Musicology," *JAMS*, IV (1951), 240–48 by Seeger; *The Place of Musicology in American Institutions of Higher Learning* by Bukofzer (New York: The Liberal Arts Press, 1957); and *Some Aspects of Musicology*, three essays by Mendel, Sachs, and Pratt (New York: The Liberal Arts Press, 1957).

5. *AM*, XXXI (1959), 25–31.

6. *AM*, XXXIII (1961), 72–79.

7. *Ibid.*, pp. 79–83.

8. (Brooklyn: The Medieval Institute).

does not directly propose a new scheme, although the point of view is clear particularly in the essays by Krohn, Dittmer and Hibberd. The other book, *Musicology*,[9] treats the field extensively in essays by Frank Ll. Harrison, Claude V. Palisca, and Mantle Hood.

The next development in this sequence took place at the 1964 annual convention of the AMS, where an entire plenary session was devoted to consideration of American musicology. The initial paper, "A Profile for American Musicology," was read by Joseph Kerman and published in the succeeding issue of *JAMS*.[10] In it Kerman proposed that American musicology should concern itself chiefly with criticism and "critical insight" in the highest sense. By following such a path, he envisaged elevation of stature and improved quality which at the same time would constitute a uniquely American contribution without dependence on European models. Brief comments on the paper were given by Victor Yellin and Barry Brook, with a lengthy reply read by Edward Lowinsky, later also published in *JAMS*.[11] Lowinsky objected to Kerman's proposal as being too limited in scope to serve as the total sphere of activity, and, furthermore, unsuited to many who might engage in musicology with profit to all the field. He also objected to nationalistic implications that might be drawn from exclusion of European scholarship.

Thus, while there was no more agreement in 1964 than in 1934, the events and documents since 1959 show widespread concern for the nature, the aim, the scope, and the future of American musicology. That self-conscious concern, contrasting sharply with the relative lack of it during the preceding fifteen years, constitutes an important recent trend in American musicology.

The four recent treatments share a common ground: they present the field of musicology as an essentially humanistic discipline, a view widely held among nonmusic scholars as well as

---

9. *The Princeton Studies: Humanistic Scholarship in America* (Englewood Cliffs, N.J.: Prentice-Hall, Inc.).

10. *JAMS*, XVIII (1965), 61–69.

11. "The Character and Purposes of American Musicology," *JAMS*, XVIII (1965), 222–34.

musicologists. Humanistic bias is exhibited in three ways: first, either they clearly state that view (Palisca), or they betray it by emphasizing the humanistic aspects of musicology; second, they accord a less prominent place to scientific elements among musicology's component parts; and third, they lay considerable stress on the relation between musicology and other humanistic disciplines.

Interrelationship with other humanities and the essentially humanistic nature of music itself were never denied or put to question among the older systems. On the contrary, these elements seem to have been assumed as integral, and therefore required little stress. It is precisely this point, more than any other, that distinguishes between the former and the present approaches. In the field as conceived by Kinkeldey or Haydon, the relation of musicology to other humanistic disciplines such as literary criticism, language and linguistics, liturgics, sociology, philosophy, cultural history, etc., was assumed, while great attention was given to musicology as a science closely connected with acoustics, physiology, psychology, etc. The matter is one of emphasis, and a considerable emphasis was placed on the scientific aspects of music in the older schematizations.

In the new systems, scientific aspects of musicology are deemphasized sharply in favor of elements that are humanistic in both their processes and end results. Hibberd, under his general classification of "Research," places all scientific and aesthetic matters within categories termed "tangential," "marginal," or "intermediate." Under "Primarily Musical," he places all those matters that are humanistic by their very nature. In addition, he discusses allied disciplines that are closely related to musicology, that are of considerable use to the field, and nearly all are generally classified as humanistic rather than scientific. The Hibberd system of classification places the humanistic aspects of musicology in a foremost position.

Spiess's *Historical Musicology* reflects the same attitudes. Through discussion and bibliographical lists, Spiess draws continual attention to books that correlate the arts and activities of man. In fact, the title of the book itself reveals its humanistic bent. Even more indicative, however, is the inclusion of a lengthy essay on linguistics by Luther Dittmer, emphasizing still further a humanistic bias. Hibberd's essay in *Historical Musicology* discusses musical research problems and organization, and casts that organization in a mold almost identical to that found in many other humanistic fields, but wholly dissimilar to the research plan common in science. No scientific subject receives extended treatment in the book.

Palisca clearly states his view that musicology is a humanistic study closely related to other humanistic disciplines. Throughout his essay he puts to question the place of science in musicology and emphasizes those aspects that can only be called humanistic.

It is obvious in the foregoing that the word *science* signifies a far different concept from that implied by Haydon, Kinkeldey, or Pratt. Especially since World War II, the two adjectives *scientific* and *systematic* have drawn farther and farther apart in meaning. By common usage *science* has come to have a more restricted significance, and its use now as practically synonymous with *systematic* would be anachronistic, while its use in a figurative sense would be confusing.[12] Central to the Palisca essay is the question of whether a procedure that is systematic is therefore necessarily scientific. But this is not merely a matter of terminology; it is a question of fundamental emphasis that has extensive ramifications. The scope of musicology is far different if one follows a humanistic emphasis, using the processes of science to attain an interpretive end, while avoiding science's repetitive experimental method. The scope becomes at once more restricted and more broad—more restricted in the sense that acoustics, physiology, psychology, aesthetics, etc., are relegated to positions among allied fields, and broader in that other humanistic disciplines (as well as interrelations between those disciplines) such as linguistics and cultural history, are included not only as attendant or allied fields but as component parts of musicology.

---

12. Professor Albert Luper made the following observation in a recent letter to the author: ". . . some of the seeming earlier emphasis on 'scientific' is partly a semantic one. . . . I believe that it was the German term *Wissenschaft* that is partly responsible, in being translated too narrowly to mean 'science,' rather than its broader meaning of 'scholarship' and scholarly investigation." There is little question that Mr. Luper is correct, and, as the paragraph above implies, that semantic difference itself is a significant development.

The normal historical process of selection and emphasis is operative here, and the currently selected attitudes are humanistic, whatever categories may be proposed as embodying the scope and purpose of musicology.

Recent scholarship in music has made copious use of linguistics, archaeology, anthropology, liturgics, literary criticism, most especially of cultural history, and many other fields—exactly those fields that are mentioned most frequently nowadays as valuable allied fields. Musicologists recognize among the humanities a community of interest, of aims, of methods, and of end results. Proof of such awareness lies in the growing number of musicologists whose names are found among the membership of the Modern Language Association, the American Historical Association, the Medieval Academy, the Renaissance Society, and the like. Contact with the sciences and attendant methodologies appears to have been less intimate. While the musicologist (particularly the ethnomusicologist) adopts apparatus originating in the electronics laboratory, he employs such devices as tools to lead him toward a humanistic, interpretive goal. In general the means he uses are much more analogous to those of scholars in other humanistic disciplines than to those of the science laboratory.

As Bukofzer suggests, each generation interprets history in its own way. Accordingly, the change that has come with the years is obvious in recent American historiography. Three attitudes are immediately apparent: first, musical historians have come to consider historiography as consisting not merely of a chronology of personalities and artifacts, but of the analysis and interpretation of those facts as well; second, they no longer consider aesthetic value as the main criterion by which suitability for scholarly inquiry is justified; third, and most significant, musical historians have come to recognize that music neither does, nor did, exist in a world apart, that to comprehend adequately the music of a time or place, one must consider also the society that provided the climate for its creation.

Waldo Selden Pratt's *History of Music* (1907) is essentially a biographical and documentary approach to the problem of music history. It contains little of musical description or criticism.

Theodore Finney's *History of Music* (1931) has a similar bio-graphical orientation, and essentially it too is a chronology of men and forms. Karl Nef's *Outline History of Music* is originally a German work, but the English translation of 1935 with notes and bibliographical references by Paul Lang was widely used as a text and reference work, and exerted considerable influence. Containing sound scholarship and extensive documentation, it was the leader in the United States for a time. Nef's book intro-duces some musical criticism and commentary on musical style, but following a strictly narrative, highly objective approach, it is basically a chronology of musical facts most often devoid of interpretation. Factual significance and relative importance some-times must be deduced largely from the way and to what length facts are presented. Of all these, Finney's book is the only one to come to grips with the problems of music in its own time, as well as the only one to mention American music or musicians.

Paul Lang's *Music in Western Civilization* (1941) represents a radically different approach. Full of symbolic reference, often impressionistic in musical description, and always assuming the reader's acquaintance with the music he discusses, Lang places music against a broad cultural and intellectual background. In an introductory chapter to each musico-historical unit, he de-scribes the milieu surrounding the music to be discussed. It is precisely this humanistic approach, joined with splendid docu-mentation, that accounts for the book's continuing utility and interest a quarter-century after publication.

Curt Sachs employs an integrative approach in *Our Musical Heritage* (1948). While the book itself concerns only music, the full comprehension of much that he says depends upon suggested additional readings, drawn mostly from his *Commonwealth of Art, World History of the Dance,* and *History of Musical Instru-ments.* Taken together they form a comprehensive and singularly humanistic combination. Sachs departs from traditional patterns also in that he lays great stress on folk and popular art forms, and upon ethnomusicology, its methods, and processes.

Concurrently, some period histories have exerted an influence that is difficult to overestimate. Gustave Reese's *Music in the Middle Ages* (1940), and *Music in the Renaissance* (1954;

1959), are among the most widely-disseminated and often-used American sources. Not only have they set superb standards of scholarship, but they also have great influence on American historiography of all eras, and, since they exhibit definite views as to the methods of musicology, they have exerted influence over a much broader area than their specific subject matter.

Manfred Bukofzer's *Music in the Baroque Era* (1947), has had a similar effect. Moreover, by opening with a discussion of considerable length devoted to the intellectual and cultural basis of the Baroque Era, and by including a later chapter treating the sociology of the Baroque Era, Bukofzer reflects the concern of musical historians with extra-musical considerations.

Donald Grout's *The History of Western Music* [13] is a history of musical styles. It represents at the same time a synthesis of former methods and a reflection of the widespread preoccupation among American scholars with stylistic matters. Significantly, instead of separate chapters for extra-musical considerations, such matters are woven into the fabric of the work as appropriate occasions warrant, the humanistic relations assimilated into the whole. Here, too, is a strong tendency to view music as a humanistic study integrated into a broad pattern of cultural history. In a not dissimilar fashion, *The History of Music and Musical Style* [14] by Homer Ulrich and Paul Pisk takes its very origin in music approached as a humanistic art. A further example is Richard Crocker's *A History of Musical Style*.[15] Not only does he employ a broadly humanistic and integrative approach throughout the book, but in the preface he specifically recommends the concurrent reading of ". . . material from social or intellectual history, literature and the other arts. . . ."

Three recent period histories demonstrate similar attitudes. Peter Hansen's *Twentieth Century Music* [16] draws most heavily upon art, particularly painting, in relating music to the general culture of our age, while Joseph Machlis in his *Introduction to*

13. (New York: W. W. Norton, 1960).
14. (New York: Appleton-Century-Crofts, 1962).
15. (New York: McGraw-Hill, 1966).
16. (Boston: Allyn and Bacon, 1961).

Contemporary Music [17] uses literature and political history to achieve a similar end. More recently William Austin's *Music in the Twentieth Century* [18] reflects the breadth of integrative viewpoint, and the depth of perceptive insight that is to be found in the best American scholarship.

The altered point of view is also obvious (particularly through comparative analysis of cultural phenomena) in recent books intended for the general student: *The Way of Music* [19] by William Brandt, *The Art of Music* [20] by Beekman Cannon, Alvin Johnson and William Waite, and *The Enjoyment of Music* [21] by Joseph Machlis. In stressing the relation of music to contemporary philosophy, aesthetics, culture, and general social climate, all three contrast sharply with such prior books as Martin Bernstein's *Introduction to Music*,[22] Theodore Finney's *Hearing Music*,[23] or Edwin Stringham's *Creative Listening*.[24] And, indeed, the latter three were a marked change from what had preceded them.

In all the recent works mentioned, whether scholarly histories or books for the general student, there is a clear effort to interpret music within the broad context of human endeavor. Their authors employ comparative analysis in the same fashion as historians in other humanistic disciplines, and demonstrate a humanistic emphasis to an extent, and in a way that was not characteristic thirty years ago. Musical historiography has become quite a different thing, and its humanistic bias is an important development in recent American musicology.

If, as Palisca states in his essay, the recent practice of musicology has served to restrict its scope, certainly it is equally true that there has been tremendous expansion in depth within those narrower limits. Centuries and geographical areas that were

---

17. (New York: W. W. Norton, 1961).
18. (New York: W. W. Norton, 1966).
19. (Boston: Allyn and Bacon, 1963).
20. (New York: Crowell Publishing Co., 1960).
21. (New York: W. W. Norton, 1957).
22. (New York: Prentice-Hall, Inc., 1937).
23. (New York: Harcourt Brace and Co., 1941).
24. (New York: Prentice-Hall, Inc., 1946).

virtually untouched even a decade ago have acquired importance
and active interest. The number of persons engaged in one or
another aspect of musicology has more than doubled in the last
ten years, and in less than twenty years the membership of the
AMS has increased 700 per cent!

Among the very most significant and important areas which
exhibit dynamic expansion is the field of Ethnomusicology.
Working both in Western folk music and in the music of oriental
peoples, American scholarship has made a genuine contribution.
The formation and rapid growth of an American society of
scholars in the field, along with increasing interest in courses at
the graduate level in various colleges and universities, is concrete
evidence of vitality. Mantle Hood, in the final essay of *Musicology,* relates some of the struggle through which ethnomusicology
has passed to establish itself firmly on the American scene. Although comparatively young and still experiencing all those
difficulties attendant to an early stage of development, little doubt
remains that ethnomusicology will claim an ever-increasing role
of importance.

Study of the music of the Western Hemisphere also has shown
dramatic growth in the past ten years, and recent scholarship has
revealed a large amount of music of high quality from the two
Americas.[25] Scholars also have discovered that in hymns and
gospel songs, whatever their aesthetic value, there lies an important source for gauging popular public taste in the United States.
Recently the area has attracted a great deal of interest and respect among informed musicologists, and no little public acceptance. Gilbert Chase's *America's Music from the Pilgrims to
the Present*[26] was recently published in its second edition—a
remarkable feat for a book on this subject. The second edition of
Chase's *Guide to Latin American Music*[27] already has been issued and a third edition employing the services of a large number
of Latin American scholars is now underway. Robert Stevenson
followed a lengthy list of important books and monographs full
of erudition and scholarly skill with a recent description of Peru-

---

25. For example, Lincoln Spiess's recent discoveries in Mexico.
26. (New York: McGraw-Hill, 1966).
27. (Washington, D.C.: The Pan American Union, 1962).

vian music.[28] And these are only exemplary of a large number of other studies which include editions of music and numerous articles by the staff of the Moravian Music Foundation.

Two University institutes especially concerned with the music of the Americas have been established recently at Tulane University and at Indiana University. This is in addition to extensive work proceeding at the University of Iowa, the University of Michigan, Michigan State University, and St. Louis University, among others. Only the surface of this broad and fertile area has been scratched and surely such expanding interest represents an important trend in American musicology.

Musical bibliography is an area of study which is not only very active, but which also has greatly expanded its scope in the last decade. Significant effort has been expended toward compiling bibliographies of all sorts, by individuals and by groups, working at local, national, and international levels. Of particular interest here is the changing attitude toward bibliography as an area of study. Recent essays and studies suggest that not only is bibliography a tool for the ends of scholarship, but it is a worthy end in itself; that it has become a full-fledged component in the field of musicology; and that it even can become a central method in the approach to problems of musical style. A dissertation completed at Yale in 1963 will serve to illustrate this latter point. Edwin Hanley's "Alessandro Scarlatti's *Cantate da Camera:* A Bibliographical Study," is concerned with stylistic matters but the central method of attack is bibliographical, as the title suggests.

The functions of bibliography in the training of young scholars have attracted considerable interest lately. The Spiess book, as has been noted, is intended as a handbook for students and teachers. Spiess not only commences his book with a chapter that is largely bibliographical, but devotes the largest part to bibliographies and lists. Constant reference is made to the use of bibliography in Hibberd's essay on *The Doctoral Dissertation in Music,* a later chapter in the same book. Hibberd's penetrating article, "The Teaching of Bibliography" in *Notes*[29] not only dis-

---

28. *The Music in Peru: Aboriginal and Viceroyal Epocs* (Washington: The Pan American Union, 1960).

29. *Notes,* XX (1962–63), 33–40.

cusses the matter of its title, but examines as well the scope, content, and aims of bibliography.

In the same issue of *Notes* [30] Vincent Duckles discusses basic textual material for teaching bibliography. He says, "Bibliography can be taught as a body of subject matter, or it can be taught as a tool." Palisca's systematization of the field of musicology seems to include bibliography among the component areas along with music history, ethnomusicology, etc. In using the term "bibliographical musicology," Spiess implies agreement with Palisca's view of bibliography's status in the field. Hibberd, in *AM*, includes lexicography and editing among the component parts of musicology, although he excludes the listing of compositions, which he classifies as bibliography or cataloguing "which are tools for, but not part of, musicology." [31]

Music theory has always occupied an equivocal position in the schematization of musicology, and there is no general agreement on the matter now. Much of the discussion revolves around who writes the theory, what kind of theory it is, and what its purpose and public are intended to be. Palisca would include some kinds of theory, particularly studies in the history of theory or any theory derived from practice (though it is sometimes difficult to know where to draw the line), but he would exclude from musicology any theory that is predictive or that is intended for the composer in the act of composing. Hibberd, on the other hand, excludes theory designed for classroom use, but includes speculative theory, and within a general category of history of music, the investigation of theoretical aspects such as harmony, rhythm, etc.

Whatever the rationale and its justification, much theory has been written and written about during the last decade, and musicologists have had no small hand in it. On the one hand are critical editions and translations of Medieval and Renaissance theorists issued by the Medieval Institute, the *Journal of Music Theory*, and the American Institute of Musicology. On the other hand several predictive theories have appeared in the *Journal of*

---

30. *Ibid.*, pp. 41–44.
31. *AM*, XXXI (1959), p. 29.

Music Theory. Activity along this line in the past decade has reached unprecedented proportions in the history of American musicology.

The large bulk of American scholarship, however, has been within the province of music history. The predilection of American scholars for music of the Renaissance has long been recognized and more contributions have dealt with problems rooted in this era than in any other. A most encouraging aspect of recent American musicology is the ever-increasing volume of studies of music before 1400 and after 1600. To cite only a few of the many notable scholars working in the earlier centuries, there are Richard Hoppin and Nino Pirrotta working in the fourteenth century, Luther Dittmer in the thirteenth, William Waite in the twelfth, Willi Apel in Gregorian Chant, Eric Werner in music of the early Christian era, and Kenneth Levy, Oliver Strunk, and Miloš Velimirović in Byzantine music. In the later eras contributions have been made to Baroque scholarship by Henry Mishkin, William Newman, and Wiley Hitchcock; in the classic era by H. C. Robbins-Landon, Barry Brook, William Newman, and Edward Downes; in the nineteenth century by Eric Werner, Alexander Ringer and Donald Mintz; in the twentieth century by William Austin, Irving Lowens, and George Perle.

However, it is in the mushrooming scholarship residing in dissertations and theses that the increasing spread of interest is most apparent and most important for present purposes, for these are the scholars who will help to redefine American musicology in 1985. There is clear vindication here for Bukofzer's prognosis that studies would be rooted in style analysis.

Another recent trend in American musicology has been so gradual in its emergence that its presence and implications are easily overlooked. In ever greater numbers musicologists are involved directly and indirectly with performance. Concern has been expressed in many ways, one being that the study of performance practice in all eras or localities has become one of the liveliest topics on the current scene. Increasingly the scholar attempts to ascertain how music sounded and how it should sound now. He tempers his scholarly investigation with considerations of practical musicianship in the creation of editions that go a step beyond the bare symbols of the original source. He seeks not merely to exhume a dead art, but to recreate a living one. Editions like those of Robert Donington, for example, of the operas of Monteverdi or Lully, are increasing in number. Similar historical-practical studies may well become one of the waves of the future. In efforts such as these the musicologist involves, along with his intellect, all the sensitive musicianship he can command; he is not only a scholar but a musician.

Interest in performance has led musicologists to a deeper study of musical instruments and their techniques which, in turn, has led to a whole field of investigation that has developed largely within the last decade: musical iconography. This, too, may become a major concern during the immediate future.

It is a small step from interest in performance practice to the establishment of performance groups. The Collegium Musicum is nowadays such a common phenomenon that its absence on a college campus arouses more surprise than its presence. There are now amateur and student groups, as well as several professional groups such as the New York Pro Musica. One of the striking features of this recent development is that often these groups are directed by musicologists, or, if not actually directing them, musicologists are intimately involved in their activities. Musicology now is involved with performance in ways and to a degree that could scarcely have been imagined when the AMS was founded in 1934, and most of the development lies in the last decade. The implications are broad, and may even require important modifications in the program of training.

Several conclusions can be drawn from this survey. First, musicology is a vital, expanding, productive discipline. Second, contemplating the enormously expanded body of knowledge already in existence, the process of "close and necessarily slow investigation" presumes a degree of painstaking care and perceptive insight that was scarcely possible to American musicology thirty years ago. Third, musicology, both quantitatively and qualitatively, has long since passed its infancy and has arrived at a stage in its vigorous youth at which it seeks to know and to interpret itself, to arrive at its own wisdom in the full sense of

Aristotelian *sophia.* Fourth, by far the largest part of American musicology has been oriented humanistically. Fifth, musicology has become intimately involved with the practice of the art.

These, then, the histories general and period, the studies ethnological, stylistic and historical, the critical editions, the translations, the bibliographies, and finally the schemes of musicology's aim and scope—all this is what American musicology has become in our time. The view of the field and its constituent parts expressed by Pratt, Seeger, Kinkeldey, Haydon, and Lang appeared in what might be called the infancy and early adolescence of American musical scholarship. In a sense these views may be likened to what Palisca calls predictive or "creative" theory which, to a certain extent, precedes subsequent practice. To illustrate: in his *Introduction to Musicology,* Haydon says, "Style-criticism is the ultimate goal of a very large portion of musicological research." [32] During the ensuing twenty-five years, stylistic matters have remained by far the largest concern of American musicologists.

On the other hand, the Hibberd, Palisca and Spiess views have appeared at a more mature stage of American musicology's development, and frankly are derived from practices and attitudes current among American scholars. As such, the recent schemes are analogous to Palisca's derivative or "analytical" theories. We must remember, however, that, historically, the practice of a style period becomes crystallized and then receives full systematization only at, or toward, its close. Does the appearance of recent schemes—does reawakened interest in the topic itself—indicate that one stage of American musicology is drawing to a close and another beginning?

---

32. (New York: Prentice-Hall, Inc., 1941), p. 297.

INDEX

Manuscripts are listed alphabetically by city and library under the heading "Manuscripts"; Masses are not listed separately by title but are arranged alphabetically by composer and title under "Masses." "Music" or "illus." following an entry or subentry locates all music examples and illustrations. The index was compiled by the editor of this volume.